THE NEW
SOFT WAR
ON WOMEN

ALSO BY CARYL RIVERS AND ROSALIND C. BARNETT

The Truth About Girls and Boys:
Challenging Toxic Stereotypes About Our Children

Same Difference: How Gender Myths Are Hurting
Our Relationships, Our Children, and Our Jobs

She Works/He Works: How Two-Income Families
Are Happy, Healthy, and Thriving

ALSO BY CARYL RIVERS

Selling Anxiety: How the News Media Scare Women

JEREMY P. TARCHER/PENGUIN

a member of Penguin Group (USA)

New York

THE NEW

SOFT WAR

ON WOMEN

How the Myth of Female Ascendance
Is Hurting Women, Men—and Our Economy

CARYL RIVERS

—— AND ——

ROSALIND C. BARNETT

JEREMY P. TARCHER/PENGUIN
Published by the Penguin Group
Penguin Group (USA) LLC
375 Hudson Street
New York, New York 10014

USA · Canada · UK · Ireland · Australia
New Zealand · India · South Africa · China

penguin.com
A Penguin Random House Company

Most Tarcher/Penguin books are available at special quantity discounts for bulk purchase
for sales promotions, premiums, fund-raising, and educational needs. Special books or book excerpts
also can be created to fit specific needs. For details, write: Special.Markets@us.penguingroup.com.

Library of Congress Cataloging-in-Publication Data

Rivers, Caryl.
The new soft war on women : how the myth of female ascendance is hurting women,
men—and our economy / Caryl Rivers, Rosalind C. Barnett.
p.   cm.
Includes index.
ISBN 978-0-399-16333-3
1. Sex discrimination against women—United States.   2. Women—United States—Social conditions.
3. Men—United States—Attitudes.   I. Barnett, Rosalind C.   II. Title.
HQ1237.5.U6R578   2013   2013017960
305.40973—dc23

Printed in the United States of America
1   3   5   7   9   10   8   6   4   2

BOOK DESIGN BY MEIGHAN CAVANAUGH

To my children, Steve and Alyssa, and to my grandchildren,
Lauren, Zuey and Azalea. And also to the memory of Alan Lupo,
my husband, soul mate and best friend

—CR

To my husband, Nat; my children, Jonathan and Amy;
and my grandchildren, Reuben and Tess

—RCB

CONTENTS

THE NEW
SOFT WAR
ON WOMEN

ONE

WHERE THE BATTLE LINES ARE

At first glance, it may seem like a wonderful time to be a woman—a time of empowerment and achievement.

But look again, more closely, and you will see an ominous truth. Women's gains in the workplace either have stalled out or are in grave danger of being rolled back. While more women than ever before are studying medicine, law and business in college and professional schools, there is a real question whether they will ever attain leadership positions in the areas in which they have been trained.

Women have made dramatic gains in higher education and employment. For the first time, women make up half the educated labor force and earn the majority of advanced degrees. But these dramatic gains have *not* translated into money and influence. Women are not getting to the top at anything like the rate one would have expected, given their education and early promise. The needle hasn't moved. It may be counterintuitive to think that education and employment don't yield the sort of money and power that they do for men. But that is indeed the case.

Despite the fact that the pipeline is getting filled with educated and talented women, their way forward is too often blocked. Under a veneer of success and progress, what we call the New Soft War on Women is growing in strength. As we will demonstrate, the war's skirmishes are less visible and predictable than the old and obvious closed doors but are in many ways at least as effective.

New barriers and old biases—which we will discuss in detail—shackle women as they try to move ahead in the arenas of business, academia, the sciences and politics. Picture, if you will, two people, a man and a woman, starting out on a lifelong path of work. Both are equally qualified, both have the same sort of dreams, and both are willing to work as hard they can to achieve their goals.

But only one of these people, the man, is unencumbered. The other, the woman, carries a fifty-pound pack on her back. He strides freely and swiftly, looking neither to the right nor to the left. She travels much more slowly, struggling with a burden that she can't seem to shed. She is carrying a history of gender discrimination that is as heavy as a pack filled with large rocks and that slows her down as she struggles to move ahead. Most of this weight has been thrust upon her by history and culture, but some of it she herself has picked up when succumbing to notions of what a woman should be. In her path are barriers that she may not even be aware of before stumbling into them. She has to muster a great deal of energy and resources to continue her journey, while the man, unimpeded, moves at a brisker pace. The farther along she goes on the path, the more formidable the barriers become, and the harder it gets for her.

Over the past forty years, much progress has been made at the beginning of the road, with women streaming into graduate and professional schools. More and more women are getting educated and saying they want lifelong careers. They start out at a sprint. But the farther they go, the greater the wear and tear of this heavy backpack. They have to expend ever more energy and struggle ever harder to keep up with the men who are moving inexorably ahead of them. In spite of the extra burdens they carry, women *are* making progress in reaching their goals. But it's slow going, and the number of women thins out as the top of the ladder comes into view.

The number of women in leadership positions has been anemic for a long time, and remains so. In many arenas, women are actually slipping backward.

This may surprise you, because the media tell us that women are taking over the world and that men are failing. For now, this "threat story" is winning the day. It argues that women have come too far too fast, and because of their success, men are faltering.

Don't believe it. In nearly all areas of work, the narrative on women's great progress is highly misleading—especially when it comes to top-level jobs. Here's the evidence:

- The gains in salary that women acquired over the 1980s and 1990s not only have leveled off, but also have, in fact, dropped off to the point where men's salaries are pulling far ahead once again.[1]

- Women's remarkable strides in education during the past three decades have not resulted in full equity in pay—even for college-educated women who work full-time. In 2011, a typical college-educated woman twenty-five years or older working full-time earned $50,000 a year, compared with $70,000 for college-educated male workers in the same age group—*a difference of $20,000 each year.*[2]

- The WAGE (Women Are Getting Even) Project, a national group that helps women close the gender gap in pay, illustrates this salary difference in a stark way. "Tina and Ted graduated from the same university, with the same degree. They work the same number of hours, in the same type of job. And yet, as they start their first jobs, Ted is making $4,000 more than Tina. In the second year, the difference has added up to almost $9,500."[3]

- Over a lifetime of work, a woman with a bachelor's degree will earn *a third less* (some $700,000) than a man with the same degree. This pattern holds in nearly all fields of endeavor.[4]

- Female physicians earn, on average, 39 percent less than male physicians.[5] Female financial analysts take in 35 percent less than male financial analysts, and female chief executives 25 percent less than male executives.[6] Female MBAs earn, on average, $4,600 less than male MBAs in their first job out of business school.[7] Women start behind and *never* catch up. This pattern holds true even among graduates from our most elite universities: Female Harvard graduates earn 30 percent less than their male counterparts.[8]

- Male chief financial officers are paid an average of 16 percent more than their female counterparts of similar age at U.S. companies with comparable market values.[9]

- Women have made few inroads into U.S. corporate boards or executive suites. In 2012, figures show glacial progress in increasing female representation, according to Catalyst, a non-profit research group studying women and business. Catalyst dubbed such progress "flat, static, immobile, inert," and its CEO, Ilene H. Lang, said, "If this trend line represented a patient's pulse—she'd be dead."[10]

- The number of women promoted to board seats in Fortune 500 companies, which had steadily increased in the late twentieth century, has dropped over the past three years. A major report by the international consulting firm McKinsey that was commissioned by the *Wall Street Journal* found that "despite the sincere efforts of major corporations, the proportion of women falls quickly as you look higher in the corporate hierarchy. Overall, this picture has not improved for years."[11]

- Only 4 percent of health care organizations have women CEOs; among those that received more than $2 million in venture funding, zero had a female CEO.[12]
- In computer science and engineering, women's earlier gains appear to have slowed or even shifted into reverse.[13] The share of women in tech fields is a meager 25 percent, and they make up a dismal 11 percent of tech executives. The percentage of women holding jobs in computer fields has declined from nearly 40 percent in 1991 to 25 percent today.[14]

ON THE BATTLEFIELD

These staggering statistics tell the story of the New Soft War.

Why do we call it *soft*? Because research finds that today's barriers are more subtle and insidious than the old ones. It's less a frontal assault than an ongoing and very effective guerrilla movement. Now, bias operates under a welcoming facade; the bombs are under the surface, but they still explode. This isn't an overt conspiracy to hold women back. Instead, it's a perfect storm of economic, political and social factors that combine to threaten women's progress.

Today, nobody says, "No women need apply." But people may say, "You're just not as likable as he is." Or, "You women have come far enough. Now we need to pay attention to the men." Or, "You've done great work, but I've got more confidence in Joe's potential. He's going to be a star!"

If you're a female in a top job and you slip up in a man's world, you're most likely out the door. If you're working on a project with a man, he'll probably get the credit you deserve. You and your male colleague may both have a mentor, but he'll get a sponsor—an advocate who will go to bat for him in a way that a woman's champion will not. You'll get more scrutiny than he will. If you are a mother who is serious about your work, you will be looked on as not really committed to that work, and not very competent to boot. A man with a résumé just like yours, however, will get a bonus for parenthood; he will be seen as serious, dedicated and responsible. If you speak up at some length at work, even if you are in a senior position, you will be seen not only as gabby but also as incompetent. A man who talks as much or more than you do will be seen as powerful and forceful.

Why do we use the term *war*? Because the statistics we've just cited about women's lack of progress are casualty figures. What was startling to us as we looked at these data was how powerful and pervasive gender stereotypes really are. Like many women, we knew there were still problems, but we had assumed that many of these stereotypes were fading and that the future looked bright indeed. It was only when we saw these issues, not one at a time, but with a wide-angle lens, that we realized how deeply disturbing the panorama is. It's not that there haven't been gains by women—there have been many. It's that the payback we expected simply hasn't materialized. In many ways, women's progress is stuck—and may even be shifting into reverse.

The small-arms fire keeps coming, but women don't see who's sniping at them, who's slamming doors and where the next land mine is planted. They're blindsided by all the rhetoric about how good they've got it. They may even believe it.

Women want to succeed and are working hard to do so. But despite their best efforts, the rewards and promotions they have every right to expect often do not materialize. The New Soft War is affecting them, and the scary fact is that women don't clearly grasp what's happening.

Recent research shows a major gap in how men and women view female success. Psychologists Michael T. Schmitt and Jennifer Spoor at Queensland University in Australia found that when men focus on the gains women have made over the past fifty years, they report high levels of anxiety as well as a strong identification with their own gender.[15] There's a tendency to circle the wagons, to exaggerate how far women have come and how far men have fallen.

In contrast, when women focus on these gains, they report low levels of threat as well as low gender-group identification. This might be a case of the "rose-colored glasses" syndrome. Too many women think that all the battles have been fought, that discrimination is a thing of the past and that the future will bring ever greater progress for them. When the media highlight token high-achieving women like Yahoo! CEO Marissa Mayer, the rest of us tend to think broad progress has been made, even when it hasn't. This may explain the current low level of feminist activism.

So, men are afraid that they will lose their status and power, and women are so delighted with their "progress" that they don't see the storm clouds overhead.

These fears feed into a national narrative that says feminism is dead, women's problems are over and in fact women may have gone too far and left men in the dust. In this narrative, there's a "mancession," in which men are losing more jobs than women are, and a "boy crisis" in education, in which boys are failing and girls are thriving. There's a belief that women are assuming more and more power and will soon take over most of the influential roles in society, while young men lack ambition and will soon drift into irrelevance. According to Philip Zimbardo and Nikita Duncan, in today's popular films "all the leading male characters are presented as expendable losers usually incapable of taking responsibility for themselves, often plotting intricate but seldom realized plans to get laid, and generally running the opposite direction of any kind of commitment. Not only do they avoid the future, sometimes they attempt to re-live past glory in order to avoid living in the present. It seems these guys don't have much value to contribute to society beyond their ability to entertain the other male characters, and of course, the audience."[16]

Even though the evidence for these beliefs is scant, they thrive in our twenty-four-hour, sound-bite-driven culture. They have become memes—those often repeated, widely spread notions that get ingrained in our everyday discourse and shape how we see the world.

In the 1970s, biologist Richard Dawkins first identified the meme as a unit of cultural change, like a virus that spreads rapidly.[17] Some memes, propelled by heavy media attention, travel at warp speed and reach ever larger audiences.

WOMEN'S CRITICAL ECONOMIC ROLE

Why is this pushback against women's success so ominous? Because now, for the first time, women have the potential to reenergize the U.S. economy, and they have started to do so. According to the *Wall Street Journal*'s McKinsey report, titled "Unlocking the Full Potential of Women in the U.S. Economy":

The productive power of women entering the workforce from 1970 until today accounts for about a quarter of current GDP. Between 1970 and 2009, women went from holding 37 percent of all jobs to nearly 48 percent. That's almost 38 million more employed women. Without them, our economy would be 25 percent smaller today—an amount equal to the combined GDP of Illinois, California and New York. . . .

About 76 percent of all American women aged 25–54 are in the workforce. That compares with about 87 percent in Sweden. Getting all U.S. states up to an 84 percent participation rate would add 5.1 million women to the workforce. This would be equivalent to adding 3–4 percent to the size of the U.S. economy.[18]

Women hold the key to the economic future. Businesses owned by women now employ 35 percent more people than do all the Fortune 500 companies combined. Women hold the majority of positions in the fields expected to grow the most over the next decade—professional and service occupations. If women's paid employment rates were raised to the same level as men's, America's GDP would be 9 percent higher.[19]

A nineteen-year study of 215 Fortune 500 firms reveals a strong correlation between aggressively promoting women to top jobs and excellent profits. The 25 Fortune 500 firms with the best record of moving women to the executive suite are between 18 and 69 percent more profitable than the median Fortune 500 companies.[20]

Women represent an increasingly large proportion of the educated workforce. Their numbers present a huge opportunity for companies that are smart enough to embrace them. To succeed, corporations need to promote the advancement of all employees; women are no longer a "special-interest" group.

The great American economic boom of the 1990s, says Richard B. Freeman, director of the National Bureau of Economic Research and the Herbert Ascherman Chair in Economics at Harvard University, was "not a story of male employment but of the large increase in female employment."[21] He notes that the employment of married women with children was a major reason why the United States outstripped the European Union economically in the 1990s.

In fact, if women's previous gains stall—as they appear to be doing—the U.S. economy will also stall. We all have a stake in keeping this from happening.

MEN'S AND WOMEN'S WORLD TODAY

More than ever before, men as well as women have an investment in women's economic success. Forty years ago, the typical man did not gain another breadwinner in his household when he married. Today, he does—giving his household increased earning power that most unmarried men do not enjoy. The superior gains of married men have enabled them to overtake and surpass unmarried men in terms of median household income.

While there have been few major changes in gender equity in corporate America, there have been stunning shifts in the attitudes of men and women toward both work and family. Today, more young women than men ages eighteen to thirty-four say that "being successful in a high-paying career or profession is 'one of the most important things' or 'very important' in their lives," according to the Pew Research Center.[22] Indeed, 66 percent of young women make this claim compared with 59 percent of young men. Over time, the number of men who have endorsed this view has remained steady, whereas 10 percent more women endorsed it in 2011 than did in 1997.

These changes have not come at the expense of people's personal lives. Today, a high percentage of men and women place great importance on marriage and family. For both women and men, being a good parent and having a successful marriage remain much more important than career success. More than 90 percent of working-age people of both sexes agree that being a good parent is of great importance, whereas more than 80 percent say the same thing about having a successful marriage.

In the past, it was assumed that women were desperate to marry and were chasing after men who were running away as fast as they could. This, it was said, was simply "nature" at work. But in another new twist, men ages eighteen to thirty-four now place a much higher priority on marriage and family than they did before. For the first time, among middle-age and older Americans, nearly equal percentages of women and men say that marriage is very important in their lives.

Unfortunately, the American workplace has yet to accommodate the changing desires of men and women, whose priorities and hopes and dreams are becoming more closely aligned. In a world where everybody's working, where most everybody's trying to raise kids, and everybody needs to succeed on the job and in private life, corporations must do everything they can to make this possible. It will no longer suffice to treat women as a special-interest group, as if their needs are different from those of their male colleagues. The fact is that corporate success increasingly depends on meeting *all* employees' needs as best as possible.

We've been tracking these changes for a number of years as a research psychologist (Rosalind) and a journalist (Caryl). Our joint work examines stereotypes of women and men, girls and boys, and how these stereotypes can limit peoples' possibilities. As both friends and colleagues, we have raised our own children while working full-time and managing our households. So we know from personal experience as well as from science and research the challenges of this kind of life.

Our individual work has provided each of us with important insights. One of the main thrusts of Roz's research has been the issues faced by full-time-employed dual-earner couples. Caryl has followed and written extensively on politics and policy in this area.

The New Soft War is as bad for the bottom line as it is for women themselves. It threatens the creation of a workplace that's good for everybody. When we treat women as a marginal group, whose needs are unique to them, we are going down the wrong path. We generate needless tensions and invidious comparisons between men and women. If, however, we avoid the trap of focusing on gender and treat all employees equally, everybody benefits.

Managers, corporate leaders and CEOs urgently need to recruit, retain and nurture the valuable asset that women have become. We must all embrace a new paradigm that places women at the center of twenty-first-century economic realities, not on the fringe.

We have to actively defang the memes about women and their "natures" that are still deeply entrenched in our society and accepted by both men and women. The burden of discrimination has to disappear.

This book offers a roadmap to achieving those goals.

TWO

DOING WELL MAY NOT WORK OUT SO WELL

We are often asked, *How can you say that women aren't getting to the top? Look at Hillary Clinton and Nancy Pelosi. What about Ginni Rometty, the IBM CEO, and Indra Nooyi, the PepsiCo CEO? The Supreme Court now has three women. A woman is the executive editor of the* New York Times. *Women are presidents of Harvard, Brown, Princeton, and the University of Pennsylvania.*

Indeed, this is all wonderful news. Some women certainly have made it to the top of their professions. Women can and do break the glass ceiling, *but*—and here's the rub—their road is full of craters, they tote an extra-heavy load on their journey and, too often, when they get to the top, they are all alone and vulnerable.

In the pages ahead, we take a hard look at the rocky road women have to travel. As we interviewed women in business, law, medicine, journalism, the arts, the sciences and academia, we heard the same stories of hard work and thwarted progress. Our interviews back up the work of many researchers who have illuminated how women get blindsided and shortchanged. We like to believe that the workplace is fair and that if we do a good job, we will be rewarded. After all, that's the American way. But this belief is less true for women than it is for men.

Indeed, too often women whose performance is stellar get fewer rewards than men do—even men who are less than outstanding. Among high-potential employees (the people companies invest significant dollars to recruit, develop and advance), "women lag men with respect to both level and compensation starting with their very first job out of business school. . . . When you start from behind, it's hard enough to keep pace, never mind catch up—regardless of what tactics you use," according to researchers at the nonprofit group Catalyst.[1]

And no, it's not that women are less ambitious; women pursue their career goals as proactively as men pursue theirs. But even when women make use of the same strategies, they don't get as far.

Doing all the right things to get ahead—using those strategies that are regularly suggested in self-help books, coaching sessions and the popular press—pays off much better for men than it does for women.[2]

PROMISE VS. PERFORMANCE

Why do we see so many young male hotshots moving up the ladder ahead of more seasoned females? Women need a longer, stronger track record because they are judged on what they have actually accomplished. For promising men, research shows, potential is enough to win the day.

The *Wall Street Journal*'s McKinsey report documents this disturbing fact, according to Vikram Malhotra, McKinsey's chairman of the Americas: "Middle-management women get promoted on performance. Many middle-management men get promoted on potential. Qualified women actually enter the work force in sufficient numbers, but they begin to plateau or drop off . . . when they are eligible for their very first management positions. And it only gets worse after that."[3]

The *Economist* notes, "Discrimination continues in subtle ways. Business schools that follow their alumni's careers find that men are promoted on their potential but women are promoted on their performance, so they advance more slowly. The women adjust to this, which slows their progress even more, and so the discrimination goes on without either side necessarily being aware of it."[4]

Catalyst, in a 2008 study, found the following:

- Women who switched jobs two or more times after earning an MBA received $53,472 *less* than women who stayed put at their first job and climbed the ranks. These women had to prove themselves again *each time* they changed employers.
- On the other hand, men who moved on from their first post-MBA job earned $13,743 *more* than those who stayed with their first employer. It seems that they were being paid for promise.
- Men were almost twice as likely as women to become CEOs or senior executives. Among the group of real go-getters, 21 percent of men advanced to leadership positions compared with 11 percent of women.[5]

Catalyst studied more than 3,000 full-time female and male MBAs and divided the participants into four "strategy profiles":

Climbers, who are actively seeking to get ahead inside a company
Hedgers, who are looking for advancement both inside and outside their current employers
Scanners, who are looking for future prospects in the job market
Coasters, who are not actively using career-enhancing tactics[6]

Male hedgers got the biggest advancement rewards for their efforts—twice as much as female hedgers.

Being proactive didn't give women anywhere near the bang for the buck that male hedgers got.

Women we talked to have had firsthand experience with the power of male advantage. At a very successful national magazine, a popular section was edited by a male senior editor, and the deputy editor was a woman in her forties. She was well respected by everybody on the staff, did the lion's share of the editing and was a go-getter who came up with new ideas all the time. So when the senior editor announced his retirement, his deputy fully expected that she would be promoted. She was shocked when he appointed a twenty-seven-year-old man to the position. When she protested, he said that the young man impressed him because "he reminded me of myself at the same age."

A senior manager with both an MBA and a Ph.D. said, "At a large, well-known consulting firm, I was hired at the same time as a man of about my age (but without the Ivy education and MBA, which I had). Our offices were next to each other, and we worked similarly ridiculous hours, including many weekends in the office. I noticed he spent a fair amount of time during the workweek bragging about how hard he was working, and generally getting in front of the 99 percent male senior consultants, while I kept my nose to the proverbial grindstone, working and working away. I thought the bosses would notice all my 'perfect' work. In my mind, my male colleague was making a mistake and marking himself as obnoxious and self-aggrandizing. I was wrong. One day, he was packing up his office and moving up an entire level. It was my first hard lesson that in the real world, politics and networking can be more important than your work ethic and conscientiousness."

Another woman told us: "I was up for a top job in my company, and I counted on my significant accomplishments in the job to win the day. But they hired a much younger man with an Ivy League degree and raved about his glowing potential—even though he'd not done much yet. My stellar track record seemed to count for less than what he might do in the future."

In Washington, D.C., the ultimate power town, women do not move up the ladder as fast as men. A 2012 *National Journal* online survey of 717 professional women found that almost three-quarters of them said that men have a greater number of opportunities to get ahead than women do.[7] Fully half said that they had had a personal experience with gender discrimination in the workplace, while 60 percent said that it is more difficult for women than for men to attain leadership positions.

The *National Journal* noted, "Women are indeed muscling their way toward the back rooms where the most important decisions are made. But the door is still closed much of the time. Even President Obama, who arguably is one of the most feminist presidents in U.S. history, is not immune to criticism." The article went on to quote Heidi Hartmann, an economist and the president of the Washington, D.C.–based Institute for Women's Policy Research: "The people he plays basketball and golf with are male. Most of his Cabinet secretaries are men. There does still seem to be a sense in which the inner circle is frequently male-dominated."

NO CREDIT WHERE CREDIT IS DUE

A thirty-six-year-old media manager we interviewed, who had been on the job for twelve years, said, "Actually, myself and two other women co-created a huge (and profitable) project, including the creation of a news-gathering database system. A male colleague took credit and is still consistently credited by our (mostly male) management as not just the creator but the 'most knowledgeable' on the system, which he never uses. The two other women have since quit and moved on."

She noted that it was "common" for males to get the lion's share of the credit in her workplace. "I was teamed with another male colleague and we were splitting projects. . . . When he turned in something he worked on with a problem, I was blamed. But when I turned in something I worked on and was great, we were praised as a team."

Another woman told us, "I coordinated and ran the network depot for a nationwide network . . . and a young male student was given a monetary and certificate award for the work that we did, and I was not mentioned. . . . And then he was given the official leadership on the next project because the boss also 'felt more comfortable' with him. They could socialize, lunch and talk guy stuff."

Cara, an attorney, reported, "I worked on a project with a young male partner, where he oversaw my work and strategy on the matter. My hard work and strategic decision making led to our client winning and to significant attorneys' fees in the case. When the young male partner reported to the shareholders of our success, I was only cc'd on the e-mail and was not given any credit. The shareholders responded to the male partner's success story with a 'well done, young man,' having no clue that it was me, and not the male partner, who should have been credited with the win."

These stories are sadly all too familiar. Women work hard and achieve the desired results—and men get the credit. New York University psychology professor Madeline Heilman and Michelle Haynes have shown that when there is ambiguity about which member of a two-member, male-female team is responsible for the team's successful joint performance, credit is far more often given to the male than the female team member.[8] Specifically, female members were rated as being less competent, less influential and less likely to have played a leadership role in work on the task. Both females and males fell into the trap of giving higher marks to the male team member.

This happened to Pamela, now a history professor at a small college. She was originally hired to work at a large, prestigious urban university, a job she was thrilled to get. In her second year, she was given the assignment to produce a major report for the department with a male colleague. Pamela did the bulk of the research and writing for the report, which was very well received in the department. But she noticed that people in her department just assumed that she had played a bit part in the process. Her colleague was a large, forceful man who had a knack for promoting his own accomplishments. He did nothing to disabuse the chair or other faculty members of their assumptions. Pamela quietly seethed.

The man rose in status and was promoted to associate professor, while her rank stayed the same. Even when she received a major national award for a paper she wrote, few of her colleagues seemed to notice. Several years later, both she and her male colleague were scheduled to go up for tenure. He was encouraged, while she was told that the department would not support her candidacy. Reluctantly, she left the large university for the small college, which is in a less desirable area. She is valued more at her new school, but her salary is much lower, and her prospects for national attention much dimmer. Plus, she misses the city that had become her home.

This situation contributes to the phenomenon of "the invisible woman." Jacki Zehner, a founding partner of Circle Financial Group and a former Goldman Sachs partner, wrote an article titled "Why Are Goldman's Women Invisible?" for the Huffington Post, in which she discusses a *Bloomberg Markets* piece with a foldout page featuring forty-two of the firm's most prized ex-partners.[9] Forty-one of the photos are of white men, as are the eight honorable mentions.

Why, Zehner asks, were the many high-ranking female ex-partners not mentioned? "The media in general, and this [*Bloomberg Markets*] article in particular, had the opportunity to make women leaders VISIBLE and they chose not to. . . . The lesson here? Our society does not merely fail to develop, reward, retain, and lift up women leaders, we have done the opposite. We perpetuate their invisibility. As Marie Wilson, head of the now closed White House Project, which promoted women in politics and business, has said over and over again, 'You cannot be what you cannot see' and we do not see women leaders, especially on Wall Street."

Other workplaces have similar problems.

Deborah, a former elected prosecutor in Missouri, told us the following story: "When I was elected prosecutor, there were a lot of subtle obstacles placed in my way. I was required to manage an office in which we were severely understaffed and underfunded. We did not even have enough money to pay for our paper. I worked ridiculous hours, sixteen to eighteen hours a day, five to six days a week, and four hours on Sunday, because we could not keep up with the crime. When I first took over, I was not allowed to shut the office down to train our people and myself on the new computer program. I was in court almost every day, so it was hard to file new cases because there were only two of us in the office. To me, it seemed like they wanted me to quit. I didn't, because I am not a quitter. I worked even harder, because that was how I knew to survive. I noticed the incredibly opposite attitude when my successor took over, and all of a sudden there was $100,000 in the budget and he could hire three more attorneys and increase the staff."

A partner in a large law firm in a major city told us about how a female colleague worked with a male colleague on a huge case for the firm, one that resulted in one of the largest jury verdicts in the country's history: "In the attendant publicity over the massive win, not only was the male colleague consistently touted as the lead attorney, but also, in many of the articles, the woman partner was not even mentioned or was mentioned in a far lesser role. The last straw came when the female partner was given far less credit for her work than her male colleague in the firm's own marketing push (internal and external) touting the victory. The woman partner left for a rival firm shortly thereafter, attended by much hand-wringing but no visible accountability for her departure."

Ashley, an engineer at a major defense contractor, said, "I have sat in meetings where I presented after doing all the work, but my male coworker next to me was asked questions. He then fumbled through answers, clearly not knowing what he was talking about."

Here's yet another horror story from Cathy, the managing director of a consulting firm: "At a previous company, I led a team that wrote a new business plan for the company. When the results were presented, I was laid off and the two men on the team were promoted."

WOMEN GET MENTORED— BUT NOT SPONSORED

All mentoring is not created equal. As the *Harvard Business Review* notes, "There is a special kind of relationship—called sponsorship—in which the mentor goes beyond giving feedback and advice and uses his or her influence with senior executives to advocate for the mentee. . . . Women are overmentored and undersponsored relative to their male peers—and so women are not advancing in their organizations. Furthermore, without sponsorship, women not only are less likely than men to be appointed to top roles but may also be more reluctant to go for them."[10]

A 2010 survey conducted by Catalyst looked at more than 4,000 high-potential women and men with excellent credentials.[11] It found that women tended to have more mentors and reported getting more mentoring—but that the men's mentors were more senior or more likely to be senior executives.

Two years later, in a follow-up study, Herminia Ibarra, a professor at the international business school INSEAD, asked how many of these women and men had received promotions since the Catalyst survey. In an interview with the *Harvard Business Review*'s IdeaCast, Ibarra said that there was "a significant relationship between having had a mentor and having received a promotion within that two-year period. For women, there was no relationship. Having a mentor had no correlation whatsoever with whether they got promoted."[12] This phenomenon could be called "mentor lite."

Ibarra said, "We had a number of actually really rather funny interviews with women who said, 'Gee, there's this mentoring program and that mentoring program. And I have this mentor who wants me to do X and that mentor who wants me to do Y. And they all have pre-work, and they all have different extracurricular activities. And yeah, I'm going to get mentored to death before I'm promoted.'"

The *Harvard Business Review* interviewed several women who found themselves in this position.[13]

Nathalie, a senior marketing executive at a multinational retailer, was a top prospect for the head position in the country where she worked. Her boss suggested that she increase her profile by becoming more visible locally. She was matched up with a high-level mentor and had almost completed the lengthy training he had assigned to her when she received an invitation to yet another training program for high-level leaders. Again, she was asked to fill out more self-review and career-goal paperwork.

Nathalie felt she was pushing the same rock up the same hill, again and again. What was all this work for? Would it really get her anywhere? She told the *Harvard Business Review* that despite all the mentoring, "I'd been here for 12 years, and nothing happened."

Amy, another manager, experienced a similar dilemma. "My mentor's idea of a development plan is how many external and internal meetings I can get exposure to, what presentations I can go to and deliver, and what meetings I can travel to," she said. "I just hate these things that add work. I hate to say it, but I am so busy. I have three kids. On top of that, what my current boss really wants me to do is to focus on 'breakthrough thinking,' and I agree. I am going to be in a wheelchair by the time I get to be vice president, because they are going to drill me into the ground with all these extra-credit projects."

Julie, a respected finance manager with star potential, also received intensive mentoring, and expressed concern "that she may be getting caught betwixt and between" two mentoring programs—one run by her boss and another run by a corporate team. Her boss felt that the corporate mentoring was getting in the way of his own program. "I'd prefer to be involved in the corporate program because it is more high-profile," she said, noting that when all is said and done, "it adds up to a lot of mentoring."

Other women agree that having many mentors can create roadblocks rather than smooth the way forward. Sallie Krawcheck, the former head of Bank of America's wealth management division, puts it this way: "If you look around Wall Street and corporate America, we're putting women on diversity councils, we're putting them in mentoring programs, we're giving them special leadership training, telling them how to ask for promotions—but we are *not* promoting them. My goodness, we are just making them busier."[14]

Is it better to have a male or a female mentor? Research is mixed on this question, but Alice Eagly, a professor of psychology at Northwestern University, and Linda Carli, a senior lecturer in psychology at Wellesley College, found that "protégés who have male mentors tend to receive more financial compensation, regardless of their own gender."[15] Since oftentimes men have more power and control more resources, they can give a woman's career a boost that women mentors can't.

A journalist for a national news organization told us, "For a while we had a male manager who took various young men under his protective wing, while treating the female staff like petulant children."

Another interviewee noted, "At a relatively young age—just over forty—I was told that I didn't need a mentor any longer and should be looking for opportunities to be a mentor instead. Men are mentored throughout their career. Women are not."

A fifty-seven-year-old manager said of her mentoring situation: "A female boss used all the 'teamwork' and 'mentoring' phrases, but when it came time for advocating for promotions and fair salary upgrades to reflect the work I was handling—and also the work of those on my team—she refused to negotiate with me or accept my recommendations for raises, etc. She and a male coworker, who was essentially at my level, made all the decisions about promotions. She was threatened by me as the other senior, smart female in the department, and she made sure that I was kept 'in my place,' working away behind the scenes and helping her look good in ways that were never credited fairly. There were two openings in other departments that I expressed interest in, and she claimed she had put in a good word for me, but I truly am not convinced that she did."

Another woman chimed in that she found the female-mentor power problem to be "completely true." She told us, "My women mentors do not support me in attempts to get promoted. Perhaps they do not feel they have sufficient power bases to do this."

These women are not atypical. Their experiences reflect a common workplace experience: having mentors who don't really mentor or who are even actively hostile to the women under their wing. Companies that have invested considerable time and resources in mentoring continue to see their pipelines leak at the middle to senior management levels, even though they are actively searching for ways to retain their best female talent. In a 2010 World Economic Forum report on corporate practices for gender diversity in 20 countries, 59 percent of the companies surveyed said that they offered internally led mentoring and networking programs, and 28 percent said they had women-specific programs.[16] But does all this effort translate into actual promotions and appointments?

In a word, no. Women have mentors up the wazoo. But they have little to show for it in terms of money, promotions or satisfaction. It makes us wonder whether company mentoring programs for women are nothing more than facades—or Potemkin villages.

In 1787, Russian minister Gregory Potemkin created a tour for Empress Catherine the Great to view newly conquered territories in the Crimea. Potemkin ordered that hollow shells of villages be constructed along riverbanks to make it seem that this desolate area included thriving and prosperous communities. Too many well-intentioned corporate mentoring programs, it seems, are in reality just window dressing to make women feel that they are appreciated. These programs may also help companies recruit the women they say they want. Even if they are in reality only Potemkin villages, they can seem impressive to female job seekers who view them from a distance, and can give upper-level managers something to say when they are asked about what they are doing to promote diversity.

As one person posted on the *Harvard Business Review* website, women are in dire need of better sponsorship: "Sponsorship is the dirty little secret that has been practiced in corporate America for decades but spoken little about. . . . Sponsorship gets the job done. One can only hope to get the 'right' sponsor for them. It's not what you know. It's who knows you and [is] willing to advocate for you that accelerates careers."[17]

According to the authors of the Catalyst report mentioned earlier in this chapter, "When there is no formal sponsorship program, individuals might reach out to others to informally play that role. As well, executives may decide on their own to sponsor someone."[18] The challenge with relying on catch-as-catch-can connections is that women are often excluded from critical informal networks, decreasing their access to potential sponsors. Moreover, when executives select someone to sponsor, chances are that they "might be drawn to someone who reminds them of themselves, which won't support the development of diverse talent."

Catalyst's conclusion: "Organizations that want to identify and develop top talent should implement formal mechanisms to ensure equal access to the process" and ensure that "diverse candidates aren't being inadvertently overlooked."

SPONSORSHIPS THAT WORK

Women need more sponsors and fewer mentors. Companies should rip down the Potemkin villages and replace them with structures that are solid and real, which will help stem the brain drain of talented women. How can they do this?

For answers, we can look at the example of men who have been successfully sponsored. One male mentee reported: "My boss said, 'You are ready for a general management job. You can do it. Now we need to find you a job: What are the tricks we need to figure out? You have to talk to this person and to that one and that one.' They are all executive committee members. My boss was a network type of a person. . . . Before he left, he put me in touch with the head of supply chain, which is how I managed to get this job."[19]

Women need this kind of vigorous coaching and strategizing from a sponsor who is really invested in their success.

Too often, policies and programs designed to help female employees focus on hand-holding or on short-term goals, such as achieving a work-family balance or setting personal objectives. While these programs are worthwhile, they do not address the long-term goal of getting women into corporate leadership positions. That is what sponsorship is all about.

Catalyst reports, "At Deutsche Bank, for example, internal research revealed that female managing directors who left the firm to work for competitors were not doing so to improve their work/life balance. Rather, they'd been offered bigger jobs externally, ones they weren't considered for internally. Deutsche Bank responded by creating a sponsorship program aimed at assigning more women to critical posts. It paired mentees with executive committee members to increase the female talent pool's exposure to the committee and ensure that the women had influential advocates for promotion. Now, one-third of the participants are in larger roles than they were in a year ago, and another third are deemed ready by senior management and HR to take on broader responsibilities."[20]

Many upper-level managers—male and female—don't know about the research (much of which we report in this book) on the ways in which gender stereotypes are a drag anchor on women; they may simply believe that discrimination is a thing of the past. Yet such stereotypes are so pervasive that women and men both have an easier time envisioning a male in a leadership position. This unconscious bias is undoubtedly reflected in the opportunities male and female employees are given and the encouragement they are provided.

Fortunately, unconscious bias can be made conscious and then uprooted, making way for new policies built from the ground up. One way to do this is to hold sponsors accountable. An employee's failure to obtain a promotion should be viewed as a failure of the sponsor, not of the candidate.

"At IBM Europe," Catalyst's Christine Silva says, "a sponsorship program designed for senior women below the executive level aims to promote selected participants within one year. Sponsors, all vice presidents or general managers, are charged with making sure that participants are indeed ready within a year. . . . If they are not, the sponsor is taken to task."

A related problem: "Sponsors typically declare victory and move on after their high potentials advance—just when they need help to successfully take charge in their new roles. We know of no programs designed to shore up participants past promotion and through the 'first 100 days' in the new position. With that extra bit of attention, sponsors could help deliver not just promotions but strong transitions."[21]

THE "HOT JOB" GAP

"Women simply aren't getting the 'hot' jobs," the *Washington Post* reported in an article based on a 2012 Catalyst study.[22] "When they're not being placed on highly visible projects, in key international roles or in critical profit-and-loss management positions, they're never going to reach the top leadership ranks to which such high-profile stretch assignments typically lead."

The numbers tell the story. In 2008, Catalyst identified 1,660 MBA graduates, female and male, who were excellent candidates for "hot jobs." Four years later, the men in the group were faring far better than the women. The men were more likely to lead projects with big budgets, be in charge of larger teams, take on more risk and have more exposure to senior managers in the C-suite.[23]

Too often women don't get offered jobs that they are clearly qualified to do. An executive in the oil and gas industry told us, "In my career, I have made it a point to say yes to opportunities, special projects and special assignments. This may involve extensive travel, long hours and making the choice of my career first and family second. For my efforts, I am routinely praised and given credit publicly.

"But due to the corporate structure, there are not many promotional opportunities. In the last three years, there have only been two. In both cases, the positions were not posted—rather, they were bestowed upon a white male. While the men appointed are bright and talented, myself as well as other women with equal qualifications and sometimes greater experience were never given the opportunity or the courtesy of an interview. After it happened the first time in 2011, I questioned one of the decision makers and was told that they didn't talk to me because they 'didn't think I'd be interested.' When I pointed out that I would have been if the position had been posted or [I had] otherwise learned of it, I was placated and told, "Don't worry. You two are making about the same money.' I said I would be interested in and would like to have the opportunity to discuss future openings. Needless to say, that did not occur with the recent opportunity, and so I am spending more time networking for my next opportunity at a new company."

The Catalyst study found that many promising women were quite satisfied with the sponsorships they had received, but that was not enough. They still had far less access than their male peers to some crucial hot jobs. For example, 42 percent of high-potential men vs. 30 percent of very promising women worked on projects with a budget of $10 million or more.

In the eighteen months following participation in a leadership development program, women were less likely than men to

- get an international assignment (14 percent of women vs. 23 percent of men);
- receive profit and loss responsibility for the first time (7 percent of women vs. 13 percent of men);
- have their budget oversight increase by 20 percent or more (15 percent of women vs. 22 percent of men); or
- receive a promotion within a year of completing the program (37 percent of women vs. 51 percent of men).

Clearly, leadership programs alone—even very good ones—are not enough to close the gender gap.

SCHOOL DAYS

What's true in corporate America and in Washington is also true in academia. A major MIT report describes what happens all too often to talented women.[24]

Having attained the distinction of a tenured professorship at the prestigious MIT School of Science, six women had no reason (and no data) to believe they were being shortchanged in several aspects key to their continued academic success or to question their status relative to their male colleagues. Yet when they got together, they found that as a group, they had smaller offices, fewer opportunities to speak at international conferences and smaller support staffs, among other things.

A committee formed to investigate the situation found that each generation of young women—including currently senior faculty members—had at one time believed that gender discrimination had been "solved" in the previous generation and that it wouldn't affect them. Gradually, however, their eyes were opened to the realization that the playing field was not level after all, and that they had paid a high price both personally and professionally as a result.

Will today's eager, talented young women, like those before them, believe that the discrimination problem is solved and wind up paying the same high price?

A similar situation to the one at MIT has been identified at the Harvard Medical School.[25] Several outstanding untenured female researchers were invited to Harvard to work with leaders in their fields. Having been courted for and feeling privileged to have these opportunities, the women did not think to question their situation. Again, when provided with the relevant information, they discovered that they were more likely than their male peers to have a shared rather than a private office, a smaller start-up package, fewer opportunities to apply for research grants and so forth. Perhaps most egregiously, senior male faculty appropriated their important research findings for internal use while prohibiting them from publishing those findings under their own names. These discriminatory practices severely limited, if not precluded, their opportunities to advance up the tenure ladder at Harvard.

Interestingly, these women had no family responsibilities; they either had no children or their children were grown. Thus, the men who created and perpetrated these inequities could not blame the women's failure to succeed on the familiar excuse that their family demands precluded their total devotion to their jobs, which was key to their success.

And it isn't only in the prestigious Ivies that women are getting the short straw. In the wake of the MIT report, many universities started to look at the situation of women on their own faculties. Nine universities—MIT, Harvard, CalTech, Princeton, Stanford, Yale, the University of Michigan, the University of Pennsylvania, and the University of California at Berkeley—concluded that "barriers still exist" to prevent progress for female academics.[26] While the original focus was on science, they found that the gender inequity problem was broader, extending "beyond science, to women in academic fields throughout higher education."

Here are some of their findings:

- Women faculty are typically slower to be promoted than men.
- Women are doing less well at attaining positions of power within their departments.
- Women, especially senior-level women, typically report more job dissatisfaction than their male counterparts.
- Female faculty report more stress associated with balancing work and family.
- Female junior faculty members generally receive less professional mentoring than their male counterparts.

Universities across the country have started to look closely at how women faculty members are treated, and the same inequalities emerge. MIT biology professor Nancy Hopkins, a longtime champion of women in science, says that women "don't have the confidence level to get to the top."[27] She notes the cumulative effect of small setbacks throughout a career and says that women are "getting undercut. People tend to think that the problem has gone away, but alas, it hasn't."

BIAS KEEPS ON TREKKING

In a 2012 article, "Bias Persists for Women of Science, a Study Finds," the *New York Times* reported:

> Science professors at American universities widely regard female undergraduates as less competent than male students with the same accomplishments and skills, a new study by researchers at Yale concluded.
>
> As a result, the report found, the professors were less likely to offer the women mentoring or a job. And even if they were willing to offer a job, the salary was lower.
>
> The bias was pervasive, the scientists said, and probably reflected subconscious cultural influences rather than overt or deliberate discrimination.
>
> Female professors were just as biased against women students as their male colleagues, and biology professors just as biased as physics professors—even though more than half of biology majors are women, whereas men far outnumber women in physics.[28]

The study was a simple one. The Yale researchers submitted résumés to professors in the biology, chemistry and physics departments at six major research universities and asked for evaluations of the candidates for a lab manager position. Each professor received the same single-page summary of a promising candidate. The only difference was that half of the résumés were from "John" and the other half from

"Jennifer." And not surprisingly, the fictitious John did much better than the fictitious Jennifer.

"I think we were all just a little bit surprised at how powerful the results were—that not only do the faculty in biology, chemistry and physics express these biases quite clearly, but the significance and strength of the results was really quite striking," Jo Handelsman, a Yale molecular, cellular and developmental biology professor, told the *Times*.

The same problems were found in Sweden, a country thought to be a paragon of gender fairness. It turns out that the Swedish Medical Research Council, which funds biomedical research, does not evaluate women and men on an equal basis when awarding prestigious fellowships.[29] When men and women were rated for scientific competence, males fared far better—even when they weren't as good as women: a female applicant had to be 2.5 times more productive than the average male applicant to receive the same competence rating that he did. The most productive group of female applicants (those with 100 points or more for publication, research, etc.) was the only group of women judged to be as competent as men. Even then, astonishingly, these female achievers were only judged to be as competent as the *least* productive group of male applicants (those with fewer than 20 points).

Why does this happen?

Often, it's because the people doing the ranking, the hiring or the promoting are not relying on the hard facts they see before them. Instead, they make decisions on quite subjective grounds. So, the woman with the great résumé and the impressive track record can wind up losing out to a less capable man because of a decision made on factors other than the objective record.

If this all sounds unfair, it's because it is. Doing well should bring rewards—for everybody. Today it doesn't, and we need to change that.

THREE

COMPETENT BUT UNLIKABLE?

When Harvard professor and consumer activist Elizabeth Warren ran against handsome jock Scott Brown for a Massachusetts Senate seat, critics claimed she wasn't warm and fuzzy enough. A *New York Times* story said, "There have also been worries that Ms. Warren comes across as a scold when she speaks directly into the camera."[1] The *Boston Globe* chided her for her TV ads, claiming that she had "wasted millions on ads that turned her into every man's worst nightmare: a smarter-than-thou older woman sporting granny glasses and sensible hair."[2] Warren quickly changed her TV campaign ads to feature other people talking about how warm and caring she was.

Researchers at Marquette Law School have found that "all political candidates are subject to attack from supporters of their opponent, but female candidates, especially in high-profile offices such as president and vice president, appear to face targeted gender attacks. Specifically for Hillary Clinton and Sarah Palin [in the 2008 campaign], these gendered attacks mirrored the two sides of the double bind; one was consistently portrayed as competent, but unlikeable and the other likeable, but incompetent, respectively.

"With Hillary Clinton, everybody agreed she was smart, but was she likable? The media generally decreed that she was not. On January 4, 2008, Neil Cavuto of Fox News' *Your World*, declared, 'Men won't vote for Hillary Clinton because she reminds them of their nagging wives. And when Hillary Clinton speaks, we hear 'Take out the garbage!'"[3]

When a reporter asked Clinton about her likability in a debate during the New Hampshire primary, she said, "I don't think I'm *that* bad." Barack Obama dismissively replied, "You're likable enough, Hillary."

But when she showed a softer side and shed a few tears, the media were equally critical. On January 4, 2008, Glenn Beck announced, "Big news from New Hampshire tonight is: It cries! After spending decades stripping away all trace of emotion, femininity, and humanity, Hillary Clinton actually broke down and actually cried yesterday on the campaign trail!"[4]

The *New York Times* headlined a Maureen Dowd column this way: "Can Hillary Clinton Cry Her Way to the White House?"[5] ABC News said, "Whether Clinton has appeared too emotional, too sensitive or too weak in her recent public appearances is still up for debate."[6]

Clinton lost the election, was appointed secretary of state, got rave reviews for her diplomacy and is now respected around the world. She's being mentioned as the frontrunner for the Democratic presidential nomination in 2016. How will she be received the next time around? If she once again goes for the top job, will she still be seen as the angry, shrill, overambitious woman of the 2008 campaign trail, or as the revered stateswoman of today?

Sarah Palin also fell into the likability-competence gap. She was caricatured as a good-looking "hottie," a caring hockey mom and a hopeless idiot—though certainly her gaffes in interviews led to much of the criticism.

After Carly Fiorina, who was pushed out as CEO of Hewlett-Packard in 2005, threw her hat into the California Senate race, the *Fiscal Times* said, "Fortunately for the three-term Democratic incumbent, Barbara Boxer, her challenger, the Silicon Valley executive Carly Fiorina, has proven to be unlikable enough to possibly lose an election that Republicans might have handily won with a stronger candidate."[7]

And when Fiorina was at HP, her gender was a constant factor. As she writes in her memoir, *Tough Choices*, "Because I was a reasonably attractive woman, some people assumed I wasn't capable."[8]

That could sound like the paranoid excuse of a fired executive, but Fiorina is far from wrong in her assessment. Being attractive and forceful is a combination that can be a double whammy for women heading for the top. As we've said, a major problem for women who are clearly competent is that they are also often judged as unlikable. Competent women violate the traditional female stereotype of passivity. And that violation can trigger a reaction of fear and loathing. In fact, the more accomplished that females become, and the higher they rise, the more they may suffer in the workplace; if they're viewed as efficient, caring and good with people, they may well be dismissed as not strong enough. Harvard Business School professor Rosabeth Moss Kanter said, "If women are seen as only glorified office facilitators but not as tough-minded risk-takers, they will be held back from the CEO jobs."[9] But if they are seen as too strong, they can also lose out.

NYU's Madeline Heilman has found that forceful women are characterized as conniving or untrustworthy—what she calls "your typical constellation of 'bitchy' characteristics."[10] She says that often, such women are seen as "not just unlikable, but downright awful."[11] Unfortunately, women frequently are not even aware of this dynamic. The Duke University *Chronicle* reported that when Heilman gave a lecture mentioning the "bitchiness cluster," her words "actually elicited gasps from her audience."[12] Those young college women who had assumed that the sky was the limit for them were stunned to imagine that they might be seen in this way. Sure, they could imagine this happening to their mothers thirty years ago, but not today, in this brave new world for women.

A stunning example of this sort of over-the-top reaction to a powerful woman occurred in April 2013, just after the *New York Times* had won four Pulitzers for its outstanding journalism. You'd think that Jill Abramson, the first female editor of the *Times*, would be basking in the golden glow of this accomplishment. But the opposite occurred.

A savage profile on the influential website Politico pictured her as stubborn, nasty, condescending, difficult to work with and too hard-driving.[13] The piece used anonymous sources to blast her: "Every editor has a story about how she's blown up in a meeting," said one. Another complained, "Jill can be impossible."

Women journalists around the country were outraged. Many remembered the praise lavished on the "tough-as-nails" male editors they had worked for. These guys could punch walls, make staffers weep, blow their stacks in meetings and make impossible demands. If Abramson was a male, they asked, would the story be the same? Would there even *be* a story?

Writer Tricia Romano explained it on the Daily Beast website: "Translation: Jill Abramson is a shrill, hysteria-fueled bitch. Why isn't she handing out cookies at the Page One meeting? . . . The most depressing thing about this article is that we've been here before, many, many times, with regard to stories about women in power. Nearly every time a woman reaches the pinnacle of her career, there is an accompanying piece about how hard she is to work with, how bitchy she is, or how she's not in keeping with the old-fashioned notions that women are lovely and amazing."[14]

One senior academic woman observed that male faculty members can be assertive—even bullying or mean—in meetings, but when a woman seems too strong-minded or assertive, she gets tuned out and becomes disliked. She told us, "I know that if I have a strong point to make—especially if I am going to be critical of what a male colleague has said—I have to make nice and toss in a lot of chunks of carrot before I resort to the stick. It's not fair, and it makes women have to work a lot harder for less power."

Sallie Krawcheck, who was ousted from her job leading Bank of America's wealth management division, told *Marie Claire*: "I've thought a lot about the issue of stereotypes, particularly on Wall Street. I can't count the number of times I have seen men slam something on a table, even throw something. You sort of do a mental eye roll and move on. I can count on one hand—on *one finger*—the number of tantrums I've seen a woman have. As she was having it, I remember thinking to myself, *Bitch*. So if *I'm* having that view, it's hard to imagine that someone else isn't having the same view. Women need to operate in narrower emotional channels than men."[15]

Women we interviewed confronted the same dilemma. Sarah, a senior urban planner, said, "I find that this happens to me on a regular basis. I am a forthright person, and I generally will go out on a limb to have the hard conversations, but I often get criticized for being aggressive when I don't think that I have been out of line."

A lawyer at a global medical device company told us, "This is a very challenging issue. Male execs here have actually hit other employees and were not held accountable in any apparent way, while I received a reprimand for much less egregious behavior. My current boss has more than once been dismissive and harsh in his commentary to me, and it has been very difficult for me to manage [his hostility] without fear of incurring additional reprimands."

Marie, a senior consultant at a management company, was given the impression that her assertiveness was valued. "They told me that I needed to be more in control of the team and that it was good that I lost my temper and told the guys to step up, as it would make them pay attention," she said. "Then I got dropped from the project when my colleague undermined me." The complaining male got the job that should have been Marie's. "He was junior to me and had never implemented the technology before, versus my ten years of experience."

And a journalist in her mid-thirties at a major news organization said, "I once made a joke about what seemed like an unfair situation at work—a joke just pointing out how ridiculous the whole thing was, thinking it could lighten the situation and get people to rethink it. I was formally reprimanded. It scared the hell out of me. I thought I was being fired. A male coworker regularly and publicly made cruel jokes about individuals, but this was ignored (my joke was not cruel or personal)."

Jacqueline, an assistant general counsel for a medical products company, said, "Bad behavior by men is rewarded at my company, at least as far as upper management is concerned. Screaming, demeaning and accusing language and throwing other team members 'under the bus' results in promotions for men. Women are promoted when they are conciliatory and work cross-functionally to meet unreasonable deadlines."

An attorney for a global technology company told us, "I have struggled to control my emotions, with limited success. I got angry and was reprimanded for it with a threat of discharge for any additional infraction, and the reprimand was to live in my personnel file for three years (it is still there, as HR would not remove it even when I asked them to do so after three years). A man actually hit someone in this organization a few years ago and was not only not reprimanded, but was ultimately promoted, with no apparent accountability or repercussions."

Geraldine, a senior consultant at an IT services company, said, "I was specifically told by my supervisor to be more forceful and in control of a project, but as soon as I called a guy out on his lack of productivity and obstructive behavior, I was 'told off' for not being collaborative and for coming across as being difficult."

It's not only men, but women as well, who have an adverse reaction to assertive female managers. Kristin, the vice president of a global public relations agency, said, "Surprisingly, I find that both men and women have this response to a female manager. It's incredible that when someone objectively screws up, I'm somehow perceived as being 'too hard' or 'too regimented' when I address it. My objective feedback is received as subjective critique—which it is not. I'm not saying 'I don't like you' if I critique your work. I'm simply saying, 'You messed up. Let's fix it and make sure it doesn't happen again.' Yet somehow, people take it personally and project it back onto me. Women do it to other women as much if not more than men, oddly."

Alicia, a marketing communications manager for a major international firm, reported, "During a time of rumored layoffs, everyone in my department was stressed out. One male coworker who was prone to outbursts frequently got away with a simple reprimand from our boss. Whereas I had a handful of outbursts, and in my performance review I was told that I was a 'bitch' and 'if I were a man [my outbursts] wouldn't be a problem.' I was laid off a few weeks later. The male coworker? Still there."

Laurie A. Rudman, a psychologist at Rutgers University, has called this issue a "double-edged sword for women."[16] Competent women often get high marks for their ability. But less able men who are seen as likable are more apt to be hired or promoted. In one Massachusetts company, a candidate for a top job impressed the firm's executives with her stellar résumé and no-nonsense manner. Her competition was a man who was older and less of a star, but he was perceived as real nice guy—someone you'd want to have a beer with. He got the nod.

One way that male leaders get ahead is by aggressively promoting their own accomplishments. You'd think women could do the same. Not so. Men are admired for tooting their own horns, if they aren't too obnoxious about it. Women are disliked for violating the feminine stereotype of modesty and subservience. Hilary Lips, director of the Center for Gender Studies at Virginia's Radford University, says, "When women promote their own accomplishments, it can cause their audience to view them as more competent—but at the cost of viewing them as less likeable."[17]

This held true for Jill Barad when she was selected to head the toy giant Mattel. Barad had been spectacularly successful in running the Barbie brand for Mattel, but when she moved into the top job, she really irritated many men. *BusinessWeek* described Barad's style this way: "Glamorous and radiant, she seems more Hollywood than corporate."[18] That rubbed people the wrong way as she politicked her way to the top. "Many men hated me," she told *BusinessWeek*. "I think it can be a tough thing for a man to lose to a woman." Early in her career, a supervisor called the young Barad into his office and took her to task for her self-promotion and outspokenness. "'You shouldn't pretend to know all the answers,'" she recalls him telling her, and warning her that she "'wouldn't go far.'"

Barad promoted herself aggressively, and some Mattel execs referred to her hard-driving, flamboyant manner as "the Jill factor."

BusinessWeek quoted Geraldine Laybourne, president of Disney/ABC Cable Networks, as saying, "These people calling her abrasive, have they met Ted Turner? Have they met Michael Eisner? Compared to most CEOs, she is not abrasive. But maybe compared to their wives she is."

The focus on her style may have been in part due to the fact that it was hard to fault her on intelligence. In *Toy Monster*, author Jerry Oppenheimer says, "*Ladies' Home Journal* bestowed upon her the honor of being one of America's 10 smartest women. How many executives can make that claim?"[19]

Along with her superior intelligence, she had spectacular looks. You'd think that the combination of looks and smarts would be a winning one. Not so for women. For a "gorgeous, vampy female," Oppenheimer says, "there is always lots of gossip about how they got to be on top, and there was such chatter about Barad. But beyond her appearance, and allure, there was a brilliant business mind at work."

One of the tenets of the New Soft War is that what works for men all too frequently undercuts women. Men who are handsome rarely raise suspicion or attract the negative personal attention that beautiful women get. Carly Fiorina noted that being an attractive woman was held against her, and that was true in spades for Barad. It probably didn't help her likability that *People* magazine named her one of its "50 Most Beautiful People" in 1994, noting, "Barad's own vibrant looks are unforgettable."[20] The article focused on her appearance and quoted her as saying, "By 16, I never left the house without lipstick or eye makeup. It was the time of Twiggy, when you did patent-leather liner and false eyelashes."

Barad's crash was as spectacular as her rise. *Fortune* put her at the top of its list of "five chiefs who need to wake up—fast." Calling her "the consummate marketer," *Fortune* said that "she has made the big mistake of using her style of promotion and hoopla (which worked so well to build Barbie into a global brand) on Wall Street. She told investors the business looked fine . . . just before Mattel revealed huge sales and earnings shortfalls."[21]

Certainly, Barad made some very bad decisions; but when she started to slip, there was no helping hand to get her back on track. She was left holding the bag for corporate decisions that were *not* all her doing. For sure, other executives and board members had a voice in these same decisions. It's reasonable to ask whether a man in the same position would have been dispatched so quickly. Maybe. But Jill Barad didn't get a second chance.

That isn't true of some top financial executives who made colossal errors in the 2008 financial crisis yet remain in their top positions. Lloyd Blankfein is still CEO at Goldman Sachs, despite accusations of corporate misbehavior. The firm agreed to pay $550 million to settle claims that it had misled investors in a mortgage security it sold. At Merrill Lynch, CEO John Thain presided over a stunning loss of $15 billion in the fourth quarter of 2008 after a merger with Bank of America. Thain was forced out, but now he is CEO of the megabank CIT Group—quite a second chance.

Barad and Fiorina probably suffered from the fact there are many more ways for a woman to be disliked than a man, plus from a double standard. When a man speaks at length and with authority, people listen. When women do the same, they are seen as talking too much and get tuned out. Hilary Lips mentions one study in which women and men were told to use the same expressions and the same words when leading a group meeting. Lips notes, "Group members responded to the male would-be leaders' comments with attention, nods, and smiles; they responded to the women by looking away and frowning. Furthermore, these group members were not aware that they were treating would-be female and male leaders differently."[22]

This pattern occurs in the real world as well as in the research lab. Field studies of small group meetings within organizations show that female leaders are more often the target of displays of negative emotion than male leaders, even when both sets of leaders are viewed as equally competent. Claire Babrowski, the former CEO of RadioShack, says that when people close their eyes and visualize the top dogs sitting around the corporate table, "we picture men in leadership roles. As a woman you already have this hurdle to overcome."[23]

On Wall Street, this problem is intensified. Catalyst CEO Ilene H. Lang explains it this way: "The Wall Street culture is characterized by what you might call really macho kinds of behavior. So what's looked up to on Wall Street are people who swagger, people who will do the deal at any cost, people who will work day and night, hour and hour, for lots and lots of money and they don't care about anything else. . . . Women who behave in those macho ways are then perceived as being very masculine, and that's considered very unattractive. While men are aggressive, women are labeled with the 'B word.' It is behavior that's admired in men but despised in women."[24]

On "the Street" and in much of corporate America, there are success stories, but way too few. Lang says, "There have been very few role models, and they haven't lasted very long."

THE ANGRY WOMAN

Anger is problematic for women. Anger expression is an effective means for attaining higher status for men; for women, it has the opposite effect. When men express anger at work, male and female evaluators judge them to be powerful, competent and worthy of a high salary. Angry women, on the other hand, are seen much less favorably. They are viewed as less competent, less powerful and less likely to be paid a high salary.

The editor of a weekly newspaper told us, "Throughout most of my journalism career, I have been regarded, to one degree or another, as a rabble-rouser and someone willing to tell bosses unpleasant truths. This has not kept me from advancing, to some degree. But I know that I am regarded by some as formidable or unapproachable. I cannot say I have seen men getting credit for getting angry, but I can tell you I have never gotten any credit for it, at least not with bosses—even when I do my best to present my objections calmly and constructively."

Another woman said, "When I get angry, I'm [seen as] overreacting or a bitch. When they get angry, it's justified."

Stephanie, the vice president of an energy association, shared this experience: "I actually had my president—upset about meeting budgets—enter my office, grab me by the shoulders, shake me and state, 'I am so mad I could just choke you . . . but I like you too much.' I lodged a formal complaint to the board of directors (his supervisors) requesting a formal apology and that he attend anger management or leadership training. They hired an attorney to do interviews about the incident and report back to the board. After all was said and done, I found out he denied the 'touch.' The formal apology? He came into my office and said, 'This is in response to your request,' and handed me an envelope with a one-sentence memo stating that he 'apologizes for the incident' without an actual signature; he copied a JPEG file of his signature and applied it to the memo. Furthermore, when the board chair called me to report on the outcome (that an apology is forthcoming and the president will get some training), he then continued on to berate me, saying, 'He is your boss! And he has financial expectations.' Regardless, it sure doesn't justify the action."

Research by psychologists Victoria Brescoll, an assistant professor at the Yale School of Management, and Eric Uhlmann, formerly a research associate at Northwestern University and now an assistant professor at HEC Paris, shows that even a women's status in the organizational hierarchy will not protect her from the harsh judgments her anger evokes. A woman who expresses anger is thought to be of lower status than a man, "regardless of whether she is a powerful executive or a lowly trainee."[25] Amazingly, evaluators were willing to pay unemotional females more money than angry females—even when the angry women were high-ranking CEOs.

For men, rank bested anger. Evaluators did not punish male CEOs who got angry, as they did with women.

Why are angry women penalized? Because women simply aren't supposed to be angry. We know that when a stereotype is violated, the tendency is to explain the violation as due to some personal failing, not to some provocation that calls for anger. So, a woman may be seen as an angry, out-of-control person, no matter what caused her reaction. "As a result, a professional woman's anger may imply that she is not competent at dealing with workplace situations," according to Brescoll and Uhlmann. Her anger may therefore lead those around her to accord her less status.

However, when men explode, the picture is very different. Their anger is seen as understandable; they're just getting mad when someone screws up or a plan falls apart. They're OK—their competence isn't questioned. They don't lose status.

How can women break the anger-incompetence link? We'll deal with that in our concluding chapter.

THE SOUND OF SILENCE— MORE IS LESS

Successful women know that powerful leaders command the airwaves, dominating the discourse to shape opinion and influence others. Yet they hold back because they fear that talking too much will be seen as a negative. And they are right. In a 2012 study, Victoria Brescoll found that the rules of the power game differ for men and women.

Using actual speech data from the U.S. Senate, she discovered a significant relationship between power and volubility (i.e., the total time senators spoke on the Senate floor). This finding was not surprising, Brescoll noted, because "the more an individual verbally participates, the more likely that individual will be seen as having power. Therefore, volubility not only plays an important role in establishing power hierarchies but also in communicating one's power to others."[26]

However, there was a twist: Male senators showed a significant relationship between power and volubility, but female senators did not.

Using additional experimental data, Brescoll found that "a female CEO who talked disproportionately longer than others in an organizational setting was rated as significantly less competent and less suitable for leadership than a male CEO who talked for an equivalent amount of time." Moreover, these ratings were similar for male and female perceivers.

In short, when men talk, people see them as powerful. When women talk, people see them as incompetent and unsuited for leading. It's the classic catch-22.

What is going on? It appears that all of us, men and women alike, share similar views about gender and power. The higher men are in the status hierarchy, the more power they are seen to have and the more others expect them to behave powerfully. A male CEO who is high in volubility is seen as more competent and suitable for leadership than his low-volubility male counterpart. For men, high status and talkativeness fit together easily. Bill Clinton, for example, is well known for continuing his speeches after the red "stop" light has flashed on. He ran over his presentation time at the 2012 Democratic National Convention, but his performance was labeled "masterful" by the press.

But the same is *not* true for women. It seems that we all like women better when they talk less. A female CEO who is low in volubility is seen as equally competent and deserving of leadership as a highly voluble male CEO. High-status behavior for women bumps up against the "nice" female stereotype.

This incongruity sets up a conflict for women—especially high-status women—that men never have to deal with. Would Hillary Clinton have talked as long as her husband did if she had been the one giving the speech? Probably not. Brescoll reported that high-power women adjust their volubility so that their talking time is virtually identical to that of low-power women and low-power men.

What's happening? In a follow-up study, Brescoll found one answer. High-power women are "concerned about the potential backlash that may result from appearing to talk too much."

If you are giving a major speech, and you have to worry not only about how to present the material clearly and logically but also about being seen as a "blabby woman," you have stress that a man would never experience.

One former judge told us, "Men seem to prefer that women speak less, and they react negatively when I voice comments or opinions; however, they then seem to assume that by speaking less, I have nothing to contribute. I have actually been verbally 'shut down' when trying to speak on behalf of other women in the workplace."

A female manager at Goldman Sachs commented, "Men seem to speak with confidence (even if it is not justified) that then instills others with confidence in that person. A man who works for me has relatively weak skills in my area of expertise. Yet he speaks confidently, and no one else in the organization seems to recognize his weaknesses."

Marge, a senior corporate trainer said, "My communication style is pretty direct and concise. So I speak up often but generally make targeted remarks. A female boss actually provided the following feed-back in a performance appraisal when addressing this tendency. 'You give the impression that you know more than you should know.'"

A business development coordinator at a major law firm told us, "Women are expected to know what to do at all times and speak very little, if at all, and asking questions is perceived as a sign of weakness."

Jenny, a director of risk management strategy, said, "I've spent my career working in historically male-dominated fields, and it's striking to me how much women are still considered 'nags' when they speak up frequently. I find it incredibly sad that this sentiment often comes from fellow women. Why do we continue to find other strong, competent women threatening? I'm proud to say that the women in senior leader-ship roles in my current organization are actively working to eliminate the tendency for women to trample each other on the way up and in-stead encourage each other to make their ideas and opinions—and *voices*—heard!"

Both women and men expect high-status individuals, men and women, to behave in ways that reflect their power—being forceful, clear and decisive. At the same time, we expect all women to be defer-ential, thoughtful and considerate of others.

So, women are stuck between a rock and a hard place, trying to be ambitious without overdoing it. According to the 2007 Work and Pow-er Survey of 60,000 people conducted by *Elle* magazine and MSNBC .com, stereotypes about sex and leadership are alive and well. The survey found that women don't want to appear too confident and aggressive for fear of being labeled bitchy. But they also don't want to be consid-ered wishy-washy or risk being called indecisive or emotional.[27]

When Lauren Stiller Rikleen interviewed female lawyers for her book about gender barriers in the legal profession, she reported how dismayed she was at "seeing strong women lose their voice entirely. It was hard to reconcile the strong and intelligent women interviewed with their frequent stories about circumstances in which they became silenced when faced with behavior they felt was threatening or which undermined their ability to succeed. Story after story emerged striking this similar theme."[28]

For example, one female partner said she was upset that the women in her firm would not speak out on issues regarding women: "It wasn't power as much as it was voice. I think there are still a lot of issues for women to be able to stand up and speak [about] and I think the problem is that we don't want to speak about them."

Other women told Rikleen that their silence was expected and that when they spoke up, they become branded. "I think it turns them [supervisors] off," one lawyer said. "I think that then you become the 'troubled person.' You become the thorn in the side and eventually they find reasons to say, 'well, you know you're not working out as well as we said you were.'"

For female lawyers, the silence imperative can start in law school. Lani Guinier, who studied students at the University of Pennsylvania Law School, reported that the competitive, hierarchical culture at such prestigious schools encouraged peers to put down female students. "Many women who complained that their voices are pushed down, suffocated early on by hostile first year classmates, described how those women who did speak out felt humiliated by male—and sometimes female—contemporaries."[29]

Women talk less, whether alone or in groups. When men and women work together to solve a problem, women speak only 75 percent as much as men do, according to researchers at Brigham Young University. Chris Karpowitz, a political scientist at the university, says, "Women have something unique and important to add to the group, and that's being lost, at least under some circumstances."[30]

Perhaps because they are so new at it, women have trouble using power.

"There is a large space between *having power* and *being powerful*," according to CEO coach Henna Inam.[31] "Women have historically had a love hate relationship with power. Personally, I am one of them. In some situations in my corporate career, I was in positions of great power but had a hard time exercising it. As women, we have fought throughout history for our rights to be empowered. Why then can we be so ambivalent about power when we get it?"

Inam recounts how her company requested that she transfer to Mexico "to turn the business around." She says, "I had P&L [profit and loss] responsibility, leadership for all functions (including a manufacturing plant and R&D), in total an organization of about 600 people. I felt energized by the challenge. Our turnaround strategy included rapid new product introductions and our team came together to make this happen."

She ran up against a local plant manager whose main agenda was cutting costs. Her plan for developing new products collided with his cost-cutting plans. Like her, he also had a direct line to top management. She asks, "Who had the power to make the call? Technically, me, as I was the P&L leader. Did I exercise that power? Not really. Not the way most men would. Make the call. Move on. Instead of asserting, I found myself negotiating, cajoling, bridge-building. It was a longer and frankly much more painful process, and I didn't necessarily feel very powerful through it."

Clearly, the issue of women and power is complex and involves the culture of the workplace as well as individual expectations and behavior. Problems around this issue are not going to vanish overnight, and the New Soft War can't be won until women can hold power without being punished by others or always second-guessing their own actions.

FOUR

THE GLASS CLIFF AND THE GLASS ESCALATOR

When you look at a major American company on the brink of crisis, what do you often see? A woman dangling by her fingertips, trying not to plunge into the dark abyss below.

It's a phenomenon that foretells danger for women who climb too high. Today, the story of women being chosen to steer companies through troubled waters is so well known that it has a catchy nickname: the "glass cliff."

We all applaud when we hear that a woman has been given a great opportunity to head a major company. But hold the cheers. Dangers may lurk in high places.

Female business leaders are more likely to be appointed to powerful positions when an organization is in crisis or in high-risk circumstances. In short, these women are perched on a glass cliff, set up for failure. Why do women end up in this position? Is it because they are viewed as more capable or because they are more easily sacrificed? Researchers Michelle K. Ryan and Alexander Haslam of England's Exeter University found that "a company's poor performance is a trigger for the appointment of women to the board."[1] Women then become lightning rods—blamed for negative outcomes that were set in motion well before they assumed their new roles.

It's typically a no-win situation for women when a company's circumstances are so precarious that only a Hail Mary pass will save the day. If the new female leader fails, people mutter, "See what happens when you put a woman in charge."

Kristin J. Anderson, an associate professor of psychology at the University of Houston–Downtown, speculates in *Psychology Today*: "One possible reason for putting women in positions with greater risk of failure is that women may be seen as more expendable and better scapegoats. If you believe that men are natural leaders, if a company fails under a man's leadership, you would look for explanations for the failure other than the man's gender. In contrast, if you believe that women don't really belong in positions of authority, and if a company fails under a woman's leadership, you might point to the leader's gender as the explanation. . . . A more cynical explanation is that organizational leadership might believe that putting women in high risk positions is a win-win strategy: If a woman succeeds after being placed in a difficult position, then the organization is better off; and if she fails, the woman can be blamed and the prior practice of appointing men can be justified and resurrected. At the same time, the organization can present itself as egalitarian and progressive."[2]

The glass cliff has become a buzzword in management circles. When Marissa Mayer got the job as Yahoo! CEO, her possible failure was one of the first things everybody talked about. *Forbes* asked, "Did Marissa Mayer just receive the job offer of a lifetime or did she just ascend to the pinnacle of the glass cliff?"[3]

The Daily Beast wondered whether Mayer was "headed toward a savage plunge off the 'glass cliff.'"[4]

Meg Whitman, named CEO of Hewlett-Packard in 2011, was number three on *Fortune*'s list of the 50 most powerful women in 2012.[5] However, *Fortune* warned, "Whitman was supposed to be HP's savior, but the hoped-for turnaround has yet to materialize."[6] Is she also teetering on the glass cliff?

There is much anecdotal evidence for the glass cliff. Indeed, Hewlett-Packard itself presents a case study of this issue. One of Whitman's predecessors, Carly Fiorina, might well be poster girl for the glass cliff. Fiorina, Kate Swann of British retailer WH Smith and Patricia Russo of Paris-based global telecommunications company Alcatel-Lucent were all appointed to top positions at a time of tumbling share prices. Not that women are uniquely drafted into crisis-ridden situations—plenty of male leaders find themselves in equally rough waters—but women can be especially at risk.

In 2007, Zoe Cruz, co-president of Morgan Stanley, was pushed out of the company after a $37 billion loss that proved to be the canary in the coal mine, foretelling the coming major recession. Jay Dweck, who at the time was a Morgan Stanley executive, told the press he was astonished by the lengths to which Morgan Stanley went to put Cruz on the skids.[7] She was obviously a scapegoat; in fact, she had suggested that the company pull out of risky subprime mortgages. The men around her failed to heed the warning and wound up behind the eight ball. But they didn't pay the price.

In 2012, Jamie Dimon, CEO of JP Morgan, made headlines when he announced that the company faced a whopping $10 billion loss on risky trades. He admitted to reporters, "We took far too much risk."[8] But did Dimon's head roll? No, it didn't. Ina Drew, the chief investment officer, was the one who stepped down. "One of the top women on Wall Street," as the *New York Times* called her, was replaced by two men.[9]

Women at the top are often going it alone. Since few other women are at their level, they don't have a cheering section to promote their successes or "old buddies" to watch their back.

Janet Hanson, a former Goldman Sachs executive, told *New York* magazine, "In a bull market, women are fine. When the shit hits the fan, these guys probably don't even trust each other. Could you theorize that more women get chucked when things start going deadly?"[10] Probably.

We don't yet know whether Melissa Mayer will succeed at Yahoo!, but the company recruited Carol Bartz as its CEO in 2008 during another rocky period and then pushed her off the cliff in 2011 when results didn't improve.

At *CBS Evening News*, Katie Couric took over the anchor chair in 2009. The *New York Times* noted that "her celebrated hiring, at a salary of $15 million a year, was part of a much larger experiment to lift the newscast out of the ratings basement in which it had languished for more than a decade."[11]

From the start, many people seemed to be rooting for Couric to fail.[12] They criticized her short skirts, leaked stories about her "diva behavior" and called her flat and automaton-like in the anchor role. Dan Rather criticized CBS's decision to bring her onto the show as an attempt to "dumb it down, tart it up in hopes of attracting a younger audience."[13]

Over the long haul, Couric wasn't able to drag *CBS Evening News* out of the ratings basement, and she departed in 2012 to host her own talk show.

That same year, when NBC's *Today* show—Couric's old stomping ground—started to founder in the morning-news ratings, it was coanchor Ann Curry who was tossed out. *Baltimore Sun* critic Susan Reimer said, "*Today* held the top spot for a remarkable 16 years before stumbling to second place behind *Good Morning America* for a week in April, and it is the woman—always the bridesmaid and never the bride on *Today*—who must take the blame."[14]

Reimer noted, "Ms. Curry's critics (always quoted anonymously) say that she is cloying and hyper-empathetic when she is interviewing the victim *du jour*. That she is not engaged when doing the fluffy fashion and food segments. She doesn't have the right chemistry with host Matt Lauer, and she hasn't meshed well with the rest of the *Today* family." Curry's dismissal is part of a discouraging trend in television to feature women who are more decorative than substantive. Fox News, for example, is noted for showing pretty, long-haired blonds with revealing necklines in news programming. If Curry was being criticized for not handling the "fluff" well, and as more and more the morning TV shows get lighter and lighter, the future for serious women journalists looks increasingly bleak.

Reimer said, "It is the typical stuff you say about a woman in a job performance review, touchy-feely language rarely used when describing a guy's shortcomings. When Mr. Lauer is criticized, for example, it is for being abrasive and combative—not particularly cozy qualities for the small screen but ones that could be construed as strength in a journalist.

"This kind of thing happens all the time in television news. If ratings falter, or fail to improve, it's the woman who takes the hit for the team. . . .

"Maybe there is some special ratings tool that measures the credibility deficit of women in television, but I doubt it. If there's a problem, the easy answer is to replace the chick. Preferably with a younger, prettier chick."

Another woman who found herself on the cliff was Cathie Black, the hypersuccessful media executive who built *USA Today* for Gannett and headed Hearst Magazines. But there was an uproar when New York mayor Michael Bloomberg appointed Black, who had no experience in education, as chancellor of the city's schools. She took a beating in the media and seemed to be undercut at every turn by the school bureaucracy. After ninety-five days of constant criticism, she was let go.

Asked if she was a victim of the glass cliff, Black said that "it was like having to learn Russian in a weekend—and then give speeches in Russian and speak Russian in budget committee and City Council meetings."[15]

Given her stellar management background, Black probably could have learned fast on the job, but she wasn't given the chance. She asked, "If I were a guy, would I have had the pounding that I did?"

Often, women perched on the glass cliff get precious little support from colleagues. *Forbes* notes that "while these women were able to rise, they may not have had the deep networks of their male counterparts to vouch for them when things went sour."[16]

Couric launched a bitter attack on her former employers at CBS and claimed that she felt "liberated" after leaving the TV network. She said that her bosses made her five years of working for the company miserable because they were "projecting their own issues onto me." Anchoring *CBS Evening News* left her feeling "constrained," Couric said, and only by biting her tongue and just getting on with it could she deal with the poisonous atmosphere.[17]

In her memoir, Fiorina writes, "When I came to HP I knew about the company and the history, but I didn't fully understand the extent to which I was an outsider: non-engineer; East Coast big company, not West Coast small start-up; telecom, not computer; and then a woman on top of that. That person was such a challenge to the established way of doing things. It wasn't just the work I was trying to do; it was who I was."[18]

Of her firing, after missing earnings goals, Fiorina says, "More CEOs [were] fired in 2005 and 2006 than ever before. . . . But no firing has been treated with the same out-of-proportion publicity as mine was. It was a very public beheading."

As a woman, Fiorina was indeed more vulnerable to the chopping block than a man would have been. Recent research points to a clear-cut difference between men's and women's ability to weather risk and failure. According to a June 2008 *Harvard Business Review* report, "When female executives wrestle with stormy weather and fail to right the ship, corporate cultures can be unforgiving. Isolated women leaders find it impossible to rally support in the wake of failure. More so than men, they crash and burn."[19]

This phenomenon may be at work in politics as well. A 2010 British study found that women are often nominated for political races when the race is difficult to win. The researchers warned, "The existence of glass cliffs in the political arena has important implications for women considering a career in politics. Merely selecting women to run as candidates does nothing to improve the underrepresentation of women in politics if these positions are unwinnable. Indeed, given the electoral failure that almost inevitably follows, casting women in the role of 'sacrificial lamb' may simply reinforce the notion that women are not suitable for political office, while at the same time discouraging potential female candidates from entering the political arena. Taken together, the results . . . suggest that simply opening the door for female candidates pays mere lip-service to equality if women are not given reasonable opportunities to be elected and then contribute to politics, government, and public decision making."[20]

Add to this problem another dilemma that female candidates face. Political Parity, a program dedicated to doubling the number of women in Congress, reports that the media and the public judge female candidates' appearances, personal lives and likability more critically than they judge male candidates.' Moreover, women running for national office still get asked inappropriate questions like the absurd *Fifty Shades of Grey* query a journalist put to Senator Kirsten Gillibrand and Republican candidate Wendy Long in their sole debate in the campaign for a New York Senate seat. During a "lightning round" of questions about issues such as prostitution, guns and politics, the two candidates were asked whether they had read *Fifty Shades of Grey*. The *Atlantic*'s David A. Graham wrote: "Yes, that's right, when you get two powerful women together for their one and only *political* debate, they're forced to discuss S&M erotica. . . . Can anyone imagine this being asked in a race with any male candidates? (For that matter, would anyone ask two male candidates if they had subscriptions to *Playboy*?) We're not talking about a laugh-line about underwear at an MTV candidate forum; it's an actual question, delivered in a real debate by an accomplished journalist. There are just 17 women in the Senate today; can you blame a prospective candidate who would rather sit it out than face this sort of questioning?"[21]

THE GLASS ESCALATOR

While women are at grave risk of tumbling off a glass cliff, men are moving in the opposite direction—up.

Once upon a time, not so very long ago, men who went into stereotypically female occupations such as nursing and elementary school teaching were seen as less than macho. In the popular 2004 movie

Meet the Fockers, the fact that Ben Stiller is a male nurse is a running gag throughout the film.

But attitudes are shifting fast in our hard-pressed economy. Men are now gravitating toward female-dominated occupations, according to a recent analysis of census data by the *New York Times*.[22] The analysis shows that over a decade, from 2000 to 2010, female-dominated occupations (those that were more than 70 percent female) constituted roughly a third of male job growth, twice as much as in the previous decade.

The men the *Times* interviewed said they found themselves enjoying what used to be considered "women's work."

> "I.T. is just killing viruses and clearing paper jams all day," said Scott Kearney, 43, who tried information technology and other fields before becoming a nurse in the pediatric intensive care unit at Children's Memorial Hermann Hospital in Houston.
>
> Daniel Wilden, a 26-year-old Army veteran and nursing student at the University of Texas Health Science Center at Houston, said he had gained respect for nursing when he saw a female medic use a Leatherman tool to save the life of his comrade.

A male dental assistant in Houston, Miguel Alquicira, age twenty-one, the *Times* said,

> graduated from high school in a desolate job market, one in which the traditional opportunities, like construction and manufacturing, for young men without a college degree had dried up. After career counselors told him that medical fields were growing, he borrowed money for an eight-month training course. Since then, he has had no trouble finding jobs that pay $12 or $13 an hour.

He gave little thought to the fact that more than 90 percent of dental assistants and hygienists are women. But then, young men like Mr. Alquicira have come of age in a world of inverted expectations, where women far outpace men in earning degrees and tend to hold jobs that have turned out to be, by and large, more stable, more difficult to outsource, and more likely to grow.

"The way I look at it," Mr. Alquicira explained, without a hint of awareness that he was turning the tables on a time-honored feminist creed, "is that anything, basically, that a woman can do, a guy can do."

Men who move into what used to be female territory are doing very well—better than women, in fact. In the twenty most common occupations for women, according to the Institute for Women's Policy Research, men outearn women in all but two.[23] For example, the median weekly earnings for a female social worker are $798, while for a male they are $902.

White men in these fields are climbing aboard what's coming to be called the "glass escalator." They get a double boost from being white and being male and rise more quickly than equally qualified women and non-white men in position, pay and benefits.[24]

This is in stark contrast to what happens to women who move into male-dominated fields. Historically, token women have faced discrimination and marginalization and are often overlooked for promotions, even when their work is stellar.

Intriguingly, the glass escalator seems to operate for white men in female-dominant jobs only when they are supervised by women or members of minority groups. (That applies to a lot of men, because women often have seniority in these fields.) This effect was published in a 2010 study by sociologist Ryan Smith at Baruch College, City University of New York.[25]

As they move up the glass escalator, white male supervisors also have a greater probability than minority men of receiving lucrative retirement benefits, thereby further widening both the gender and color wage gaps. Smith suggests three possible explanations for why female and minority managers favor white men:

- "White men bring their privileges with them when they enter female-dominated occupations, and women and minority supervisors may simply yield to the weight of these societal stereotypes."
- "Women and minority supervisors may cater to white male subordinates to bolster the perception that they are fair and unbiased and perhaps to ward off any accusations of reverse discrimination."
- "They may favor white male subordinates to increase their own status in the eyes of their white male peers and superiors." As Smith says, "Just as some mentors are partial to their most promising protégés, women and minority mentors may take a special interest in white male protégés because they possess two socially valued statuses."

In the process, of course, women and minority males may be reinforcing job barriers that were built on a foundation of bias. By buying into the legitimacy of white male privilege, they make it harder for others to rise up the ranks and enjoy top pay, promotions and benefits.

Christine Williams, chair of the Department of Sociology of the University of Texas, Austin, says, "Men are effectively being 'kicked upstairs.' . . . Those specialties considered more legitimate practice areas for men also tend to be the most prestigious, better paying ones. A distinguished kindergarten teacher, who had been voted city-wide 'Teacher of the Year,' told me that even though people were pleased to see him in the classroom, 'there's been some encouragement to think about administration, and there's been some encouragement to think about teaching at the university level or something like that, or supervisory-type position.'"[26]

How many female kindergarten teachers, even those known to be excellent at what they do, are encouraged to move up the ladder to administration or to college teaching?

One stunning fact that Williams uncovered is that women tend to downplay their gender because it might be "a source of scorn and derision," while men emphasize their maleness and find that doing so pays off. When asked whether his male professors explicitly encouraged him, one librarian said, "Definitely." Two male professors and the dean were solidly in his corner. "It wasn't in the classroom, and it wasn't in front of the group, or if we were in the student lounge or something like that. It was . . . just myself or maybe another one of the guys just talking in the office." He called it "kind of an opening up and saying, 'You know, you are really lucky that you're in the profession because you'll really go to the top real quick, and you'll be able to make real definite improvements and changes. And you'll have a real influence,' I can remember [that happening] several times."

The same man described how his female classmates were excluded from these informal chats: "A lot of times in the classroom there would be discussions about a particular topic or issue, and the conversation would spill over into their office hours, after the class was over. And even though there were . . . a couple of the other women that had been in on the discussion, they weren't there. And I don't know if that was preferential or not. . . . It certainly carried over into personal life as well. Not just at the school and that sort of thing. I mean, we would get together for dinner."

Such on-the-job friendships have positive consequences for men in "female" jobs. Men found that they were well accepted by both male and female supervisors. But their female colleagues had a harder time. One male nurse told Williams, "I think the women seem like they have a lot more trouble with the physicians treating them in a derogatory manner—or if not derogatory, then in a very paternalistic way—than the men. Usually if a physician is mad at a male nurse, he just kind of yells at him . . . like an employee. And if they're mad at a female nurse, rather than treat them on an equal basis, in terms of just letting their anger out at them as an employee, they're more paternalistic or there's some sexual harassment component to it."

One male Massachusetts teacher admitted that his friendship with his principal helped him get his current job. They shared activities— music and running—and "just seemed to get along real well right off the bat." The teacher said, "It is just kind of a guy thing; we just liked each other."

Ironically, the more "female" the occupation, the better men do in it. When asked whether he had encountered any problem getting a job in pediatrics, a male Massachusetts nurse said, "No, no, none. . . . I've heard this from managers and supervisory-type people with men in pediatrics: 'It's nice to have a man because it's such a female dominated profession.'"

A male teacher commented, "I am extremely marketable in special education. That's not why I got into the field. But I am extremely marketable because I am a man."

For men, it's a win-win-win situation. Their male professors and bosses encourage and promote them, their female supervisors put them on the glass escalator, they advance quickly to supervisory positions that pay well and they generally don't get the same kind of dismissive treatment that women frequently receive.

Men are indeed moving into these fields, but not fast enough.

Maybe the stereotypes about what men "ought" to be doing are keeping them from getting into sectors of the economy that offer stable and well-paid jobs.

On the plus side, having men move into the "pink ghetto" could heighten the prestige of these fields and increase benefits for everybody. But this good effect could be blunted if white men on the glass escalator leave everybody else behind. Today we face the prospect of a large influx of men crowding out female coworkers, enjoying favorable treatment and further widening the wage gap.[27]

SEX-SEGREGATED LABOR

The U.S. labor market is so highly sex-segregated that almost 30 percent of full-time female employees work in only ten occupations:[28]

- Secretaries and administrative assistants
- Elementary and middle school teachers
- Nursing, psychiatric and home health aides
- Customer service representatives
- First-line supervisors/managers of retail sales workers
- Cashiers
- First-line supervisors/managers of office and administrative workers
- Receptionists and information clerks

- Accountants and auditors
- Secretaries and administrative assistants

In each of these female-dominated occupations, women earn less than men. Strikingly, women earn less than men in almost *all* occupations, whether female-dominated or not. Hispanic/Latina women have the lowest median earnings, earning just 55 percent of the median weekly earnings of white men; black women have median weekly earnings of 64 percent of those of white men.

Even before men started moving into female-dominated jobs in any significant numbers, those few who did make the choice outearned their female peers. The glass escalator isn't new, but now more men are on it.

At one time, people hoped that as men moved into female jobs, the prestige of those jobs would rise.

But it's usually not women who reap the benefits. Men are moved into top spots in such fields as health care, nursing, social work and teaching. Taboos that have prevented men from entering these fields are fading. The U.S. Bureau of Labor Statistics predicts that nursing, other health care work and elementary school teaching will be among the occupations that will have the greatest number of job openings through 2018.[29] Men are already heading into these areas, and unless women find a way onto the glass escalator, they will be left in the basement—looking up.

FIVE

HARD-WON AND EASILY LOST

When they land a good job, most women think they have soared over the toughest hurdle. They're wrong.

Simply getting a job with high status isn't enough; you have to keep it. And keeping a high-level job is easier for men than for women. Men are often forgiven their mistakes. Not so with women, who after one error might find themselves on the skids. For women in typically "male" occupations, any mistake they make may well be magnified, resulting in a loss of status and a decrease in perceived competence.

Intriguing research suggests that males and females are rated as having equivalent status regardless of whether they are in a "male" or "female" occupation. If—and it's a big *if*—they don't make any mistakes.

However, gender does matter when you slip up. When you do make a mistake, the consequences depend on whether you are in a job typical for someone of your gender.

It turns out that if you are in an atypical job for your sex and you make a mistake, you are seen as notably less competent and less worthy of esteem than an employee in a gender-typical job. In other words, if you're female and you are an elementary school teacher or a secretary, a mistake won't spell doom. But if you're an engineer, a pilot or a police officer, watch out. Someone may lower the boom.

Though these results hold for both sexes, serious consequences are much more likely to be felt by women than men. Why? Because many more women are likely to aspire to "male" occupations than men are to seek "female" occupations.

For a woman, the higher up the job ladder you climb, the more you are venturing into male territory. A slip-up that would be only a temporary glitch for a man can be disastrous for a woman. Women need this information so that they can protect themselves—find allies, build networks of support and watch out for potholes. Many women believe that if they simply do a good job, they will be rewarded and that one mistake won't end a career. Not so.

To study people's attitudes, Victoria Brescoll and her coauthors created scenarios for the actions of fictitious female and male police chiefs and women's college presidents.[1] (Police chiefs, of course, are typically male, and presidents of women's colleges are usually female.) When the fictitious chiefs and women's college presidents didn't make any mistakes, they were accorded the same status, whether male or female. "However, when female police chiefs and male women's college presidents made a mistake, they were accorded significantly less status, and viewed as less competent" than their counterparts, according to their report. "Any mistakes that they make, even very minor ones, could be magnified and seen as even greater mistakes." This problem is more acute for women, since high-ranking jobs tend to be typically male, and more women want to get into them.

Brescoll and her colleagues repeated the study, focusing on a fictitious CEO of an aerospace engineering firm and a chief judge. Guess what? Same results. Women who succeed in "male" jobs lose status big-time after making a single mistake. This can make them "vulnerable, and ultimately fragile."[2]

NO SECOND CHANCES

Many women in science, engineering and technology believe that when they fail, they won't get a second chance. This fear was uncovered by the Athena Factor research project.[3] In 2008, IBM, Microsoft, Dell, Cisco and others sponsored studies to better understand how to retain women in technology. Data from this project show that a significant proportion of women in science, engineering and technology (SET) believe that for them, one slip and they're done.

The report noted, "In the private sector, the female talent pipeline in SET is surprisingly deep and rich. Athena Factor survey data show that 41% of highly qualified scientists, engineers, and technologists on the lower rungs of corporate career ladders are female. Despite the challenges they face at school and in our culture, a significant number of girls begin careers in science. Their dedication is impressive: Two thirds of female scientists choose their fields to contribute to the well-being of society.

"But there are some serious challenges. The female drop-out rate is huge. Over time, fully 52% of highly qualified females working for SET companies quit their jobs, driven out by hostile work environments and extreme job pressures. Powerful 'antigens' in SET corporate cultures contribute to the exodus of female talent."

Sylvia Ann Hewlett, a member of the Athena Factor research team, noted, "We found, particularly in the tech firms, that the way to get promoted is to do a diving catch: some system is crashing in Bulgaria, so you get on the plane in the middle of the night and dash off and spend the weekend wrestling with routers and come back a hero."

According to the Athena Factor report, "Tech women talked about this 'diving catch' behavior that is center stage at technology companies. Alpha male techies come to the rescue—zooming in at the eleventh hour like Superman or the Lone Ranger to save a system that is threatening to crash. Women find it extremely difficult to take the kinds of risks involved in making these saves—their buddy system just isn't strong enough to save them if they were to fail. They resent the fact that making a diving catch is often the only way to get promoted at a tech company."

But what if you don't make the catch? Hewlett said, "Women have a hard time taking on those assignments because you can dive and fail to catch. If a man fails, his buddies dust him off and say, 'It's not your fault; try again next time.' A woman fails and is never seen again."

It's not just in the tech world that a single failure can doom a woman, but it's especially dangerous in science, technology, engineering and math (STEM) fields. Because women often lack mentors and sponsors, they feel that it is much more difficult to find "cover" if things don't go smoothly. As a result, they tend to be risk averse. For them, the downside to taking risks is just too great. In focus groups, women were vocal about the gendered nature of risk taking in tech companies. One female engineer said, "Men play differently. . . . Men will make decisions to move forward and do things that are high risk. That's because men are able to walk away unscathed from a mistake—women aren't."

This quandary puts enormous stress on women. Jillian, a young engineer at a major tech company, admitted that she's now on medication and in therapy to help her function in her job: "One night I had to go to the ER because I was shaking uncontrollably." The combination of several project deadlines, pressure to outperform just so she could be considered an equal by her male colleagues and an upcoming performance review had pushed her over the edge. She said that the ER doctor told her, "Oh, you're from [X firm]. We see one or two of you women engineers a week."

Sally, a computer engineer at a top high-tech company, was recently promoted to vice president. She has managed to find her way in a tough environment. "It is fast-paced—we are a company full of type A personalities [and it is] a testosterone-heavy workplace. The way to get ahead at this company is to raise your hand for every risky assignment . . . and attempt the diving catches." Every time she tries a diving catch, she asks herself, "What's the worst that can happen to me?"—a question she remembers her mother asking throughout her childhood and a phrase that helps her reduce her stress level. While she has learned to do the diving catch, she understands that most women find it really tough and that the environment gets in the way.

Women typically don't get the easy acceptance that men do. Ashley, the engineer at a major defense contractor whom we heard from in Chapter 2, told us, "I am always slower to be trusted. I get it, I am a female in engineering, and that extra little X chromosome clearly leads to issues knowing what all those magical electrons are going to do. . . . But when it has been years and I can clearly run the show myself, and the guy who has been here just as long is already running some things, I am starting to sense something is up when you insist I be babysat, have things done for me or be trained as if I had just started."

The Athena Factor project asked nine tech women, "How many of you are seriously thinking about leaving in, say, a year?" Five raised their hands. So women wind up in a lose-lose situation that they didn't see coming.

Women in a variety of other fields agree. "In my company, mistakes and missteps are rarely tolerated to the same degree for women as for men, said a mid-level manager. "A promising male may have two to three opportunities . . . and will be tagged as 'ballsy' for taking on difficult projects, even if he fails. Women will be tagged as incapable or 'not yet ready' when they fail in the same situation. We are always so out on the limb and so alone. Even the most supportive executive will not stand side by side with a female in this situation."

Geraldine, the senior IT consultant we met in Chapter 3, said, "I was blacklisted from ever working on a particular type of project when my first one went south after I expressed from the pre-planning stage how complex and challenging it would be." Her male colleagues, however, never admitted up front that they had reservations about the project's chance of success. "The guys on my team would behave perfectly in front of visitors and influencers," she said, but when the outsiders left, the men would reveal their real worries about the project.

THE GENDER TRIGGER

Books for women about how to get ahead in business often propose what we call the Nike solution: Just do it. Go in with guns blazing, ask for what you want, be tough, take command. But sometimes, that doesn't work. When women step on a gender trigger—or perhaps more accurately, a gender "trip wire," the whole situation can explode. The woman didn't see the wire, pushed ahead as she had been advised to do, and *kaboom!* Not a great result.

Is it fair that women have to tiptoe around gender stereotypes as if they were wired with explosives? Of course not. But who said life was fair.

"Hard-won and easily lost" is about more than losing a job. It's about the fact that women are put in—and put themselves into—positions that do not bode well for their advancement and for getting their just deserts. Steeped in a culture that says men receive—and deserve—the lion's share of rewards, women defer to the inevitable. They don't ask for as much as they think they're worth, they don't push for the promotion they've earned, they don't complain when they're shortchanged in an unfair performance review and they don't press for the challenging work that they deserve. It's not that women are masochistic; they have simply internalized the messages of the culture in which they have grown up—as have the men around them.

Commenting on her book on leadership cowritten with Hannah Riley Bowles, Professor Kathleen L. McGinn said, "We could argue for a long time where these [gender] triggers come from, but they tell women 'You're worth less,' or 'This isn't a situation where you should push.' Or, 'Why don't you let the guy do this one?'"[4]

In our corporate culture, men feel much more entitled to rewards than do women. It's been dubbed the "entitlement effect." Riley Bowles said, "If you bring men and women into a lab and you say either one of two things: 'Work until you think you've earned the $10 we just gave you,' or 'Work and then tell us how much you think you deserve,' women work longer hours with fewer errors for comparable pay, and pay themselves less for comparable work."

Both men and women buy into the idea—often subconsciously—that men are entitled to the good stuff while women are not. Why? Because, historically, men have indeed gotten all the "good stuff" at work.

"And with those triggers present," McGinn said, "the environment tells you who should be claiming more resources. It's him."

Since men usually compare themselves with other men, while women compare themselves with other women, female employees (and their bosses and peers) get an idea in their heads about what women do or do not deserve. Too often, women don't even realize the full extent to which they are limiting their horizons. If you look only at the women around you, you may feel you are doing pretty well. But since we know that women generally don't do as well as men at the same level, you are comparing apples and oranges. It's a losing strategy for you to look only at women, because you aren't getting a true picture of what your level of talent really is earning for others in your company.

In addition, if you're watching how other women behave, you may get a skewed idea about your own behavior. You may think you're being too "unfeminine" and too pushy, a conclusion you'd never draw if you compared yourself with men at your level.

McGinn said, "When I look around and see what other women are doing . . . well, I actually look like I'm being quite aggressive." A woman in this situation might then hesitate to demand resources she needs to get the job done. "So even if I am feeling entitled to those resources, I might put a check on my own behavior because of the triggers in the environment. It is possible that at some point in time these triggers will be gone. But not yet."

So until these triggers are disarmed, women have to be on guard against them. "There are barriers along the way," Riley Bowles said. "But we think this is a good news story in the sense that there are many things people can do. You don't have to wait for society to change. You're part of changing society. We don't presume that the answer is necessarily that women need to imitate the men. This may be about developing women's voice in a new way."

TOOTING YOUR OWN HORN

You've worked hard to get where you are. You're competent, you're a good team player, you're good leadership material—you may have even won awards, written books, produced a play, authored an often-cited journal article, received a major grant, procured a patent and so forth. Who knows about it? That's an important question, because others need this information to develop an accurate picture of who you are and how valuable you are to them.

Men automatically get the benefit of the doubt. In the absence of evidence to the contrary, they are assumed to be hardworking, success-oriented and dedicated to the welfare of the organization.

Not so for women, who don't get that automatic pass. They have to demonstrate their competence; it's not taken for granted.

So, it's especially important for women to self-promote. Without specific information, people fall back on the female stereotype and assume that a woman is not competent, not fully committed, not productive, a "junior" employee and certainly not leadership material.

This isn't just conjecture. NYU's Madeline Heilman (with Michelle Haynes) has shown that this bias actually operates in the workplace and sets up yet another no-win situation for women.[5] To be taken seriously, women have to provide information about their accomplishments. But if they do so, they run the risk of being seen as boastful and aggressive. However, women who self-promote are seen as more competent than those who are self-effacing. But as we've noted, the price of competence may be unlikability. So, female self-promoters are often *less likely* to be hired—a burden men simply don't have to carry.

Cara, the attorney quoted in Chapter 2, said, "Men boast all the time about their accomplishments, yet women tend to be more shy about such accomplishments. I even saw an e-mail from a male colleague boasting about his recent success on a case, which was sent to the entire office! No woman would ever *think* about doing that, for it would be seen as tacky and shameless self-promotion. Prideful women seem to leave a bad taste in people's mouth."

Given this, should women take the risk? Absolutely. It works. In a 2011 report, Catalyst noted, "Among the career advancement tactics we studied, one stood out as having greatest impact. The women who did more to make their achievements known advanced further, were more satisfied with their careers, and had greater compensation growth. . . . The implication for women is obvious. They should continue to ensure that their managers are aware of their accomplishments, seek feedback and credit as appropriate, and ask for promotions when they are deserved . . . Helping others recognize their contributions will help women get ahead further and faster."[6]

Still, this can be hard for women, who typically don't want to be seen as boastful, egocentric, pompous, self-important and, most of all, selfish. Many women have spent their whole lives learning to be thoughtful, deferential and considerate of other people. So now, do they have to reverse all of this learned behavior to toot their own horn?

Yes, yes and yes. Women have to realize that being self-interested is not the same as being selfish. In fact, you are *not* hurting anyone else by providing information about what you can do. You are actually helping your employer, your coworkers and your organization by enabling them to use your talents effectively.

DON'T PUT ME UP ON THAT PEDESTAL

Gayle Tzemach Lemmon, a seasoned political and business reporter, wrote about her experience at a Harvard Business School scholarship dinner in the *Atlantic*. "I thanked a distinguished alumnus for supporting academic achievement and he answered by asking me how old I was. When I told him 32, he leaned over and generously advised,

'Well, you better hurry up and get married because you don't have much time left.'"[7]

He was perhaps typical of many senior executives in American corporations today. Such men likely have traditional, stay-at-home wives, and they may have trouble taking professional women seriously.

Researchers at Harvard, NYU, and the University of Utah found that "husbands in traditional marriages . . . exhibit attitudes, beliefs, and behaviors that undermine the role of women in the workplace" and that such men can create "a pocket of resistance" to female advancement.[8]

Harvard researcher Sreedhari Desai has found that so many of the gender attitudes her work unveils are of an "unconscious nature," which makes beating them back particularly difficult. She said that male leaders may think they are honoring women, not stifling them.

"You think of women in a very positive light, you tend to put them on a pedestal—you don't think you are discriminating against them, you just think you are protecting them," Desai said of senior male leaders who may be part of that pocket of resistance. "Without realizing it you are preferring men over women when it comes to [challenging] positions."[9]

SEXUAL DYNAMICS—
OR DYNAMITE?

Kiri Blakeley tells the story of Megan McFeely at Forbes.com: "When her hotel room phone rang at two a.m., Megan McFeely [a management professional] assumed it was an emergency. Maybe a friend or family member was hurt or in trouble. Worried, she sleepily picked it up, only to hear a male co-worker on the other end. Not a superior, he was someone with 'definitely more power than I had,' urging her to come back down to the hotel bar. It was obvious he was drunk.

"'I was astounded,' says McFeely, who was in New York with several colleagues for a work conference. 'He asked me what I was doing in bed, why wasn't I down there partying with them.' McFeely told the man she needed to get some sleep and hung up the phone. But the call continued to weigh on her. 'When you're not the one in power, and someone does something like that, you just feel unsafe.'

"Welcome to the new sexual harassment," writes Blakeley. "It's (usually) not about the stuff you see on *Mad Men*, it's not chasing the secretary around the desk."[10]

The blatant sexism of the bad old days is fading somewhat. Sure, sometimes a male employee will push a female against a file cabinet for a quick grope, or a boss will send a note to his secretary demanding that she has to sleep with him or be fired. But the issue is usually more subtle—and harder to combat, like the two a.m. phone call mentioned above. As more women move up in companies, as they travel with male colleagues, attend high-level meetings and spend long hours working with them on major projects, issues about what is—and what is not—sexual harassment become more complicated.

But overall, the problem is not going away.

The *Cornell Law Review* reported that between 40 and 90 percent of women in the U.S. workforce have been the victims of some form of sexual harassment on the job.[11] "As even conservative Ninth Circuit Judge [Alex] Kozinski recognized: 'It is a sobering revelation that every woman—*every* woman—who has spent time in the workforce in the last two decades can tell at least one story about being the object of sexual harassment.'"

Sexual harassment harms companies as well as victims. For the year

2011, claims filed with the Equal Economic Opportunity Commission cost employers over $52.3 million.[12]

In the military, the problem is especially acute—and not so subtle. Military.com reports, "Sexual assault in the military has launched into the national spotlight as rates rise, especially after the release of *The Invisible War*, an award-winning documentary on the spree of sexual assaults female service members endure. The documentary highlights the statistic that one-in-five U.S. female veterans have sustained some form of sexual assault."[13]

And while the armed forces have ramped up their anti-harassment campaigns, women still too often face skepticism about their charges. Michael Waddington, a military defense lawyer, told Military.com, "There's almost a presumption that the girl is a liar. The juries want to see some physical evidence. The guys in three of my past four [sexual assault] cases have been found not guilty."

A new issue has arisen as more and more lesbian, gay and transgender individuals become less secretive.[14] Close to 40 percent of "out" lesbian, gay and bisexual workers report that they have experienced harassment or discrimination based on their sexual orientation— and nearly all transgender employees (97 percent) have experienced harassment.

In a few sectors, sexual harassment claims are dropping, but the reason may be the terrible economy, not real progress. Fatima Graves, vice president for education and employment at the National Women's Law Center, notes that finance is one area in which claims are down.[15] But statistics may not tell the whole story. "We must also take the unpredictable economy into account. Being afraid of retaliation after filing a sexual harassment complaint is by no means a new fear for women, but in an industry where layoffs have become quite common, it can seal your fate as another victim of the finance industry—in more ways than one."

Men, too, have problems in this area. Not only can they be victims themselves, but they can also face other issues with female employees. A man may hesitate before he decides to mentor a woman for fear that his overtures could be misunderstood as being sexual in nature. He may monitor his own behavior, with the result that she sees him as aloof or uninterested in her career. Perhaps the best solution to this problem is to talk openly and frankly about this mentoring relationship and what it means. One woman remembers such a conversation with her male mentor. Both were married and both talked about their happy family lives, while admitting that they found each other attractive and that they weren't going to act on it. The conversation defused the situation and turned what might have been a tense relationship into a very open and productive one.

Whether it's blatant or subtle, sexual harassment is not vanishing. And it's just another way that the hard-won progress women have made may be too easily lost.

REPRODUCTIVE ROULETTE

The "Republican War on Women" was a mega-story in the 2012 election campaign. Its major surprise was a full-throated war cry against contraception, which many—if not most—Americans regarded as settled law.

In a CNN op-ed, Pulitzer Prize–winning journalist Laura Sessions Stepp wrote: "Here's what the world is really about when it comes to using birth control: Women, notably millennials, the largest generation ever, are pursuing higher education, jobs and careers, having sex and bearing children, all according to a timetable that works best for them, their partners and their babies. They couldn't do this if birth control wasn't accessible, affordable and safe. Demonizing it amounts to telling these women to throw out their briefcases and take up their vacuum cleaners."[16]

The battle for reproductive freedom was one of the most difficult ones women have fought, but now it's yet another glaring example of hard-won rights being quietly lost. States had a patchwork quilt of laws opposing forms of artificial birth control until 1965, when the Supreme Court handed down its *Griswold v. Connecticut* decision. This action made it unlawful for states to prohibit married couples from using contraceptives on the ground of privacy rights. In 2012, the contraceptive battle erupted over a provision of the Affordable Health Care Act, which required religiously affiliated institutions, such as Catholic hospitals, to pay for birth control coverage for employees. Conservatives raised questions about religious liberty, and the Obama administration fashioned a compromise. Insurance companies, not the hospitals, would pay for the coverage.

And then the attack on birth control began in earnest. Republican presidential candidate Rick Santorum decreed, "It's not OK, because it's a license to do things in a sexual realm that is counter to how things are supposed to be."[17]

In the Senate, Missouri Republican Roy Blunt introduced an amendment that would have allowed not only religious groups but also any employer with moral objections to opt out of the coverage requirement. It would have allowed employers to do so for contraception as well as *any* health service mandated by "Obamacare."

Democrats argued angrily that the amendment was so extreme that employers might use it to refuse to cover HIV screenings for gay employees, prenatal care for children conceived out of wedlock or immunizations for children. "It would simply give every boss in America the right to make the health-care decisions for their workers and their families," said Washington senator Patty Murray.[18] "It is a radical assault."

Radio talk-show host Rush Limbaugh jumped into the fray and made the contraception story a major cause célèbre. A Georgetown University law student, Sandra Fluke, was invited by Congressional Democrats to speak at a hearing by the House Committee on Oversight and Government Reform on the importance of mandating insurance coverage of contraception for women. She explained that many women used birth control drugs to control medical conditions such as the growth of abnormal ovarian cysts.

Limbaugh roared, "What does it say about the college coed Susan [*sic*] Fluke who goes before a congressional committee and essentially says that she must be paid to have sex, what does that make her? It makes her a slut, right? It makes her a prostitute. She wants to be paid to have sex. She's having so much sex she can't afford the contraception. She wants you and me and the taxpayers to pay her to have sex. What does that make us? We're the pimps. . . . So, Ms. Fluke and the rest of you feminazis, here's the deal. If we are going to pay for your contraceptives, and thus pay for you to have sex, we want something for it, and I'll tell you what it is. We want you to post the videos online so we can all watch."[19]

Millions of women and men were astonished and furious that an articulate young woman could present scientific facts to a congressional committee in a professional manner—and then be labeled on national radio as a slut and a prostitute. The outcry was so enormous that even the perpetually outrageous Limbaugh was forced to apologize.

The Blunt amendment was finally killed by the U.S. Senate by an uncomfortably close margin, 51 to 48.

But shortly afterward, Arizona passed a similar law. Employers there can now opt out of paying for contraception for their workers. The law does require companies to pay for contraceptive drugs if they are being used for a reason *other* than preventing pregnancy. But it makes women vulnerable to invasions of their privacy. A female employee will have to first pay for the drugs and then provide proof of the medical reason to the employer's insurance company. She can be asked invasive questions about her private medical issues as well as her sexual practices. And the law does not prevent a woman from being fired for using birth control if the practice is disapproved of by her employer.

Missouri also passed an anti-contraception law in 2012. Employers or insurance companies there can now legally refuse to cover the birth control pill. Though Governor Jay Nixon vetoed the bill, calling it a step backward for Missouri, the legislature, determined to take that giant step backward, overrode the governor's veto.

More such initiatives are brewing in Alabama, Arizona, Texas and other states.

For those who thought that a woman's right to control her body was an accomplished right that could not be overturned, the 2012 campaign was a specter of things to come. The Guttmacher Institute, a nonprofit group dedicated to reproductive health, sees steady growth in opposition to women's rights. In 2000, the institute called thirteen states "hostile" to reproductive rights; it now gives twenty-six states that label. "We're seeing states that go in and make their laws worse, and we're seeing states that are adopting more extreme, more onerous, and more creative laws," said Elizabeth Nash, manager of state issues at the institute.[20]

Could this be yet another crucial hard-won battle that is now being lost?

With a growing number of "hostile" states, with a U.S. Senate bill restricting women's access to contraception failing by a mere three votes and with *Roe v. Wade* only one Supreme Court nomination away from being overturned, the answer to that question is a thunderous and frightening *yes!*

SIX

FEMALES AND MATH: STRANGE BEDFELLOWS?

I t is both the best of times and the worst of times for women in science, technology, engineering and math (STEM). The good news is that innovation, especially in the energy area, is transforming the U.S. economy.

New York Times columnist Roger Cohen says, "The self-image and economic prospects of an energy independent United States are going to see a sharp uptick. . . . The National Intelligence Council estimates as many as 3 million jobs added by 2030."[1]

And females are stepping up to the plate. Girls won in all three age categories (13–14, 15–16, 17–18) in the first-ever Google Science Fair in 2011, quite a difference from years past, when males dominated science fairs.[2] In 2012, women made up 45 percent of MIT undergraduates. In 1965, less than five percent were women, and in 1989, less than 30 percent of undergrads were women.[3]

Two women have won the prestigious Turing Award, first established in 1966 and considered the Nobel Prize for computer scientists. And according to a *Washington Post* headline, "Women in Tech

Dominate *Fortune*'s Annual Power Ranking."[4] Four of the top ten most powerful women head tech companies.[5]

On the other hand, here's the argument for the worst of times: The National Center for Women and Information Technology has found that a mere 18 percent of 2010 computer and information sciences undergraduate degree recipients were female, and that just a quarter of the computing workforce was female in 2011.[6]

Too many women are *not* turning to the careers that will shape the U.S. economic future—even though they have the ability to succeed. Girls who are taking and excelling in STEM courses are still not choosing those fields. It seems old stereotypes about women's "inborn" lack of ability to handle complex math and science material are continuing to exert a tidal pull on our culture.

The high-water mark of this mythology about women and math came in 2005, when Harvard president Larry Summers stepped to the podium to address a conference on the underrepresentation of women and minorities in the science and engineering professions. He undoubtedly had no idea of the firestorm he was about to set off.

Summers told the elite gathering of academics that perhaps an "innate" lack of aptitude for math in women was a factor behind their low numbers in the top jobs in the sciences and engineering.[7] In other words, women just don't have the right stuff to compete successfully with high-achieving males. In his audience were dozens of the nation's top female scientists, who couldn't believe their ears.

Nancy Hopkins, a biologist and tenured professor at MIT, walked out on Summers's talk, telling the *Boston Globe* that if she hadn't left, she "would've either blacked out or thrown up."[8] Denice C. Denton, then the outgoing dean of the College of Engineering at the University of Washington, said, "Here was this economist lecturing pompously [to] this room full of the country's most accomplished scholars on women's issues in science and engineering, and he kept saying things we had refuted in the first half of the day."

Summer's remarks ignited an international frenzy focused on the natural ability—or lack of it—of women in science and math. The *New York Times* ran nineteen major stories that year on the subject, *Newsweek* profiled the Harvard president as "the guy in the eye of the storm" and liberal and conservative columnists arm-wrestled in print, online and on television.[9]

When female scientists objected to the remarks, the media had a field day, chortling about how "feminists" had taken a sock in the jaw. The *Atlantic* fulminated, "The hysteria about Summers furthers the career agendas of feminists who seek quotas for themselves and their friends. Unlike most religious fundamentalists, these feminists were pursuing a careerist, self-serving agenda. This cause can put money in their pockets."[10] *Washington Post* columnist Kathleen Parker called the women "thought police."[11] George Will called those who didn't accept Summers's statements "hysterics."[12] (Why is it that men are never called "hysterical" when they discuss an issue?)

In the end, Summers not only admitted that he got the science wrong but also launched a $50 million initiative at Harvard to boost the training, recruitment and advancement of women, from undergraduates to senior faculty.

The Summers brouhaha pulled the scab off a long-standing issue in American education. Are girls and women "naturally" equipped for math? Do they have what it takes to reach the highest levels in math and science careers? Can women be Einsteins?

How we answer these questions is critical to the career advancement of women in an age when math-related skills are essential to so many high-paying jobs. So many women still don't realize how they've been steered away from math at an early age and how much they've bought into the stereotype that males are good at math and females are not. This belief is a real drag on women's attitudes, performance and career choices. How can you compete successfully in a world where math and science literacy is required but you don't feel you can achieve it?

To fully grasp the problem, we have to go back to its roots—to the ancient Greeks, in fact. They saw a universe divided by the finite and the infinite, by reason and unreason. As Natalie Angier wrote in the *New York Times*, "On Pythagoras' Table of Opposites, 'the finite' was listed along with masculinity and other good things in life, while 'the infinite' topped the column of bad traits like femininity."[13]

The Greeks saw this as a cosmic struggle. The finite (read male) constantly had to struggle to dominate the infinite (read female).

In much of the nineteenth century, it was accepted medical belief that women's reproductive organs could not develop at the same time as their brains. That's why women's education consisted of a little knitting, a little French, no math and science; otherwise, the brain would siphon off precious bodily fluids needed by those all-important ovaries, and those little eggs were greedy!

"Woman is less under the influence of the brain than the uterine system," Dr. J. G. Mulligan wrote in 1848.[14] And G. Stanley Hall, the president of Clark University and the first president of the American Psychological Association, warned in 1906 that "over-activity of the brain during the critical period of the middle and late teens will interfere with the full development of mammary power and of the functions essential for the full transmission of life generally."[15]

Echoes of these old beliefs surfaced in the early 1980s, when the question of girls' lack of ability in math became a national issue.

A team of scientists from Johns Hopkins University examined the math SAT scores of 9,927 very gifted seventh- and eighth-graders.[16] The boys outperformed the girls on the test, which prompted the researchers to draw a startling conclusion. Since the children were exposed to the same curricula, their experiences must have been the same. Therefore, the difference could not be due to environmental factors; it had to be genetic. In discussing their findings in the influential journal *Science*, the researchers suggested that perhaps girls should accept their differences from boys and not even *try* to succeed at math. Their plight was compared to that of a short boy thinking he could make the varsity basketball team.

Science also published a commentary on the study under the headline "Math and Sex: Are Girls Born with Less Ability?"[17] The mainstream media picked up the cry. The *New York Times* asked, "Are Boys Better at Math?"[18] *Time* looked at "The Gender Factor in Math."[19] Many parents worried that their daughters wouldn't be able to compete with their male peers in math. Sadly, some even started to look at their daughters differently. One longitudinal study about ten years later reported that mothers who knew about the articles lowered their expectations of their daughters' math capabilities.[20] One mother remembers breathing a sigh of relief when her daughter nearly flunked chemistry; she was glad that her daughter wouldn't have to compete in that arena. She herself had performed well in math and science on her College Boards but thought her scores were a fluke.

The "math gene" is another wave in the sea of flawed ideas about gender that has been flooding the mass media and the popular imagination. Not long after the first headlines appeared, one of the first talking Barbie dolls burbled, "Math class is hard!" Lost in the maelstrom was the quieter voice of reason. "Just because seventh-grade boys sat the same number of hours in the same classroom doesn't mean they got the same mathematical education," the late Alice T. Schafer of Wellesley College, chair of the Women in Math Committee of the American Mathematical Society, said at the time.[21] Indeed, as it turned out, the kids who took the test showed marked differences in their attitudes about—and experiences with—math. When another Hopkins scientist interviewed the same group of students, she found that gifted boys' parents picked up on their sons' talents at an early age, bought them math books and talked with them about their future careers.[22] Gifted girls' parents took little notice of their ability. Worse, nearly half of the girls interested in math careers had actually been discouraged from taking advanced math courses. One high school guidance counselor told a visiting math professor, "I'll be honest with you. I don't encourage girls to go into mathematics. They wouldn't be good at it, and in any case, what would they do with it?"

Clearly, from the earliest years, girls' experience with math has been very different from that of boys. Teachers, parents and girls themselves frequently buy into the notion that math is a "boy" thing, and they turn their attention elsewhere. This has nothing to do with girls' actual ability. In fact, Elizabeth Spelke, a professor of cognitive psychology at Harvard and co-director of the school's Laboratory for Developmental Studies, showed conclusively, in a series of extraordinary studies, that girls and boys develop the five basic cognitive skills for math at the same age.[23]

- First, a system for representing small exact numbers of objects—the difference between one, two, and three. This system emerges in infants at about five months of age.
- Second, a system for discriminating large, approximate numerical magnitudes—the difference between a set of about ten things and a set of about twenty things.
- Third, a system of natural number concepts that children construct as they learn verbal counting. This takes place between about the ages of two and a half and four years.

- Fourth and fifth, systems first seen in children when they navigate—understanding the geometry of the surrounding layout and identifying landmark objects.

There is, Spelke has found, a biological foundation to mathematical and scientific reasoning that emerges in children before any formal instruction. These systems develop *equally* in males and females. "There's not a hint of an advantage for boys over girls in any of these five basic systems," she reported.

Despite the definitive science, the narrative of girls' inability in math keeps being repeated, and has important effects. Children learn that boys are supposed to be better at math than girls, and the downward spiral begins.

Research from the 1980s through the mid-2000s found the following:

- In the third and fourth grades, boys and girls like math equally. There's no change in fifth and sixth grade for boys, but girls' preference declines.[24]
- Between fourth and twelfth grades, the percentage of girls who say they like science decreases from 66 percent to 48 percent.[25]
- Also between fourth and twelfth grades, the percentage of girls who say they would prefer not to study math anymore increases from 9 percent to a whopping 50 percent.[26]

MATH ANXIETY

We are learning that from their earliest years, girls get harmful "math messages," making it hard for them to fully embrace the subject, even when they are good at it. Because early learning is hard to undo, the effects of these messages can linger well into adulthood.

A 2010 study of students in first and second grade led by Sian L. Beilock, a psychology professor at the University of Chicago, found that little girls may learn to fear math from the women who are their first teachers.[27] Female elementary school teachers who lack confidence in their own math skills could be passing their anxiety along to the girls they teach. The more anxious teachers were about their own math skills, the more likely their female (but not their male) students were to agree that "boys are good at math and girls are good at reading" and the lower these girls' math achievement was at the end of the school year. And disturbingly, elementary education majors at the college level have the highest math anxiety level of students in any major. These teachers will soon be unwittingly passing along a virus of math underachievement to girls.

But there is a silver lining in this story. Even if a young girl has a teacher with high math anxiety, it's not inevitable that she will have problems with math. It turns out that parents and other adults can "vaccinate" girls against their teachers' math anxiety. Teachers' anxiety alone doesn't do the damage. If girls already have a belief that "girls aren't good at math," then their achievement suffers.

However, the girls who don't buy into that stereotype, who think, *Of course I can be good at math*, don't tumble into an achievement gulf.

TOO LITTLE, TOO LATE?

The stereotypes girls have absorbed all of their lives limit their choices as adults. We have to make sure those stereotypes are defanged—and that the remedies we devise are not too little, too late. Perhaps most frustrating, some of the very programs designed to help girls get ahead may be holding them back—or simply may be misguided.

Take single-sex math and science classes. While they seem like a logical way to give girls a jump start in these subjects, new research suggests that this initiative—championed over the past two decades as a possible solution—may backfire.

In a study published in 2010, Howard Glasser, then a researcher at Bryn Mawr College, examined teacher-student interaction in sex-segregated science classes.[28] As it turned out, teachers behaved differently toward boys and girls, in a way that gave boys an advantage in scientific thinking. While both sexes did equally well overall, there were important differences in *how* they were taught. The same teachers taught all-boy and all-girl classes, but they used different teaching strategies: Boys were encouraged to engage in back-and-forth questioning with the teacher and fellow students, while girls had many fewer such experiences. Girls didn't learn to argue in the same way as did boys, and argument is key to scientific thinking—as well as to promoting one's ideas in many workplace settings. Glasser's study suggests that sex-segregated classrooms can construct differences between the sexes by giving them unequal experiences. Ominously, such differences can impact kids' choices about future courses and careers.

New research shows that kids are affected by stereotypes much earlier than we had once thought, and educators and parents may well be ignoring—and sometimes even inadvertently promoting—the spread of these stereotypes. By first or second grade, both girls and boys already have the notion that math is a "boy thing."

It is a step forward that many middle school girls are getting the message that "of course girls can do math and science." Still, these messages are way too late. Research has shown that even when girls say they believe this message, they don't *really* believe it. Too often, they just know what parents and teachers want them to say.[29]

Fortunately, there is a window of opportunity that we shouldn't ignore. A team led by psychologist Anthony Greenwald at the University of Washington discovered that although girls in the early grades see math as a largely male preserve, they haven't yet made the connection that "because I am a girl, math is not for me."[30] So there is a short period of time in elementary school during which girls are relatively open to the idea that they can enjoy, and do well in, math. They can learn that math *is* for them. But too often, they don't. By middle school, the cause is lost for many girls.

Why? Because "stereotype threat" has already set in.

What is stereotype threat? Certain groups—such as girls, women and African Americans—can suffer an extra burden of anxiety because they are aware of the negative stereotype of the group to which they belong. Those women who are told that females aren't good at math do much worse on a math test than those who are told nothing at all before the test.[31] Without the negative information, they score roughly the same as men.

Many of the classic studies of stereotype threat were done with college students and adults. We've recently started to understand that the chilling effects of stereotype threat can be seen much earlier in life.

In a 2007 study in France, psychologists Pascal Huguet and Isabelle Régner looked at how middle school girls scored on tests measuring visual-spatial abilities.[32] Not surprisingly, when the girls were told that boys do better on these tasks, they did poorly. When they were told there were no gender differences, the girls did better.

But here's the surprise: When the girls were given *no* information about which sex performed better, they also did poorly. Stereotype threat was already at work. Even girls who denied holding a belief in girls' inferiority did poorly. Huguet and Régner noted, "Here we offer first evidence that ST [stereotype threat] does operate even in middle-school girls who deny the negative gender stereotype."

Clearly, we need to intervene much earlier than we thought, and we need to be creative about how we do it. Rather than simply stating "Girls can be scientists," we should be talking about what scientists do, and asking girls if these are things they would be good at and would like to do. For example, children may not know that scientists study how the things kids are interested in really work—how planes fly, for example, or how dolphins communicate. When children are encouraged to think this way, they are much more likely to retain this information than they would be if they were just given the generic girls-can-do-science message.[33]

FEMALE EINSTEINS?

Some people still argue that while girls can do OK at the middle levels of math and science, "Only Men Can Be Geniuses," as a 2007 London *Daily Mail* headline put it.[34] The newspaper declared, "The stubborn facts of history remain. Very few truly original scientific discoveries have been made by women. There are no women geniuses in physics or mathematics to rival Newton or Einstein."

It's a hard argument to refute.

Ethan Siegel, a theoretical astrophysicist in Portland, Oregon, noted: "The argument goes something like, 'Even though men and women are equal on average in math ability, men have a greater variance in their abilities. So there are more very dumb men, but also more very smart men, and those are the ones who become scientists.'"[35]

This indeed was the idea that Larry Summers bought when he said that women were not advancing to top jobs because of a "different availability" of aptitude at the high end. But is it true?

Not according to a huge study by Jonathan M. Kane and Janet E. Mertz of the University of Wisconsin.[36] They analyzed scores from more than half a million fourth- and eighth-graders from more than sixty countries. Their conclusion: There were essentially no gender differences between girls and boys in math performance. In the few instances where a slight difference did occur, Mertz said that it "is not a matter of biology: None of our findings suggest that an innate biological difference between the sexes is the primary reason for a gender gap in math performance."

If the "variance" argument were true, you'd find boys at the higher end of the distribution across all countries, because we're talking innate abilities here. Kane and Mertz found no evidence to support that claim. In some countries, as predicted, boys' variance was higher than girls'. In other countries, there was no difference, and in yet others, girls' scores showed more variance than boys' scores. Still, the idea that there can be no female Einsteins is hard to dislodge from many people's minds. Maybe this is because stellar female scientists get little media attention.

For example, when Frances Allen won the 2006 Turing Award, the U.S. media yawned. She was the first woman ever to receive the prize since it was founded years earlier. And Allen was an American. Lexis-Nexis turned up only six stories that mentioned Allen's breakthrough accomplishment, three in the U.S. press: full-length articles in *USA Today* and the *Los Angeles Times* and a three-sentence item in a Columbus, Ohio, newspaper. Then there was a brief article in the *Irish Times* that was focused primarily on another computer scientist and didn't even mention that Allen was the first woman to win the prize, and an item in the English *Guardian*.

In 2008, a second woman won the prize: Barbara Liskov of MIT. And she's hardly a household name.

WHERE WE ARE TODAY

Against all odds, a large number of girls are now expressing interest in STEM fields. A 2012 study by the Girl Scout Research Institute offers encouraging news. Nearly three-quarters of teen girls are interested in STEM subjects.[37] Of those interested, 92 percent of girls see themselves as smart enough to have a career in STEM. Additionally, 85 percent said they like to solve problems; 67 percent like to build things and put things together; 83 percent like to do hands-on science projects; and 80 percent ask questions (and seek answers) about how things work.

The girls' confidence and optimism about their intelligence is mirrored by the fact that nearly all the girls (98 percent) expect to graduate from college and 92 percent expect to go to graduate school.

All the ideas about women not being hardwired to do math are falling like dominos. In elementary, middle and high school, girls and boys take math and science courses in roughly equal numbers, and girls perform at least as well as boys.

But will they take the steps needed to pursue STEM careers?

As they leave high school, about as many girls as boys are academically prepared to pursue science and engineering majors in college. But fewer women than men actually pursue these majors. Among first-year college students, women are much less likely than men to say that they intend to major in STEM subjects. By graduation, men outnumber women in nearly every science and engineering field, and in some, such as physics, engineering and computer science, the difference is dramatic, with women earning only 20 percent of bachelor's degrees.[38] Women's representation in science and engineering declines further at the graduate level and yet again in the transition to the workplace. Even though they have the ability to succeed, women all too frequently avoid the very careers that will reap the most economic rewards in the future. This is a troubling trend, because people with math and science backgrounds will undoubtedly be in high demand and richly rewarded as our knowledge-based economy grows.

Even more discouraging is the reality that fewer women than men who earn these degrees will go into these fields. One survey of 2,213 college seniors found that among men and women who were taking both physics and calculus, the proportion of men choosing a career in science or engineering was much greater than the proportion of women doing the same.[39] So, girls who are taking and excelling in courses that will supposedly allow them to enter high-paying math and science careers are still not choosing those fields. This is a huge loss of brain power for the United States, according to researcher Shannon Dawn Bryant of the University of Massachusetts–Amherst.[40] "Even the girls who are succeeding in the mathematics classroom are not happy to be there, and very few see themselves entering a math or science career in the future." Keeping the door of opportunity open to these careers does not guarantee that they will pass through it.

A 2011 U.S. Department of Commerce report said that women are vastly underrepresented in STEM jobs and among STEM degree holders.[41] Although women fill close to half of all jobs in the U.S. economy, they hold less than 25 percent of STEM jobs. This has been the case throughout the past decade, even as the share of college-educated women has increased in the overall workforce. Women hold a dispro-portionately low share of STEM undergraduate degrees, particularly in engineering.

Unfortunately, when American girls head off to the colleges of their choice, they may not see paths to interesting and lucrative careers. According to the American Association of University Women (AAUW) report "Why So Few?" the number of women in science and engineering is growing, yet men continue to outnumber women, especially at the upper levels of these professions.[42] This is important for women's financial futures, because women with STEM jobs earned considerably more than women in non-STEM jobs.

Although the women in the AAUW study, on average, rejected the stereotype that men are mathematically superior to women, a quarter of them indicated some belief that the stereotype might be true. And the women who tended to endorse the stereotype were significantly less confident in their ability to perform well in their major, and had significantly lower performance self-esteem in general, than the women who rejected the stereotype. Moreover, these attitudes predicted career intentions: Women who tended to endorse the stereotype reported less desire to attend graduate school.

And a study of Carnegie Mellon University computer science Ph.D. students found that even when male and female students were doing equally well in terms of grades, female students reported feeling less comfortable than males.[43] Fifty-three percent of males rated themselves as "highly prepared" in contrast to *zero percent* of females.

Women's representation in science and engineering declines further at the graduate level and yet again in the transition to the workplace. Women with a STEM degree are less likely than their male counterparts to work in a STEM occupation; they are more likely to work in education or health care. From 2000 to 2012, the percentage of women in all STEM jobs did not change from 24 percent.[44]

THINKING ABOUT MATH

How women and men think about their math ability can have a strong impact on how far they go not only in math and science but also in business areas like finance, where a firm grasp of math is crucial. Males are likely to attribute math-related success to ability—a stable and reliable factor. After all, if you're good on day 1, you're going to be good on day 15—because ability doesn't wax and wane; it's just *there*. And men are likely to attribute failure in math-related tasks to lack of effort—a correctible cause. Since men get second chances more often than women do, the price of failure is relatively low. Men may be more likely to take on challenging tasks and be less fearful of failure. In contrast, women (and their supervisors) tend to attribute female math-related successes to hard work—but you can't always go all-out on every project. So, today's success is not a basis for predicting tomorrow's performance. For women without a strong sense that their solid quantitative ability will see them through, every new task could be seen as a challenge to mount a gargantuan effort.

But it's not only STEM fields that are experiencing a lack of women. The world of high-level corporate finance isn't attracting women the way it should, either. One female manager at a fund that handles more than $1.3 billion of assets said, "I'll often have meetings with a group of fund managers where I'll be the only female in the room."

According to *BusinessWeek*, "At nine of the 10 largest U.S. private-equity firms, women account for an average 8.1 percent of managing directors and senior executives, the highest-ranking and best-paying jobs, according to data compiled from the companies and their web-sites. The comparable figure for the country's six biggest investment and commercial banks is 30 percent, while women make up 13 percent of the senior ranks at 10 of the largest traditional-asset managers."[45] Women represent more than 50 percent of the workers in the financial industry but are chief executives at fewer than 3 percent of American financial companies, says Catalyst.[46]

High-paying positions in the financial sector are attracting increasing numbers of MBAs; jobs in these fields require a strong quantitative background. More and more, graduates of the best universities and colleges are pursuing the needed MBA. In 1970, only 4 percent of women earned MBAs, compared with a whopping 43 percent in 2006. Despite the narrowing of the gender gap in business education, there is a growing sense that women are not getting ahead fast enough in the corporate and financial worlds. For example, since the 2008 recession, women in the financial sector suffered the majority of layoffs (78 percent), according to the *Wall Street Journal*.[47]

The highly competitive environment in top finance is typically the breeding ground for promotions to the C-suite. And women are underrepresented in this sector. Why? One answer is suggested by the results of a survey of 1,856 men and women from the graduating classes of 1990 to 2006 from the University of Chicago's Booth School of Business. Although more women are completing their MBAs, there are clear gender differences in their areas of specialization. Compared with men, women take relatively fewer finance and accounting classes but take relatively more marketing classes, too often handicapping them in their climb to the top.

The gender gap is growing. *BusinessWeek* reported, "In 2002, 29 percent of women went into finance positions; by 2012 that number had dropped by nearly half, to 16 percent. The portion of women taking high-paying investment banking jobs slipped even more, from 6 percent in 2002 to 2 percent today. The number of men heading into finance has dipped too, but not so precipitously. A decade ago, 32 percent of men went into finance, vs. 23 percent this year, while 9.4 percent went into investment banking, vs. 6.9 in 2002."[48]

Women told us that they believed finance wasn't welcoming to them. A senior corporate trainer said, "Finance continues to be male dominated. And it is difficult to maintain strong self-esteem in the face of regular reminders that information is 'really complex' and frustrated efforts to be recognized for having value. This is an industry largely entrenched in the power and control models that have disadvantaged women for a long time."

A manager at an institutional investment consulting firm said that there is "still a bias against women in finance. . . . Women [are] still largely perceived as less competent and having more to prove than men, maybe because of the conservative, resistant-to-change culture."

A senior vice president in the power industry tells us, "Despite all the evidence that women take controlled risks and see best results in hedge funds and other financial organizations, men hire others who look like themselves and value high testosterone."

FEMALES AND STEM: A GOOD MARRIAGE?

The evidence is overwhelming. Girls are every bit as able to do math and science as are boys. Yet why is it that so many girls are going gangbusters in the classroom but not moving into STEM? Maybe because the image of what a female *should* be in our society does not yet include being a math whiz and having a good job in a mathematically demanding field. The "no female Einstein" refrain is still very much with us; girls are discouraged early, and thus as adults they shrink from lucrative fields where they could excel.

Clearly, the new challenge is to change these images and get talented women interested in these careers. One roadblock is that scientists and mathematicians and their work are stereotyped in ways that make careers in math and science unattractive to many women. Danica McKellar, the former *Wonder Years* child star who is now a mathematician and the author of *Math Doesn't Suck: How to Survive Middle School Math*, thinks this idea starts in middle school. That's when, she said in an interview, kids "for the first time become worried about what others will think of them. It's an issue for both boys and girls, but especially girls. Who am I? What kind of person am I going to be when I grow up? Am I popular? Do people like me? These things become really important at that age. And when math has a reputation of being just for nerds, it becomes less desirable. They'll think, Who am I? I'm not sure, but I certainly don't want to be a 'math person.'"[49]

You'd never guess from the stereotypes that engineering and science are typically collaborative efforts—teams working closely on complex problems. The image of the socially awkward nerd, working alone with test tubes in a dingy lab, is a far cry from reality.

And we know that women often look to jobs that have a social impact—where they can do good while they do well financially. Scientific teams have drastically reduced childhood leukemia, helped restore the Everglades, preserved sea turtles in the Caribbean, reduced AIDS in Africa, learned how to save lives by predicting volcanic eruptions and solved crimes through forensic science. Such activities are often *not* what women think when they hear the words "math and science."

New evidence suggests that young women are beginning to see

success in math as more congruent with their image of themselves as female. But progress has been way too slow, given what we know about girls' natural abilities.

Raytheon chairman and CEO William H. Swanson said at a 2012 Massachusetts STEM Summit, "Too many students and adults are training for jobs in which labor surpluses exist and demand is low, while high-demand jobs, particularly those in STEM fields, go unfilled."[50] Three million of them, to be exact. STEM skills lead to jobs that pay very well. The Georgetown University Center on Education and the Workforce found that 65 percent of those with bachelor's degrees in STEM fields earn more than those with master's degrees in non-STEM occupations.[51] In fact, 47 percent of those with bachelor's degrees in STEM occupations earn more than those with Ph.D.s in non-STEM occupations. Over the past ten years, growth in STEM jobs was three times that of other sectors. STEM jobs are projected to grow by 17 percent over the next ten years, compared with 9.8 percent growth for non-STEM jobs.

The good news is that the widely held belief that boys are naturally better than girls at math and science is unraveling. Evidence is mounting that girls are every bit as competent as boys in these areas:

- Psychology professor Janet Hyde of the University of Wisconsin–Madison has strong U.S. data showing no meaningful differences in math performance among more than seven million boys and girls in grades two through twelve.[52]
- Women now head many prestigious research universities, including Harvard, MIT and Brown. Six of the 15 female university presidents in the United States head some of the "world's top 20 universities, and 10 are within the top 50 group."[53]

- The International Monetary Fund of 188 countries that works "to foster global monetary cooperation, secure financial stability, facilitate international trade, promote high employment and sustainable economic growth, and reduce poverty" is for the first time headed by a woman, France's Christine Lagarde.[54]

It might be tempting to write off these achievements as the triumphs of a few "outliers." Their accomplishments may be spectacular, but generally, women are no match for men in math, so the argument goes.

Harder to dismiss are the results of several large-scale international testing programs that find girls closing the gender gap in math and in some cases outscoring the boys. In general, gender differences are small in the lower grades but become more pronounced at higher grades. In France, for example, third-grade girls actually do as well in math as boys. By sixth grade, however, the boys start to outperform the girls.[55]

Attitudes toward math and science are also shifting. Results of the 2007 French study of fifth- and seventh-grade boys and girls we mentioned earlier indicate that girls in both age groups and seventh-grade boys believed that girls do better in math than boys do.[56]

The task ahead is to convey a more reality-based picture of who scientists and mathematicians are and what they actually do. We also have to find the tangled roots of the issues keeping women away from STEM careers and rip them up, starting very early in girls' lives, so we aren't always playing catch-up. We need to understand the past to improve the future.

SEVEN

RISK TAKERS, NO; CARETAKERS, YES

One major narrative about the sexes is that women are getting too powerful; another is that women don't have the right stuff to be powerful. A contradiction? Sure. No matter. Both are compelling and find wide audiences.

The first story is gaining mass popularity now; the second has been around for a very long time. It directs women away from jobs that demand taking risks, exerting leadership or using quantitative analysis, and it directs them toward supportive "people" jobs. By discouraging women from a wider range of positions, it has a corrosive impact on how women select their careers.

According to Harvard psychology professor Steven Pinker (and others), men, but not women, are naturally suited for competition, risk taking, leadership, understanding systems and analytical thinking.[1]

In this scenario, successful women are seen as unnatural, pushing their innate abilities in unrealistic and unsustainable ways. Pinker sees men and women as having very different goals in life. Here is what Pinker says that men want: "having lots of money; inventing or creating something; having a full-time career; and being successful in one's line of work." In contrast, these are the things women want: "the ability to have a part-time career for a limited time in one's life; living close to parents and relatives; having a meaningful spiritual life; and having strong friendships."

In his widely reviewed 2002 book, *The Blank Slate*, Pinker writes that men are risk takers but women "are more likely to choose administrative support jobs that offer lower pay in air-conditioned offices."[2] If women are not by nature fit for leadership roles, why would any male manager consider promoting a woman to a position for which she lacks the very abilities that are key to success?

Pinker agrees with evolutionary psychologists who believe that men and women evolved differently in prehistory because they had distinct challenges to meet. Women had to nurture children, and men had to hunt to provide resources for them.

The problem with this vision is that there's no real data to back it up, and many scientists regard it as a simplistic fantasy. In our prehistoric past, evidence suggests that foraging and scavenging by men *and* women provided most of the food that our ancestors ate. In the Pleistocene era, women were as active as men in providing food for the group.

And in regard to women being uninterested in money and careers, as we noted in Chapter 1, more women ages eighteen to thirty-four than men say that having a successful, high-paying career is very important, or the most important thing, in their lives," according to the Pew Research Center.

Syndicated columnist George Will writes that women "cheerfully choose" low-paying jobs.[3] In a *New Republic* article, journalist Robert Wright flatly declares that women have less drive than men do, not bothering to cite any evidence.[4] A *Fortune* cover story in October 2003 questioned women's ambition with the headline "Power: Do Women Really Want It?"[5] Nine years later, in 2012, *Forbes* asked the same question: "Do Women Fear Power and Success?"[6]

While women's lack of risk-taking ability was being decreed as dogma, one woman sailed around the world solo, setting a world record; another rowed 4,000 miles alone across the Pacific Ocean; a female A-10 pilot flew her bullet-riddled plane across the Iraqi desert to make a perfect landing at her home base; a woman commanded the space shuttle; women mountaineers conquered the planet's highest peaks; women regularly won the grueling Iditarod dogsled race; and most recently, a female CIA agent spearheaded a five-year investigation that led to the secret mission in which Navy SEALs found and killed Osama bin Laden. These facts seem not to impress the cadre of pundits who simply repeat over and over the idea that women lack risk-taking ability. Why should facts get in the way of a sexy argument?

The notion that risk is unnatural for girls is now appearing *everywhere*. The bestselling *Dangerous Book for Boys* argues that we should return to a world where little boys brave risk and danger in childhood games while girls are content with sugar and spice and everything nice.[7] The authors even say that boys should carry handkerchiefs to dry girls' tears when they cry. Little girls are surrounded by a "princess culture," as author Peggy Orenstein puts it in *Cinderella Ate My Daughter*.[8] It's a world of pink tulle dresses, rhinestone tiaras and magic wands, in which girls obsess about their looks, clothes and budding sex appeal. Orenstein says, "It's not just being the fairest of them all, it's being the hottest of them all, the most Paris Hilton of them all, the most Kim Kardashian of them all." In other words, superficial, self-absorbed and oversexed.

Halloween costumes for girls are all about sparkles, fairies and princesses—nary an astronaut, police officer or superhero among them. Risk and accomplishment have no part in the Cinderella kiddie world.

HARDWIRED DIFFERENCES?

The idea that men are the "systematizers," the thinkers and the doers, while women merely empathize and care for others is one of those pieces of misinformation that gets repeated over and over again. People come to accept it as fact even though they have no idea where it comes from.

One version of this notion was set out by psychologist Simon Baron-Cohen of the University of Cambridge in his influential book *The Essential Difference.*[9] He has been quoted in the *New York Times*, in a *Newsweek* cover story, in a PBS documentary and in many other major media outlets. And he is a frequent keynote speaker at important conferences.

Male brains, Simon Baron-Cohen says, are hardwired for mastery of hunting and tracking, trading, achieving and maintaining power, gaining expertise, tolerating solitude, using aggression and taking on leadership roles. The female brain? It is specialized for four functions: making friends, mothering, gossiping and "reading" a partner.

In this scenario, girls and women are so focused on others that they have little interest in figuring out how the world works, or in any of the other activities that presumably occupy the male brain. As a result, these are the jobs that Baron-Cohen suggests for women: "counselors, primary school teachers, nurses, carers [caregivers], therapists, social workers, mediators, group facilitators or personnel staff." Note that these are the typically low-paid female-ghetto jobs with little power. If we buy this argument, women will have lost an important battle in the New Soft War.

Baron-Cohen's whole theory is based on one study of day-old babies done in his lab. He claims that baby boys looked longer at a mobile while baby girls looked longer at people's faces. But Harvard's Elizabeth Spelke says the study is virtually worthless: Female and male infants were propped up in a parent's lap, and since newborns can't hold their heads up independently, their visual preferences could well have been determined by the way their parents held them.[10]

A large body of literature flat-out contradicts Baron-Cohen's study, providing evidence that male and female infants respond equally to people and objects.

As for women being unsuited for leadership:

- A meta-analysis of studies of managers, conducted by Gary Powell of the University of Connecticut, found female managers as motivated as male managers.[11]
- A study of 2,000 managers found female managers more hard-driving than men.[12]
- Women are more likely than men to use an autocratic style (35 vs. 31 percent), according to a fifteen-year survey of 41,000 executives, a quarter of them female, at 5,000 firms, cited in *BusinessWeek*.[13]

There is simply no scientific evidence that women lack what it takes to be forceful and assertive. But the narrative may be steering millions of women into careers that don't really utilize their strongest skills.

And if women are best suited for low-level jobs that don't involve risk or competition, they should be pretty satisfied in those kinds of jobs, right? They're not. Catalyst has found that "women are not intentionally seeking out slower career tracks."[14] And they are less satisfied than men with their career growth. If women were intentionally seeking slower tracks, Catalyst says, "we would expect them to be as satisfied as men with their advancement and compensation growth."

Baron-Cohen has argued that women's brains are wired solely for cooperation and caring, so it stands to reason not only that females would be terrible at negotiating a better deal for themselves, but also that they wouldn't even be interested in doing so.

Again, Catalyst disagrees: "Women *do* ask." Men and women, in their first post-MBA jobs, were equally more likely to negotiate for better jobs (19 percent of women vs. 17 percent of men), and higher pay (63 percent of women vs. 54 percent of men).

OPTING OUT?

Here is an ongoing media narrative: Drawn by the appeal of domesticity, the best and the brightest women are going home. Smart women are fed up with working and are leaving in droves for the place they really belong—home. The subtext: Feminism is eroding and women want to return to more traditional lives. There's a chorus of crocodile tears in the New Soft War—*Poor dears, we know how much you yearn to be home, so you should go there.*

Perhaps the best example of this narrative is the 2003 *New York Times Magazine* cover article by Lisa Belkin titled "The Opt-Out Revolution": Many high-powered women today don't ever hit the glass ceiling, choosing to leave the workplace for motherhood. Is this the failure of one movement and the beginning of another?[15] (The failed movement is undoubtedly feminism.)

A dramatic Q&A graced the cover of the *Times Magazine*: "Q: Why Don't More Women Get to the Top? A: They Choose Not To." Women, the newspaper announced, are "Abandoning the Climb and Heading Home." The sweeping nature of the title and the placement of the article on the cover implied that the magazine was examining a pervasive national trend.

But was it? Even though the term "opt-out revolution" is an oft-quoted media staple, this article was based on no systematic research; rather, it was a collection of anecdotes from small, nonrepresentative groups of female Princeton graduates. These women were members of book groups in several cities and had husbands affluent enough to finance a comfortable lifestyle on one income.

And even though these women were presented as "opting out by choice," that's not quite an accurate picture. One television news reporter, for example, had asked her station for a part-time contract but was refused. Management said it was all or nothing, so she left—and called it a wrenching decision. "It kills me that I'm not contributing to my 401(k) anymore," she told Belkin.

Another woman, a lawyer, "worked a crushing schedule, up to 15-hour days, seven days a week, while still nursing her daughter, who was not sleeping through the night." On the morning of a trial, she was prepared, but the judge postponed the case and later in the week took it off the calendar entirely to go fishing. Earlier, the lawyer had tried to go part-time, but her request was ignored. She found that the workload was simply impossible for a new mother when there was no "give" at the firm, so she left, reluctantly.

Are these women really opting out? Belkin quotes one woman as saying, "It's not black or white; it's gray. You're working. Then you're not working. Then you're working part-time or consulting. Then you go back. This is a chapter, not the whole book." Another told Belkin,

"I'm doing what is right for me at the moment. Not necessarily what is right for me forever."

Are women in general running home? No. More than 78 percent of mothers with a graduate or professional degree are in the paid workforce, and they are three times as likely to work full-time as part-time, according to the U.S. Census Bureau.[16] One major study of high-level women failed to uncover any opt-out trend. Linda Stroh and Anne Reilly of Loyola University and Jeanne Brett of Northwestern University compared 1,029 male and female managers who had the same level of jobs and the same levels of education and time in the workforce.[17] These women *did not* opt out of demanding jobs, and they were also as devoted to their jobs as the men were to theirs. When the women left their jobs, it wasn't because of some mystical tug of motherhood. It was for the same reason men left: better jobs and more opportunity for advancement.

Joan Williams, director of the Center for WorkLife Law at the University of California, Hastings College of the Law, says, "Most mothers do not opt out. They are pushed out by workplace inflexibility, the lack of supports and a workplace bias against mothers."[18] In one recent survey, 86 percent of women cited obstacles such as inflexible jobs as a key reason behind their decision to leave.

And as author Linda Hirshman points out, "Once they leave, they usually cannot regain the income or status they had. The Center for Work-Life Policy, a research organization founded by Sylvia Ann Hewlett of Columbia, found that women lose an average of 18 percent of their earning power when they temporarily leave the workforce. Women in business sectors lose 28 percent."[19]

As the *New York Times* notes, "Despite the happy talk of 'on ramps,' only 40 percent of even high-powered professionals get back to full-time work."[20] Ninety-three percent of very competent professional women who have left the workforce want to return but can't, according to one recent study. When they have children, U.S. women experience a 10 to 15 percent decrease in future earnings—a drop that men do not suffer.[21] The Working Mother Research Institute found that women want one lifestyle, but often end up with another. Fifty-five percent of mothers who are currently at home but are career-oriented would rather return to work.[22]

In a *Times* op-ed, Harvard economics professor Claudia Goldin says that reliable data prove that "a greater fraction of college women today are mixing family and career than ever before. There is no opt-out revolution. Denying that reality is ignoring the facts."[23]

But the message from the media is clear: If even the smartest women want to rush home to 1950s domesticity, why bother with policies that support women in the workforce? Why call for federally funded child care, universal early education and paid parental leave when what women really want is to be at home? How do you build a constituency for family-friendly workplace policies when you believe that women not only *should* be home but also *want* to be there?

Unfortunately, employers may well heed the message of "The Opt-Out Revolution" when they consider whether to promote or hire well-qualified women, whom they see as likely to abandon the workplace and dash home. The perpetuation of the dewy-eyed, sentimental notion that women just want to retreat to the rose-covered cottage of yesteryear is a mainstay of the New Soft War. For example, the classy, upscale *Atlantic*, through the writings of regular contributor Caitlin Flanagan, is an ardent promoter of this myth. Flanagan is endlessly effusive on the joys of home and hearth, writing, for example, that "no woman with a beating heart and an ounce of femininity" can resist such domestic ephemera as a freshly laundered fluffy white towel or the sight of "a child's lawn pinafore draped across a painted rocking chair."[24]

But are mothers so enamored of this domestic dream that to get it they will take part-time, dead-end, pin-money jobs with mommy hours? Hardly. What they really want is a good job with reasonable hours and enough flexibility so that they can spend time with their families. As NYU sociology professor Kathleen Gerson reports, "Full time work has come to mean 50 hours or more." That overload is what mothers are rejecting. [25]

Today, Gerson finds, both men and women value work and economic self-sufficiency above all else. For young women, working and earning is part of their reality—never mind the back-to-home myth. Gerson interviewed 120 young men and women, whose average age was twenty-four. She found that both women and men want to be in dual-earner families. If they are unable to find a mate who wants what they want, however, the strategies the sexes envision for coping are very different. Many women who can't find the right partner to combine work and family will forgo marriage and choose work. Some will remain childless; others will have children outside of marriage, believing they can provide for their children's financial and emotional well-being.

Men, too, prioritize their ability to earn a living. If they are unable to find a mate who wants to be part of a dual-earner couple, then they expect to settle for marrying a traditional woman who will assume the primary nurturing role.

Again, the numbers are revealing. More than 70 percent of the women Gerson studied endorsed a self-reliant fallback position, compared with 30 percent of the men. In contrast, 70 percent of the men endorsed a neo-traditional fallback position, which was endorsed by less than 30 percent of the women.

Gerson says that today's young people are in the midst of an "unfinished" revolution. Family-friendly policies in the workplace, which should be at the forefront of our national agenda, are decidedly not there. If young adults can't create the equality they really desire, their fallback positions almost guarantee stress and unhappiness. Women will forfeit the joys of marriage, while men will probably wind up being the workaholic, distant fathers they so clearly don't want to be.

SUGAR AND SPICE AND EVERYTHING NICE

It may be forty years since the second wave of feminism rolled across the American landscape, but some things never change—like the "sugar and spice" adage about females and niceness.

As the title of a Catalyst report puts it, "Women 'Take Care,' Men 'Take Charge.'" The think tank calls this stereotype one of the most formidable barriers to women's advancement in the workplace. It "can misrepresent the true talents of women leaders, potentially undermining women's leadership and posing serious challenges to their career advancement."[26]

Catalyst points out that reviews of more than forty previous studies on gender differences in leadership demonstrate that men and women often lead in very similar ways. Yet "perception often trumps reality in evaluating the leadership capabilities of both women and men, turning both into stereotypes."[27] To make matters worse, both men and women show the same biases. Both sexes believe that more women than men are effective at "take care" skills and that more men than women are better at "take charge" skills. In recent years, some have even gone so far as to argue that women's niceness and caring should be touted as a more human style of managing, one that would enhance women's prospects. A plethora of what could be called "niceness lit" grew up, arguing that moral, nice, democratic women could be better leaders than men.

In her major—and much acclaimed—book *In a Different Voice*, Carol Gilligan, now a professor at New York University, argues that women were programmed to make moral decisions differently than men.[28] Males use a chilly "justice" standard for making such decisions, while women use a rationale of "caring." She proposes a new theory of human development based on the experiences of women and articulates the idea that women have a "relational self," which sees reality in terms of connections with other people. Moreover, this relational self is innate only to women. The idea blossomed that women have ways of knowing, ways of thinking and ways of feeling that would always be inaccessible to the male mind.

In the popular book *Women's Ways of Knowing: The Development of Self, Voice, and Mind*, the authors argue that women are violating their essential feminine natures when they try to lead.[29] They claim that men value excellence and mastery in intellectual matters and evaluate arguments in terms of logic and evidence. Women, in contrast, are spiritual, relational, inclusive and credulous.

No wonder droves of women embraced this message. Gilligan and others appeared to be elevating women from the "second sex" to the "better sex." It sounded so positive: women as better than men. Better as friends, better as parents, better at everything having to do with relationships and even in the workplace.

Sounds wonderful, right? But hold on. This line of reasoning, while very popular, offers up a highly questionable strategy, feeding into stereotypes rather than challenging them. Rutgers psychology professor

Laurie Rudman notes, "Women may not recognize that a prescription for female niceness underscores their subordinate status in society. Instead, they may view it as a means of positively distinguishing themselves from men [being more caring, more democratic] as well as a means of receiving positive reinforcement."[30]

More important, "niceness lit" had—and still has—a big problem. Science doesn't support it. As we've noted, reams of peer-reviewed data find that female and male managers have leadership styles that are more similar than different. And in actual comparisons of men and women leaders in organizational settings, few differences in leadership style emerge. *BusinessWeek* reported that a 2000 study of 41,000 executives, 25 percent of them female, at 5,000 companies, found that women are slightly more high-handed than men when making decisions.[31] "In situations where an autocratic style was deemed appropriate, women chose 'my-way-or-the-highway' 35 percent of the time, guys only 31.5 percent." More women than men (37 percent vs. 32 percent) said they would go it alone in making decisions, excluding other key people. "If your boss is a Ms., don't automatically expect her decision-making to be warm and fuzzy."

Also, scholars have deconstructed Gilligan's arguments and concluded that her research doesn't show what she says it shows. Her study, they say, was badly designed, and she had an unscientific sample and poor methodology. She overgeneralized her findings, and as one scholar noted, "If educational and occupational backgrounds of subjects are controlled, there are no sex differences in moral judgment."[32] In other words, when you look at the education people have and the jobs they do, you discover that those two factors—not their sex—account for the differences that had been erroneously attributed to sex.

FALSE CARING

Maybe one reason we all believe women are caring by nature is that women themselves believe it—even when it isn't true. Often, female caring behavior comes more from fear than from a genuine connection to others.

Since almost everybody not only expects but also *demands* that women be caring, women fear the consequences of *not* being seen that way. As a result, they may act as if they care, even when they really don't. So, not only do bosses and managers misjudge their employees' caring abilities, but women themselves can also feel fake and inauthentic when they aren't acting on the basis of who they really are, but rather on the way they are expected to be. One woman in a senior academic position has said that when students have a crisis, such as a family emergency, the men dive under the desks and the women are sent out to cope. When this happens day after day, the women get exhausted—as well as bitter and angry.

Surprisingly, men's caring behavior is often *more* authentic than women's.[33] Why? Men, more often than women, have power and therefore do not have to resort to manipulation and deception. If you don't have to worry that people will think less of you because you are not always caring, you are free to act the way you really feel. You don't have to pretend you care, because you don't fear retribution.

A kinder, gentler image of managers brings additional hidden costs to women. They get judged on their caring abilities, while men do not. Suzanne, a sales representative for a large pharmaceutical company, was to be promoted to regional manager—but her promotion hinged on a performance review. Even though her technical competence was rated very high, she got a low grade on "interpersonal skills" and lost the promotion.[34] But how do you measure these touchy-feely skills? When is enough caring *enough*? It puts women in a terrible bind.

As one high-level manager put it, "Women are expected to walk an extremely fine line between being caring and being a hard-nosed business professional. We are judged harshly by other women if we come off as too callous, but are judged equally harshly by men if we appear too soft."

The caring imperative becomes a "should" for women at work. It's regarded as discretionary for men but mandatory for women. The male stereotype—emotionally detached, unable to connect and uncaring—means that when men step out of their stereotype to offer a helping hand or a shoulder to cry on, they get heaps of praise. (Oh, what a wonderful guy!)

But when women violate the "caring" norm, they are harshly penalized. In one study, when employees did not engage in helping behavior, those who were asked to rate them (male and female) did not mark the men down, but they severely marked down the women.[35]

On the other side of the coin, when the men helped, the judges rated them very highly. The women who helped got no benefit for caring.

The raters were asked to evaluate the performance of the male and female workers on three factors: likelihood of success, likelihood of advancement in the company and overall performance. They were also asked to give recommendations for the workers, including salary increase and promotion. Finally, they rated the workers on competence and likability.

When the workers did *not* help, the men's job performance score did not suffer. But the women's performance was rated significantly lower. They were also judged as nasty, selfish and manipulative.

In contrast, when men engaged in helping behavior, their performance ratings were very high. Women who helped got *no* benefit. Overall, women who don't help pay a huge price that men never have to pay. Even more galling, when women help, they get no bump in approval. It is a huge lose-lose for women.

It's stunning to discover how powerful and pervasive this "caring imperative" is in the lives of women. From the kindergarten teacher who is tougher on the girl who snatches away a block from another child than she is on the boy who does the same, to the parent who steers a daughter away from pursuits that seem risky and competitive, to the boss who discriminates against women who aren't caring enough, this imperative affects women powerfully throughout their lives.

Until we retire "sugar and spice" to the scrap heap of history, women will never be equal.

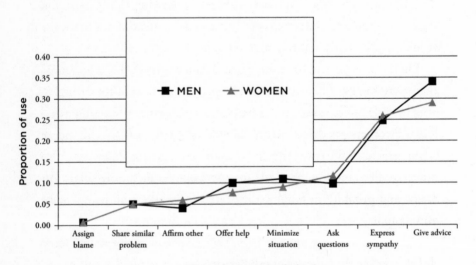

EIGHT

MISERABLE ACHIEVERS?

One of the hallmarks of the New Soft War is that threats come in a gentle wrapping of concern for women. *Yes indeed, you can do it all, and often better than men. But do be careful. You could pay too high a price for achieving. Do you really want to end up alone, miserable and childless?*

These messages affect women as they try to compete in the marketplace. As hard as it is to succeed, the road becomes even rougher for women when they are weighed down by the need to conform to media-fueled images of how they should look and behave. Being really smart is not on the list of attributes women are told to advertise.

In one form or another, the "Men don't like smart women" message has been around for many years. What's new is the idea that it's cool for young women to be smart and aim high, but *only* if they're really "hot" as well.

So, we hear that women should put ambition on hold and grab the first man willing to marry them, because otherwise they might lead unhappy, lonely lives. This is the advice of Lori Gottlieb in her 2008

Atlantic article "Marry Him: The Case for Settling for Mr. Good Enough," which garnered a lot of media buzz.[1]

Then, in 2011, *Atlantic* ran a story titled "All the Single Ladies," which offered an even grimmer prospect for single women based on a dim view of men: "Recent years have seen an explosion of male joblessness and a steep decline in men's life prospects that have disrupted the 'romantic market' in ways that narrow a marriage-minded woman's options: increasingly, her choice is between deadbeats (whose numbers are rising) and playboys (whose power is growing).[2]

In a similar vein, we hear that women have abandoned happiness and pleasure and become work-centered drones. That's the belief critic Camille Paglia expresses in her *New York Times* opinion piece "No Sex, Please, We're Middle Class," claiming that a sexual malaise has consumed the country.[3] The culprit: "the anxious, overachieving, white upper middle class." Women in this group, says Paglia, postpone childbearing, and "men and women are interchangeable, doing the same, mind-based work. Physicality is suppressed; voices are lowered and gestures curtailed in sanitized office space. Men must neuter themselves, while ambitious women postpone procreation. Androgyny is bewitching in art, but in real life it can lead to stagnation and boredom, which no pill can cure." These brainy female drones certainly don't turn men on, Paglia believes, calling to mind the old saw that "men don't make passes at girls who wear glasses."

No matter how many times researchers debunk that "misery" story with real facts, it refuses to die. Feminism is always the culprit for women's alleged unhappiness. They can't find men, they can't have children—or if they do have them, their ambitions make their kids miserable. On and on it goes. We've tracked this story over the years and its hardiness is astonishing. The media never tire of the saga of the wretched achieving woman.

For example, in his 2009 op-ed piece for the *New York Times*, "Liberated and Unhappy," Ross Douthat claims, "All the achievements of the feminist era may have delivered women to greater unhappiness. In the 1960s, when Betty Friedan diagnosed her fellow wives and daughters as the victims of 'the problem with no name,' American women reported themselves happier, on average, than did men. Today, that gender gap has reversed. Male happiness has inched up, and female happiness has dropped. In post-feminist America, men are happier than women."[4]

He is referring to a study by Professors Betsey Stevenson and Justin Wolfers, researchers at the Wharton School of the University of Pennsylvania.[5] Their report was based on data collected each year since 1972 by the U.S. General Social Survey, which asks men and women, "How happy are you, on a scale of 1 to 3?" Over the years, some 50,000 men and women have participated, making it a huge study.

However, there's less to this story than meets the eye. In large-scale studies, very small differences can rise to the level of statistical significance. And in this study, the differences between the sexes are so small that, generally, they are less than one half of 1 percent.

Hurrah, men! You are one half of 1 percent happier than women! Cause for great celebration? Of course this tiny difference tells you nothing about men, women or happiness.

And when the researchers looked at particular groups of men and women—employed, married, single, etc.—they found virtually no differences in overall happiness levels between men and women. It was only when they looked at the sample as a whole that very small differences emerged. Journalists hyped these findings far beyond their true meaning. It's a recurring problem. Even the faintest whiff of misery for modern women results in front-page headlines or talk-show sound bites.

In 2005, the *Atlantic* published an ominous headline about bright women, "Too Smart to Marry?"[6] The sentiment was echoed in the *New York Times*, the *Chicago Sun-Times* and the *Toronto Star* and on *60 Minutes*.

This drumbeat reached its zenith in Maureen Dowd's now classic *New York Times Magazine* piece, "What's a Modern Girl to Do?"[7] This 2005 article became the most e-mailed story from the *Times* website the week it was published, and it left Dowd fielding readers' mail on the past and future of feminism.

"Decades after the feminist movement promised equality with men," Dowd says, especially pessimistic about the prospects for romantic love, lamenting that "it was becoming increasingly apparent that many women would have to brush up on the venerable tricks of the trade: an absurdly charming little laugh, a pert toss of the head, an air of saucy triumph, dewy eyes and a full knowledge of music, drawing, elegant note writing and geography. It would once more be considered captivating to lie on a chaise lounge, pass a lacy handkerchief across the eyelids and complain of a case of springtime giddiness."

What a waste of such a powerful platform. If Dowd—capable of such wit, charm and political insight—had only bothered to check her social science data, she would have discovered a different story. For this surreal description of contemporary men and women, Dowd cites a study conducted by investigators at four British universities (Edinburgh, Glasgow, Bristol and Aberdeen) claiming that for every 15-point increase in IQ score above the average, women's likelihood of marrying fell by almost 60 percent. This same study led to the *Atlantic* headline mentioned earlier, "Too Smart to Marry?"[8]

Really bad news for bright women, right?

Not. Neither Dowd nor the *Atlantic* bothered to emphasize that the data were gathered from men and women born in 1921; the women, if they were still alive at the time, would have been in their nineties. When they were smart young women, the only life choices open to them were staying single or entering a restrictive traditional marriage, one that would have surely stymied their intellectual pursuits. Is it any wonder they chose to remain unmarried? Does a very antiquated study tell us anything about the marrying habits of today's men and women? Of course not.

But the drumbeat continued. Economist Sylvia Ann Hewlett, president of the Center for Talent Innovation, argues in her book, *Creating a Life: Professional Women and the Quest for Children*, that high-achieving women tend to be miserable and often childless.[9] This notion actually inspired the *Sex and the City* episode in which Miranda, the high-powered lawyer, tells a man she meets at a speed-dating party that she's a flight attendant so he won't bolt in fear.

Garance Franke-Ruta notes in the *American Prospect* the firestorm of fear this book ignited: "*Time* magazine produced a worry-inducing cover package centering on Hewlett's book and posing its message in the starkest possible terms: 'Babies vs. Career.' In *The New Republic Online*, Michelle Cottle described how a friend of hers 'burst into tears halfway through the *Time* article and had to stop reading.' It wasn't long before a full-fledged 'Baby Panic' was declared on the cover of *New York* magazine. 'Honestly,' Dina Wise, 29, told *New York*, since Hewlett's book came out, 'I've never felt worse.'"[10]

Hitting this same theme, author Penelope Trunk says in a 2008 *Boston Globe* article, "If you are past your early twenties, and you're single and want to have children, you need to find a partner now. Take that career drive and direct it toward mating—your ovaries will not last longer than your career."[11]

The London *Daily Mail* decreed in 2011, "Thousands of women regret not having more children after putting off motherhood for their careers, official figures suggested. A generation is suffering agonising 'baby hunger' after waiting into their late 30s and 40s, often leaving it too late because of declining fertility."[12]

But should young women abandon their careers in their twenties to give birth early? Is there indeed an epidemic of childlessness?

Actually, no. In Hewlett's own survey of 1,168 high-achieving women, two-thirds of them had children, while one-third did not. Why isn't the story that two-thirds of high achievers *do* manage to have kids—even in a society that has few family-friendly policies?

The fact that women over age forty face declining fertility is hardly a news story. The biological clock is a huge worry factor for women. Hewlett thinks that many women follow a male career model, blithely cruising along, assuming they will be able to have kids. They awake at about age forty-five and realize, "Oops, I forgot to have kids," and are stunned to find they are having trouble conceiving. Perhaps some women do this—but you wonder what planet they're living on.

And are childless women inevitably miserable? No. Our study of women ages thirty-five to fifty-five, funded by the National Science Foundation, found that childlessness did *not* have a significant impact on a woman's well-being.[13] (Marriage was far more important.) The childless women in our sample typically went through a period of adjustment—and sometimes asked "What if?"—but by their mid-forties they were mostly happy and feeling good about themselves. Hewlett focused on women who did not have their own biological children and presented them as universally unhappy.

Indeed, when Franke-Ruta asked Heather Boushey, chief economist of the Center for American Progress, to look at a broader set of data than what Hewlett used, the picture turned out to be quite different regarding both marriage and children.[14] "High-achieving women between 28 and 35 are just as likely to be successfully married as other women who work full time, according to the national data. Fully 81 percent of high-achieving women between ages 36 and 40 had married at least once, as had 83 percent of all other working women, though only 62 percent of high-achieving and 60 percent of all other working women remained married, thanks to America's high divorce rate. In other words, there is no achievement-related marriage gap. When Hewlett writes that 'the more a woman succeeds in her career, the less likely it is she will ever have a partner,' she is dead wrong."

Also, are empty wombs the fate of high achievers? "Not only is there no significant achievement-related marriage drought among women 36 to 40, there isn't a baby bust, either. . . . Many high-achieving women who marry and have children delay childbearing until after age 35 and then successfully start families. Because of this late-thirties baby boomlet, married high-achieving women are exactly as likely to have had kids by ages 36 to 40 as are all other married women who work full time." And women twenty-eight to thirty-five with advanced degrees who earn more than $55,000 are as likely to be happily married and to have children as women who earn less.

But the "childless" theme keeps being played by the media as a headline-grabbing scare story. Don't expect this to change.

What about the idea that educated women are doomed to spinsterhood? Nonsense. Nowadays, the more education a woman has, the *more* likely she is to marry. Men rank intelligence and education way above cooking and housekeeping as desirable traits in a partner, according to family historian Stephanie Coontz.[15]

The fact is that men are not avoiding smart women. Valerie Oppenheimer, a sociologist at the University of California, Los Angeles, reported that contemporary men are choosing as mates women who have completed their education.[16] Elaina Rose, an associate economics professor at the University of Washington in Seattle, has followed the diminishing marriage "success penalty" that women once suffered.[17] Twenty-five years ago, a woman with a graduate degree was 13.5 percent less likely to have married by forty to forty-four years of age than a woman with only a high school diploma. By the 2000 U.S. census, however, that penalty had largely disappeared. And educated and high-earning women are now *less* likely to divorce than other women.

But if you get your views about gender and marriage from the media—especially from television—you come away with a very different idea. Try to find high achievers who are happily married. The supersmart TV writer played by Tina Fey in *30 Rock* has a miserable track record with men. In *Grey's Anatomy*, only one of the leading female surgeons is happily married; the rest are divorced, have been left by their husbands or are fighting with their significant others. On the perennial favorite *House* (now in syndication), the dean of medicine is single and miserable, while several other female doctors are either divorced or unhappily looking for men. The high-powered lawyer played by Glenn Close on *Damages* is divorced and estranged from her child, and on *Law & Order: SVU*, detective Olivia Benson is a single, childless woman. On *Homeland*, CIA operative Carrie Mathison, played by Claire Danes, has a failed romance with a man who turns out to be a spy, and winds up getting electroshock therapy after a breakdown . . . on and on it goes.

What of men who marry achieving women? According to the media, they are doomed to be unhappy. "Don't Marry Career Women," editor Michael Noer advises on Forbes.com in an article subtitled "How Do Women, Careers and Marriage Mix? Not Well, Say Social Scientists."[18]

Indeed, women in great numbers did not believe the Forbes.com story and, moreover, found it insulting. By week's end, *Forbes* had been flooded with so many e-mails from furious women (some urging a boycott of the magazine) and had been chastised by so many bloggers that the publication quickly sprinted away from its own story. Publisher Steve Forbes publicly apologized for insulting working women with the article. ABC ran the apology story on the evening news. Female readers and bloggers had made a difference.

But why did the website run such a misleading story in the first place? The *New York Times* suggested a possible business motivation behind the article.[19] A provider of third-party Web traffic data told the *Times* that visits to Forbes.com had "tumbled" and were only about half of the 15.3 million a month the company had been advertising. The *Times* story noted that Forbes.com was featuring glitzy, lifestyle stories, raising the question of whether the career-women story was simply a cynical attempt to get "buzz." Sensationalizing like this happens all the time in our frenetic twenty-four-hour media. This fracas mattered because it added to the growing myth of a "scientific" consensus that ambitious women create bad marriages and that only by returning to traditional roles can the sexes be at peace.

As for men with high-earning wives, solid data suggest just the opposite of misery. One longitudinal study of 500 couples by the University of Wisconsin–Madison's Janet Hyde found that for both men and women, the highest sexual satisfaction was reported by couples who both worked and experienced high rewards from their jobs. A good job, it seems, is good for your sex life.[20]

What does the science really say? A major analysis of data from our study of dual-earner couples contradicts the Forbes.com thesis that men will be unhappy if they marry career women.

Our study—which looked at men's marital happiness—found that, overall, as a woman earns more relative to her husband, his marital quality goes *up*. Why so? Probably for a number of reasons. Men's wages have been stagnant or declining for at least thirty years, so their wives' income may be easing financial tensions and making it possible for the couple to pay their bills. Her enhanced earnings may be heightening her self-esteem, and so she brings these good feelings about herself into the marriage. He may want to spend more time with the family, and her work eases the breadwinning burden. Research tells us that men today do want more family time and are actually spending more time with their families than they used to.

RETURN TO "FEMININITY"?

A recurring theme in the New Soft War is the notion that women must instantly return to traditional (read subservient) behavior so they can be happy and men will not be destroyed. This idea pops up regularly and sells like hotcakes. In the 1970s there was Marabel Morgan's *The Total Woman*—which sold more than 10 million copies.[21] It tells women that to get the washer and dryer they really want, they should greet their husbands at the door wearing only Saran wrap. John Gray's seemingly omnipresent Mars and Venus volumes—which have outsold every other book except the Bible—instruct women that they are responsible for the happiness of their spouses.[22] In 2001, Laura Doyle's *The Surrendered Wife: A Practical Guide to Finding Intimacy, Passion and Peace with a Man* became a bestseller.[23] Her advice to women:

- Relinquish control of the household finances and rely on your husband to give you what you need.
- Apologize for being disrespectful whenever you contradict, criticize or dismiss your husband's thoughts and ideas.
- Make yourself sexually available to your husband (at least once a week).

- Defer to your husband's thinking when you have conflicting opinions.
- Most of all, practice saying the following line: "Whatever you think, dear." Say it with a smile. Try it now. Feels good, doesn't it?

Starting in the mid-1990s, Laura Schlessinger hit the same theme regularly on her popular radio show, the *Dr. Laura Program*.

The newest femininity manifesto was written in 2012 for Fox News by Suzanne Venker, niece of veteran culture warrior Phyllis Schlafly:

> Women aren't women anymore. . . .
>
> Women have changed dramatically. In a nutshell, women are angry. They're also defensive, though often unknowingly. That's because they've been raised to think of men as the enemy. Armed with this new attitude, women pushed men off their pedestal (women had their own pedestal, but feminists convinced them otherwise) and climbed up to take what they were taught to believe was rightfully theirs.
>
> Now the men have nowhere to go.[24]

But there can be a happy ending. "Fortunately, there is good news: women have the power to turn everything around," Venker says. "All they have to do is surrender to their nature—their femininity—and let men surrender to theirs. If they do, marriageable men will come out of the woodwork."

Many of these books and screeds are mawkish, over-the-top and simplistic, perhaps even chuckled at by sophisticated readers. Indeed, they could be easily dismissed as down-market nonsense for the masses, but that would be a mistake. Because they sell so many copies, and because they are so often featured in the mass media, they can't be laughed away. First of all, they are marketed to vulnerable women who have few resources and have trouble putting their own needs front and center. Even more important, these stories support the confirmation bias that still pervades our culture and acts as a growth hormone for the stereotypes that cause women so much grief. The idea that women are caretakers who do best when they focus on home and hearth sits inside the heads of women who don't even know it's there. It also lodges unconsciously inside the heads of men in the workplace who hire, fire and promote—or do *not* promote—women.

HOT—OR NOT?

Meanwhile, the new message that women can be smart, and can achieve—but they have to be hot while doing it—is growing. It seems to affect the best and brightest young women. In a *New York Times* profile of girls in the affluent, achievement-oriented suburb of New-ton, Massachusetts, girls were well aware of this imperative.[25] As au-thor Sara Rimer says,

> To spend several months in a pressure cooker like Newton North [High School] is to see what a girl can be—what any young person can be—when encouraged by committed teachers and by engaged parents who can give them wide-ranging opportunities.
>
> It is also to see these girls struggle to navigate the conflicting mes-sages they have been absorbing, if not from their parents then from the culture, since elementary school. The first message: Bring home A's. Do everything. Get into a top college—which doesn't have to be

in the Ivy League, or one of the other elites like Williams, Tufts or Bowdoin, but should be a "name" school.

The second message: Be yourself. Have fun. Don't work too hard.

And, for all their accomplishments and ambitions, the amazing girls, as their teachers and classmates call them, are not immune to the third message: While it is now cool to be smart, it is not enough to be smart. . . .

Kat Jiang, a go-to stage manager for student theater who has a perfect 2,400 score on her SATs, wrote in an e-mail message, "It's out of style to admit it, but it is more important to be hot than smart."

"Effortlessly hot," Kat added.

At Princeton, comments on the Web that female students on campus weren't "hot" enough brought complaints. One girl wrote in the *Daily Princetonian*, "I was sitting innocently in the dining hall, attempting to get through the 400 pages of reading for my politics class in the half-hour left before precept, as a young, likely freshman and quite pretty girl sauntered by. Seconds later, I heard the two boys sitting in the booth behind me whisper the following conversation:

"'She's hot.'

"'Princeton hot or actually hot?'

"'Actually hot.'

"'Nah, she's not that great . . .'

"It's become ingrained into the Princeton consciousness that our female students are, to put it plainly, just not that attractive. 'Public school hot,' 'actually hot' and 'hot for Princeton' have become recognized categories and adjectives. Even my own boyfriend—after first frantically reassuring me that, of course, I alone break the mold—admitted that he believes that the general caliber of female appearance is somewhat lower here than at big public universities. Follow-up conversations with my male friends have confirmed the widespread nature of this belief."[26]

The pressure to be supersmart, accomplished and hot at the same time takes a toll on young women. Facing a bad economy and diminished prospects, all college freshmen are experiencing the poorest mental health in twenty-five years. But women, it seems, have a harder struggle toward self-esteem than men.

One senior-level female manager tells us, "Women today are expected to meet the same standards as men in terms of intelligence, competency and enthusiasm for their work, but they are absolutely judged more harshly on appearance, even in a professional setting. We are expected to be professional, conservative and beautiful in the office, then sexy and uninhibited out at happy hour, then demure and housewife-y upon returning home. How on earth can a woman keep up with all of those pressures and still be a top performer in the areas that actually matter? It's a Sisyphean battle."

Appearance was a factor when a banker sued Citibank in 2010 for firing her because she was too curvy. Debrahlee Lorenzana, an attractive young Puerto Rican woman, was hired to be a business banker at a New York Citibank branch office. According to her lawsuit, her bosses told her that "as a result of the shape of her figure, such clothes were purportedly 'too distracting' for her male colleagues and supervisors to bear."

She claims that her male managers gave her a list of clothing items she was not allowed to wear: turtlenecks, pencil skirts, and fitted suits. And three-inch heels.

After trying to change her appearance to look more conservative, even wearing no makeup, she was told she looked "sickly," and when she left her hair curly instead of straightening it, they told her she should go ahead and straighten it every day. She finally got the message that there was no way she could win.

"I could have worn a paper bag, and it would not have mattered," she told the *Village Voice*.[27] "If it wasn't my shirt, it was my pants. If it wasn't my pants, it was my shoes. They picked on me every single day." (The case went to arbitration, and the results were not publicly revealed.)

Every year, women have a less positive view of their emotional health than men do, and the gap has widened. A *Seventeen* magazine/Yahoo! survey found that 74 percent of girls and young women felt constant pressure to be perfect. [28]

(As we'll see in Chapter 10, such pressures may be causing Ivy League women to step back from on-campus positions that could lead to good jobs.)

Of course, there has always been pressure on women to be attractive, but for the first time in history, we are getting to see far more "perfect" people than ordinary people. With twenty-four-hour media, the Internet, films, cable TV, movies, and so on, we constantly see people who are not just young and attractive, but impossibly so. Slim, beautiful models are Photoshopped to be even thinner. Body doubles are used in films if a star just isn't trim or buff enough. Computer imaging produces perfection in a nanosecond. As the Social Issues Research Centre, in Oxford, England, has noted: "We see 'beautiful people' all the time, more often than members of our own family, making exceptional good looks seem real, normal and attainable. Standards of beauty have in fact become harder and harder to attain, particularly for women. The current media ideal of thinness for women is achievable by less than 5% of the female population."[29]

And as a nation, we are spending more and more time consuming media. The website VideoMind says, "To put this in perspective, consider the following (admittedly rough) back-of-the-envelope math: If the typical American's day is broken up into thirds (sleep, work and free time), then roughly three-quarters of free time, or about 6 hours, is spent being social online and watching TV and video."[30]

And what are we seeing? Mostly women in their twenties and thirties, in television and in film. Martha M. Lauzen, executive director of the Center for the Study of Women in Television and Film at San Diego State University, says, "This is just a huge misrepresentation of reality and that really skews our perceptions. . . . Women in their teens, twenties and thirties are 39 percent of the population, yet are 71 percent of women on TV. Women 40 and older are 47 percent of the population, yet are 26 percent of women on TV."[31] The real world is very different from the way it's portrayed on television, where doctors, lawyers, high-level academics, news anchors and the like are mainly young and beautiful.

Lauzen adds, "When any group is not featured in the media, well, what part do I play in this culture? . . . There's actually an academic term for that. It's called 'symbolic annihilation.'"

The message to women and girls in all these media is that their appearance should be, above all, tailored to "the male gaze." You exist at all times in a world where men are looking at you, and you must please them.

According to the noted sociologist Erving Goffman, "Women are often posed bending their heads or bodies at an angle, with the level of the head lowered relative to that of others, including, indirectly, the viewer of the picture. The resulting configurations can be read as an acceptance of subordination, an expression of integration, submissiveness, and appeasement."[32]

Men "act" and women "appear." Men look at women. Women watch themselves being looked at.

"Most women make less money and have less power than most men," Goffman says, "and the message that goes out to women without power is that to get some, you need to gain control of a male view of women—which means to get power through male power, rather than on your own."

When you understand the politics of the male gaze, you also understand why marketing this behavior to young women is so destructive, especially to their ambitions and sense of self.

This pressure can lead young women to focus heavily on how others view them. New research tells us that college women who focus on others rather than on themselves have low self-esteem and high levels of anxiety and depression. No wonder. If you are always worrying about being perfect, you have little time for much else.[33]

PORN AND ROMANCE: AN ODD COUPLE?

Some future media historian may refer to the present era as the "age of hypersexuality." Never before have there been so many images of women in sexual poses that are demeaning, violent and subservient.

A continuing extreme sexualization of women and girls dominates the media and the culture. As cultural critic Gail Dines notes, "Something has shifted so profoundly in our society that the idealized, pop culture image of women in today's pornified world is no longer a Stepford Wife but rather a plasticized, scripted, hyper-sexualized, surgically enhanced young woman. The media world we live in today has replaced the stereotyped Stepford Wife with the equally limiting and controlling stereotype of a Stepford Slut."[34]

In October 2010, fraternity pledges at Yale chanted as they marched across the campus. This is what they shouted:

My name is Jack,
I'm a necrophiliac.
I fuck dead women,
and fill them with my semen.
No means yes,
Yes means anal.
[Repeated]
Fuck al-Qaeda
Fuck al-Qaeda
[Repeated]
Fucking sluts
Fucking sluts
[Repeated]
USA
USA[35]

The oversexualization of young women is taking a major toll, leading to severe mental and physical health problems. Some of these include risky sexual behavior and high rates of eating disorders, depression and low self-esteem. In a 2007 major report on girls, the American Psychological Association found the media emphasizing young women's sexuality "to a stunning degree."[36] A University of Buffalo study found that females are eleven times more likely to be sexualized in the popular media than males are.[37]

At the same time, the romance genre is booming; Prince Charming is alive and well, even when he arrives in peculiar forms—such as the hunky vampire and werewolf in the monumentally successful Twilight books and film. Romance fiction is a huge business, whose revenue actually increased from $1.355 billion in 2010 to $1.368 billion in 2011, and it remains the largest share of the consumer market, at 14.3 percent. Readership continues to grow.

While romance novels may seem to be harmless entertainment, they have a darker side. One study found that women who buy into romantic fantasies tend to choose occupations with reduced economic rewards that require less education after high school.

Such women also show little interest in high-status occupations. Living too fully in an unreal world of fantasy and romance can undermine your economic prospects in the real world.[38]

Both hypersexuality and the romance genre of books and movies are part of the New Soft War, because both have negative effects on one very important part of a woman's anatomy according to the American Psychological Association: her brain.

- The APA found that girls' preoccupation with appearance ties up cognitive resources, "meaning girls will have less time and mental energy for other pursuits. . . . Girls may be learning to prioritize certain rewards (male attention) over other rewards (academic accomplishment), thus limiting their future educational and occupational opportunities."
- This obsession may even interfere with their interest in science, technology, engineering and math (STEM). The APA notes, "If they perceive occupations relating to [STEM] as less consistent with a sexy self-image, they may be induced to want to be a model, fashion designer, or pop star in order to embody the sexualized look that they know is valued for women rather than choose to be a chemist, computer programmer, or engineer. If girls perceive what research shows—that women

who choose male-identified professions are least preferred (in college samples) as romantic partners—then they will perceive some social costs to choosing careers that are not consistent with a 'sexy' image."

- Research finds that women in situations in which they are aware that they are being seen as sexualized actually show a drop in cognitive ability. (The same does not happen with men.)

- Men who often view explicit sexual content tend to think less of women's intelligence and are more prone to harass.

A new, popular literary form dubbed "fratire" debases women— under the guise of satire. It has been spearheaded by Tucker Max, the wildly successful Duke Law School graduate who rates women on a scale from "common-stock pig" to "super hottie." He boasts to a wide and adoring audience about his sexual conquests, which include humiliating and insulting women. Max is making a fortune from a genre that Melissa Lafsky of the *New York Times* has called "misogyny for sale."[39] She says that fratire authors are profiting by fueling young male anger concerning societal demands for equality. Max's book, *I Hope They Sell Beer in Hell*, has sold more than a million copies and has been on the *New York Times* bestseller list for more than a hundred weeks.

Max not only has a huge following among college students but also has attracted the attention of TV producers who want to make a show based on his exploits. He claims that his writings are simply "nothing more than men writing about being men in an honest and authentic way" and "a literary reaction to the feminization of masculinity."[40] If he actually reflects what many men his age are thinking about women, then the path to mutual respect and regard between the sexes will be much harder than many have thought.

Another star in this new genre, who uses the name Maddox, told National Public Radio that the woman bashing associated with fratire was now acceptable because "women are stronger than they've ever been in society, and that singling out women as the only group not OK to lampoon is a sexist act in itself."[41] (Someone should give him a copy of the APA report on the effects of hypersexualization on girls.)

For women, paying too much attention to whether they are desirable enough, or getting mired down in romantic fantasies, can be toxic when it comes to achievement. When the narrative of "Men don't like smart women" meets the obsession of the modern media with women's appearance, it can create a perfect storm of discouragement for female empowerment. If women indeed do pull back on their ambitions, they will have lost an important battle in the New Soft War.

NINE

STRAW WOMEN, STRAW MEN?

Are women really on track to become the richer sex and to replace men as the primary breadwinners in American families? Is the United States becoming a middle-class matriarchy? Are we seeing the end of men as women take over the reins of power in the nation and become the ascendant sex? Is it time for women to step back and let men catch up?

The highly successful woman wielding power over the hapless man is now a media staple. This woman is part of the middle-class matriarchy, outearning her husband and marching to the top of the world order. She has torn down the barriers that kept her foremothers back, and now the sky is the limit.

This narrative is fast becoming the major news frame of the story of men and women, boys and girls. It's all over newspapers, magazines and the web. Despite the fact that this narrative is totally at odds with our everyday experience and with a mountain of solid contradictory data, it is replayed so often and in so many venues that you can hardly blame women and men for believing it's true.

Don't be fooled. These straw men and straw women can blow your house down. If you take in this message, you may never fulfill your potential. Why? If you believe that all the barriers to your advancement have been knocked down, and that your heavy backpack has been emptied, only *you* are responsible if—despite all your hard work and effort—you don't advance.

Nonsense. We need to put up some red flags before this runaway train gets too far down the track.

More men than women lost their jobs after the 2008 financial crisis, fueling the decline-of-men narrative. But guess what happened next? In 2012 the Bureau of Labor Statistics revealed that, in fact, we're in the middle of a "mancovery"—men are getting back on their feet while women are slipping backward.[1] Between June 2009 and June 2011, women lost close to 300,000 jobs, while men gained more than 800,000. "We've never seen a recovery like this," the National Women's Law Center's Joan Entmacher told NPR, "where two years into the recovery, women are doing so much worse than men and are actually losing ground."[2]

Still, the popular perception is that women are soaring. Much is made of the "fact" that more than 40 percent of American women are their family's breadwinner. In a 2012 *Time* magazine cover piece (adapted from her book *The Richer Sex*), journalist Liza Mundy cites 2009 Bureau of Labor Statistics data saying that one in four women outearn their spouses.[3] This claim was picked up by scores of media outlets.

But look a bit more closely at the numbers, and the picture isn't so rosy for women. *Which* women are advancing? And *which* men are backsliding? The answers are important if you are going to talk about who's getting "rich."

In fact, the only segment of society in which a substantial percentage of wives significantly outearn their husbands is low-income workers, according to two respected scholars who looked at large national data sets. Economist Heather Boushey says that in 2010, among couples whose earnings were in the bottom 20 percent (averaging some $20,000 a year per household), 70 percent of women outearned their husbands.[4] And Anne Winkler, a professor of economics and public policy administration at the University of Missouri, in her detailed 2005 analysis, has found that the wealthier the couple, the *less* likely that the wife will outearn her husband.[5]

Indeed, as family income goes up, fewer and fewer women outearn their husbands, Winkler reports. When you look at women who really *are* the breadwinners—who earn at least 60 percent of the family income—the figure drops to about 10 percent. So, when you talk about women who are making appreciably more than their husbands, it's only one woman in ten. And since that is true primarily among couples earning the lowest salaries, the term "rich" doesn't describe what's really happening for most women.

In addition, the 40 percent figure widely cited today drops dramatically when more sophisticated analyses are used. You can get to that figure *only* in this way:

- If you define a woman as the breadwinner if she outearns her working husband by as little as a dollar a day.
- *And* if you include single mothers who are sole providers. (How on earth could single mothers be included in a statistic that's supposed to be about wives outearning husbands? Only by looking at "family income," which includes single mothers.)

In Mundy's *Time* article, the only family shown in a photograph is a middle-class white family with five adult children.[6] One son is a college graduate working in finance, and the husband of one daughter was expected to be a "hot-shot corporate lawyer." Another sister is her company's global director of marketing, and her restaurant manager husband cut back his work hours. Two other sisters also earn more than their husbands.

Readers get the idea that this pattern of women making more than their husbands is common among the educated middle class. That's not so. The more typical scenario is that of the hotel maid who ekes out $12,000 a year scrubbing toilets and making beds, while her handyman husband fixes porches and repairs windows when he can get work but brings in only $8,000 per year.

Certainly, women have made significant gains in the past four decades, and there are indeed educated middle-class women who are the primary breadwinners, but they are far from taking over American homes.

Mundy wonders about the consequences of what she sees as "The Big Flip," women earning more than men. She wonders whether women who are the major breadwinners will want more control of discretionary spending. Since women make more money, will they be hesitant to let their spouses into that action? Numerous articles about *The Richer Sex* deal with that question, as if it were a big issue. However, it may not be much of a problem, because the "Flip" won't be all that big. Some couples will experience it, but not that many, since couples where the wife is the major earner and there's money to burn are not all that numerous, even among high earners. Women at the low end of the income scale who do significantly outearn their husbands won't have to grapple with this problem, because in those families there's next to no money left after the basics are paid for.

The real economic story behind headlines touting women's rise is that men, especially at the lower end of the wage scale, were doing poorly at the beginning of the recession. Even then, women weren't doing great, but men were losing their jobs at a faster clip and their wages were declining. Now, women are sliding backward. But will the "mancovery" story have legs, or will it lose out to the "richer sex" and the "end of men" narratives, which are on their way to becoming cultural memes, believed without much evidence?

THE END OF MEN?

Hanna Rosin's 2012 book, *The End of Men: And the Rise of Women*, is just the latest in this ongoing media story. *New York* magazine published an article in 2010 asking if boys are now the second sex.[7] A 2012 book by David Benatar, *The Second Sexism: Discrimination Against Men and Boys*, got a great deal of media play.[8] And Rosin went so far as to suggest that women will replace men in the "broad striving middle class" that defines society and provides leaders.

Rosin's book became a media phenomenon, inspiring university colloquia, passionate op-ed columns and lots of coverage from tiny sound bites to hourlong NPR segments. Economist Nancy Folbre, writing in the *New York Times* business section, notes that the book's title "now serves as shorthand for . . . the end of male economic advantage."[9]

Of course, a quick reality check raises some questions on that score. The American president is male, the chief justice of the Supreme Court is male and the fifty highest-paid CEOs are male. Nearly all American billionaires are male, or widows of males, with the exception of Oprah Winfrey. Only twenty U.S. senators are female—a mere 20 percent.

These end-of-men stories not only exaggerate women's progress and success but also present the worst possible scenarios for men. Worries about fewer boys going to college became another huge national story within the past few years, and it still resonates. In 2011 *NBC Nightly News* ran a story headlined "Men Falling Behind Women," which asked, "Where are male college students?"[10]

Newsweek called declining male college attendance part of a "Boy Crisis."[11]

A *USA Today* headline proclaimed, "College Gender Gap Widens: 57% Are Women."[12]

On NPR, writer Richard Whitmire voiced concern "about boys falling behind in school."[13]

But men and boys have never been one homogeneous mass. White boys from the economic class that has always held power aren't dropping out of college. They are where they always have been: in the Ivies, which still have more male than female students. Suburban boys do not avoid college—but lower-middle-class boys too often do, and the latter are the ones who may need college desperately in the emerging information economy. Poor boys are, of course, in real trouble.

This media blitz has probably convinced people that young women have fast outpaced young men when it comes to going to college. Not so. Today, among college-age whites, the gender gap is very small (51 percent women vs. 49 percent men).[14]

Given the drumbeat of our national worries about boys not going to college, many readers will find this fact astonishing. It turns out that the central tenet of the "ascendance of women" argument is based on bogus statistics. There is not now—and never was—a startling 15 percent gender gap in college enrollments.

How did that figure emerge? You can get that number only by factoring in older, nontraditional students. Researcher Jacqueline King, author of a study on gender disparity in college attendance, emphasizes that the gap is widest among blacks (63 percent women vs. 37 percent men).[15] Among Hispanics, the gap is 14 percent (57 women percent vs. 43 percent men). Among lower-income whites, it is 8 percent (54 percent to 46 percent). "It's not middle-class white young men who aren't going vs. college," King says. And an enrollment boom among older women is further skewing the numbers.

Despite the end-of-men scare stories predicated on the female edge in college classes, "women lead in college but not in the workforce," according to a report funded by the Alfred P. Sloan Foundation.[16] "Women's earnings, relative to those of men, have not kept up with their gains in educational attainment.... Part of this difference reflects the higher concentration of men in higher-paying fields, including the natural and physical sciences, mathematics, and engineering. At the college level, fewer women than men take courses in science-related fields."

If the past is any guide, women will continue to lead in college, but not in the workforce. In her book, Rosin interviewed girls about their expectations. One young undergraduate who wants to go to medical school told Rosin that she will be the "hotshot" surgeon and her future husband will be "at home playing with the kiddies."

There's a realistic scenario. (Since when are anecdotes considered data?)

As critic Ann Friedman says in the *American Prospect*, "Sure, college-age women tell [Rosin] they hope to become surgeons and marry men who will be primary caregivers.[17] But research shows that few women actually *realize* this domestic arrangement—they tend to marry other high-achieving men who expect their own careers to take precedence."

Rosin claims that today, women are the major breadwinners and make most decisions in the family. But this conclusion is based on a tiny, atypical sample of men and women in a small Alabama town largely populated by evangelical Christians with very traditional ideas about male and female roles. These men had worked in textile mills that had closed down, but they admitted they would never consider taking a "female" job. You can't say much of anything about the United States as a whole from this sample.

The research group Catalyst tells a different story. It finds women no closer to closing the gender gap at the top ranks than they were six years ago.[18] Consider these facts:

- In no area of thirteen industrial sectors studied did women earn more than men.
- At no educational level did women earn more than men.
- In no racial group did women earn more than men.
- In none of the twenty-two countries studied did women earn more than men.

Disturbingly, Rosin paints the picture of a "matriarchy" in which women will use their power against men both at home and in the workplace. But when the Pew Research Center conducted a study of 1,260 couples, it found striking equality in decision making in finances, weekend activities and big-ticket purchases.[19] Women made the decisions 43 percent of the time, men 26 percent of the time, and couples made decisions equally in 31 percent of the cases.

In the Pew survey, men and women weren't specifically asked whether they generally share decision making. However, this information *was* recorded if it was volunteered. Indeed, about half of all respondents said that they jointly decide—a real surprise.

Andrew Cherlin, a sociology and public policy professor at Johns Hopkins University, said, "I think the big story over time is the rise in shared decision making. It's not the same as the '50s and '60s, where father knew best . . . and some wives didn't even know what their husbands were making."[20]

Moreover, there was no relationship between wives' decision making and their earnings. Regardless of how much money they earn, women have a major say, singly or jointly. So, Pew notes, for men "earning more money doesn't necessarily mean making more decisions at home. . . . And for women, earning less doesn't always mean making fewer decisions."

As for wrathful women refusing to hire men, research finds just the opposite. Female supervisors hire white men *more often* than they hire other females or members of minority groups (part of the glass escalator phenomenon we discussed in Chapter 4).

CARDBOARD MEN, PLASTIC WOMEN

Hanna Rosin creates the images of "cardboard men" and "plastic women" in her tale of male decline. She says that men do not possess the skills for social intelligence and communication (so necessary for tomorrow's economy) that women do. Women, she claims, are flexible, making them perfect for the new information age. Men, on the other hand, are static, silent, stubborn and clueless—heading for the junk heap.

New York Times columnist David Brooks buys Rosin's idea that women are adapting to today's economy more flexibly and resiliently than men: "If she's right, then men will have to be less like Achilles, imposing their will on the world, and more like Odysseus, the crafty, many-sided sojourner. They'll have to acknowledge that they are strangers in a strange land."[21]

Men are allegedly as sensitive as bricks. In *The Female Brain*, author Louann Brizendine claims, "A woman knows what people are feeling, while a man can't spot an emotion unless somebody cries or threatens bodily harm."[22] In *The First Sex: The Natural Talents of Women and How They Are Changing the World*, anthropologist Helen Fisher claims that women have web brains that integrate many sides of an argument, while men are stuck with plodding linear thinking.[23] "The future belongs to women," she argues.

It's become the conventional wisdom that men and women speak so differently that they virtually inhabit separate cultures. This idea has become so widely accepted in the business world that popular speakers focus on such "differences" at well-attended management seminars. (Much of what is passed on is misinformation.)

Men are supposedly more likely than women to respond to a coworker's problems by giving advice, joking, changing the subject or giving no response. Men, it's said, tend to relate to other men on a one-up, one-down basis. Status and dominance are important. Women supposedly respond to a colleague's problem by sharing a similar problem or expressing sympathy.

Not true.

When confronted with other people's problems, men and women use essentially the *same* types of responses.[24] Both men and women largely provide support by giving advice and expressing sympathy. The sexes are remarkably alike in the types of support they provide. The clear conclusion: Gender differences in communication, especially giving support to others, are relatively small in magnitude. Men are fully able to both offer and receive supportive communications. Women have no special "communication" style.

In resolving conflicts, men and women are supposed to communicate very differently. Men allegedly focus on themselves at the expense of connection. Women supposedly focus on connection at the expense of themselves.

Not so. In a study of more than 3,000 adults, most men and women reported having a mutual style, a balanced integration of concerns for autonomy and connection. A manager who thinks a woman ought not to be promoted because she is too "tuned in" to connection to be a strong leader is probably making a mistake. The same is true when a manager rejects a male candidate, thinking that the man is inherently unable to relate well to others.

We also believe that women are kinder and more cooperative than men. Untrue. Research published in the *Psychological Bulletin* suggests that this commonly held belief needs a rethink.[25] Daniel Balliet, an assistant psychology professor at VU University in Amsterdam, and his colleagues analyzed data from 272 studies spanning fifty years. They were surprised to find that men and women do *not* differ in their overall amounts of cooperation. That's right—women are not the "helpful" sex. Also, context matters. Some situations are more conducive to male cooperation; others, to female cooperation. Women cooperate more than men in mixed-sex interactions. Maybe that's why we get the idea that women don't put themselves first; they don't need to have the last word or to push their own agendas.

But when females get together, it's a different story; there's not much cooperation going on. Less, in fact, than when men congregate.

The cardboard man is as much a fiction as the plastic woman is. But the fictions live on. *The End of Men* was soundly trashed by social scientists—just as the "Opt-Out Revolution" story was. Nevertheless, these terms have entered the popular vernacular and are cited all the time and discussed as if they were real. Unfortunately, they continue to powerfully shape our thoughts and opinions.

THE TRUE STORY

As we've noted, the real story is not the end of men; it is that under a veneer of success and progress, women are in fact at risk of sliding backward. In a recent speech, Harvard law professor Nancy Gertner said about women, "You're supposed to say: 'Things are fabulous.' But they are not. Advancement has stalled."[26] She notes that roughly 50 percent of all new lawyers are female, but only 16 percent of law firm partners are women. Also, of those lawyers who leave the profession, the majority are women, and they do so because of family or social issues. We see the same problems in other fields.

The idea that women are rapidly moving into the high-level career tracks that used to belong solely to men was debunked by a 2012 report from the Council on Contemporary Families.[27] It said flatly that the rapid progress toward gender equality that America experienced in the 1980s and early 1990s has stalled. Occupational segregation, which declined sharply from the 1960s through the 1980s, has not changed since 2000. Working-class occupations have actually become more gender-segregated since 1990 and are now back to the same level as they were in 1950.

And in the field of media, the number of women working as writers and directors on prime-time broadcast programs took a big tumble in the 2010–11 season and has stayed basically flat, says a recent report from the Center for the Study of Women in Television and Film at San Diego State University.[28] Women held only 26 percent of powerful creative positions during the 2011–12 prime-time season. The website TheWrap.com notes, "For the most part, the number of females working behind the camera remains clustered around a few select programs. For example, 90 percent of primetime programs employed no female directors, while the majority of writers' rooms remain male-dominated, with 68 percent of shows employing not a single female scribe."[29]

All across the board, in jobs that lead upward—to the law firm partnership, the CEO's office, the board of directors or the head writer job on a popular TV drama, the ranks of women are thinning. Meanwhile, many female-dominated industries, which do not require a college education, are among the fastest-growing and the lowest-paying.

If this represents male decline, it's a story that's hard to find in the real world beyond the sound bite, the magazine "trend story" or the popular book.

Why is this narrative worrisome? If the end-of-men story were just a passing notion, a bit of media fluff that vanished with the evening wind, nobody would much care. But the media today create the ideas that get repeated, passed around and believed.

Viewed in this light, the decline-of-men narrative spells bad news for women. Remember, as we noted in Chapter 1, men reported high levels of anxiety after reading census data that showcased the gains women have made over the past fifty years. Seemingly threatened by this progress, they may take the end-of-men story to heart and oppose any efforts to help women advance. For example, it's been argued that too many resources have been allotted to helping girls in math, while boys have languished in schools. College admissions officers admit to giving preference to white male students. A male movie reviewer for the *Niagara Falls Reporter* got an e-mail from his editor complaining about his review of *Snow White and the Huntsman*.[30] The e-mail said, "I don't want to publish reviews of films where women are alpha and men are beta. Where women are heroes and villains and men are just lesser versions or shadows of females. I believe in manliness."

The critic says he left the paper after being banned from reviewing films that featured strong women.

It's understandable that men may be feeling greater anxiety in to-day's economy, where so many of the traditional male jobs in manufac-turing have been outsourced and may never come back, and the new knowledge economy will require high levels of skill that many workers don't have and can't attain.

Equally troubling: the "rose-colored glasses" syndrome among women we noted earlier. Too many young women think that all the battles for gender equality have been fought and the future will just bring more progress. (This perception likely explains current low levels of feminist activism; as Barbara Epstein, a history professor at the Univer-sity of California, Santa Cruz, says unequivocally, "There is no longer an organized feminist movement in the United States."[31])

If women buy the message that all the gender battles are over, but they still aren't advancing as fast as they should be, then they may well believe there's no one to blame but themselves. What to do? Take more courses, beef up your credentials with more degrees, work harder, join company sponsored self- esteem-building programs and on and on. But if the problem is subtle discrimination, along with deeply en-trenched gender stereotypes, self-improvement will make only a lim-ited contribution to getting into the C-suite.

If you put all your eggs into the self-improvement basket and forgo any concerted action with other women, your stall will be permanent. Too often, we have met the enemy, and *she* is *us*.

TEN

LEADING THE WAY

I n the second debate of the 2012 presidential campaign, Barack Obama and Mitt Romney went toe-to-toe in a classic male slugfest. As *Forbes* put it, "There was a lot of testosterone in the room; the two men stalked around the stage and each other doing their best to take up space and intimidate the other debater. Romney walked stiffly, visibly tense, uneasy in his body, like an arthritic flamingo. Obama prowled like an angry, predatory cat, waiting to pounce, and when he did, the effect was devastating."[1]

This is our classic image of leadership: strong, dominant men marking out the territory like jungle animals. How do women fit into this picture?

Not very easily.

Because of all the stereotypes we've discussed—that women are built for caring, not for leadership; that their hormones incline them away from taking charge; that they are naturally low in ambition—we have trouble seeing women as leaders.

No matter how many times the stereotypes are debunked, no

matter how many scientific studies say they are false and out-of-date, they still ring true to us. "Confirmation bias" is at work.

We are constantly bombarded with new information about gender—more information than we can possibly absorb. Confirmation bias, first identified in the 1960s and studied ever since, has generated mountains of data. It leads us to pay attention to those bits of information that are consistent with our beliefs and to ignore those that aren't. Accurate information about strong women leaders is everywhere, but powerful filters keep that information out of our awareness.

Moreover, confirmation bias leads to self-fulfilling prophecies. If I expect *him* to be a good leader, I will pay attention to how he operates. If I expect *her* not to be a good leader, I won't see her leadership qualities—even if they are identical to his.

Confirmation bias works because people don't want to admit that their beliefs are wrong. It's far easier to reaffirm old beliefs than to perform major surgery to change them. That's why rooting out stereotypes is so very difficult. This bias adds to the weight on the backs of women who aspire to leadership positions. No matter how difficult the road, however, women need to soldier on. Why?

Having women leaders is very important for society as well as for women themselves. Hillary Clinton explained this in a major speech at Wellesley College: "If you're trying to solve a problem, whether it is fighting corruption or strengthening the rule of law or sparking economic growth, you are more likely to succeed if you widen the circle to include a broader range of expertise, experience, and ideas. So as we work to solve our problems, we need more women at the table and in the halls of parliament and government ministries where these debates are occurring."[2]

But, she went on to say, "today we have a global politics in which the voices of women often go unheard. Women occupy less than 20 percent

of seats in parliaments and legislatures around the world." Clinton talked about the role of women in American politics. "We know we've got
to keep pushing at that glass ceiling. We have to try to break it. . . .
Obviously, I hope to live long enough to see a woman elected president
of the United States," Clinton said to thunderous applause.

Over and over again, studies of the private sector have shown that
companies with more women in power do better financially. An extensive nineteen-year study of 215 Fortune 500 companies found a strong
correlation between a good record of promoting women into the executive suite and high profitability.[3] Fortune 500 companies with the
highest representation of women board directors achieved significantly
higher financial performance, on average, than those with the lowest
representation of women board directors. But as we reported earlier,
progress in getting women to the top is still far too slow.

Why so? One reason is that "because gender is a fundamental distinction of human life, categorization of people by sex is instant, automatic, and pervasive," according to Alice Eagly and Linda Carli.[4] Men
are automatically thought to have traits associated with leadership,
while women are not. The forthright, go-getting woman is as much an
anomaly as the shy, nonassertive man.

Because men don't have to prove that they have "natural" leadership
potential, they can climb without excess baggage toward success in the
workplace. That possibility doesn't yet exist for women. Eagly and Carli
say that the road to the top for women is a "labyrinth"—a series of
blind curves and unexpected jogs that can make a traveler confused and
lost. You may remember that in Greek mythology, a maze was used to
keep the dreaded Minotaur wandering aimlessly, preventing him from
being able to find his way out to wreak havoc on the community.

The shortest route to get where you want to go is a straight line. If
you are blocked from that path, you have to find another, which is

bound to be longer and harder and likely full of ruts and potholes. The going is tough, especially if you are carrying a heavy pack. It can be done—but it is so difficult that many women get discouraged along the way. Some drop out, some question their own abilities, some follow Archie Bunker's advice to his wife, Edith, in the old sitcom *All in the Family*: "Stifle yourself!"

Also, women—who are just as prone to gender stereotypes as men— may simply take themselves out of the running. At a time when women make up the majority of the educated workforce and have the talent and desire to contribute, these limiting beliefs need to be uprooted.

In the New Soft War, it's often the invisible barbed wire that can tear you up. Powerful men may also fail to recognize the difficult path that their female colleagues have to navigate. For example, at a 2012 Florida panel on women in the economy, former General Electric CEO Jack Welch told women all they had to do to succeed was "overdeliver."[5]

That statement made McKinsey director Joanna Barsh, also on the panel, fume. In a *Wall Street Journal* online chat forum she said, "Jack Welch, now I had a hard time not talking during his interview! I had to glue my mouth shut. The problem is that women ARE overdelivering and not getting noticed. Let's take it as an ante that women work hard and have grit—but without being in the network, getting sponsored, or finding opportunities, overdelivering results in happy bosses and not much more."[6]

Many women we talked to agreed with Barsh. Tamara, an independent mediator, says, "Unfortunately, women are conditioned to 'overdeliver' in many professions, and as the economy has worsened, this is the accepted expectation, to work overtime without pay, to take work home, and still not receive equal compensation or recognition for their contributions. When I personally see women CEOs in male dominated professions, I recognize that this woman has probably had to work three times as hard as her male counterparts and at least work twice as smart."

Stephanie, a senior manager, told us, "I have been a vice president in the energy field for six years, and I have been with the company for seventeen. My counterpart has been here for fifteen years. I manage more meetings annually, including our three largest events, bring in more revenue annually and manage more people than he does—yet I am paid $10,000 less."

One company finance director said, "I firmly believe that 'overdelivering' is a recipe for failure. I think back to a chapter in the great book *Nice Girls Don't Get the Corner Office*, which addresses this very topic. Women striving for advancement by quietly doing much more than expected of them simply get taken advantage of."

Overdelivering without getting credit gets you nowhere. As Rachel, a manager at a major investment bank, said: "To get promoted, you need to let people know what you are doing. Men who get promoted tend to be excellent delegators who then free themselves up to spend time promoting themselves and their agenda. Women spend so much time doing tasks and managing the people who work for them that they don't spend enough time letting others know what they are doing for their organization. As a result, they can inhibit their ability to get promoted. This is especially true at organizations that have a so-called 'democratic' promotion process."

MEN TAKE CHARGE, WOMEN TAKE CARE

As we've noted, cultural stereotypes link men with leadership and power and link women with caring and community. These linkages still have a strong grip on our world. A 2005 Catalyst report surveyed 296 corporate leaders (128 men, 168 women) on their attitudes about men and women in business. It found that senior managers perceive differences between women and men leaders *that may not exist.*[7]

Even though analyses of more than forty studies find very few differences between women's and men's leadership, Catalyst notes, "misleading perceptions about gender differences in leadership exist—and are even held by corporate executives."

When they think about corporate leadership, senior managers seem to be applying the same old stereotypes that women "take care" and men "take charge."

Women, Catalyst found, are judged superior to men at "supporting and rewarding subordinates, behaviors that relate to the caretaker stereotype of women. Men leaders are judged superior to women at delegating and influencing superiors, behaviors that relate to the 'take charge' stereotype of men."

The following comments from managers illuminate such attitudes:

"Men have a natural tendency for leadership," said a late-fifties male in top management.

"Men trust in themselves, it creates a more relaxed and natural leadership," said a late-thirties male in middle management.

"Men can be naturally tough and very results-oriented," said a mid-thirties male in middle management.

"Women were so obsessed with trying to outperform their male counterparts that they often neglected the needs of their team," said a male professional in his early forties.

"Sometimes I get the impression that they [women] are playing 'tough,' though this is not their natural preference. This can be perceived as artificial and a bit unnerving, especially when they are quite caring and soft in private," said a male middle manager in his late thirties.

"My experience with women is that they are 'turf tenders' because they have had to adapt that behavior to get where they are and do not know how to get out of that mode," said a female top manager in her late forties.

Since we expect only men to be leaders, men get an automatic leg up in the leadership game just by being male. They don't have to earn that edge; they just have it. We don't expect women to possess the "right stuff." Women start behind, through no fault of their own, and never catch up. Both male and female supervisors give men an edge in promotion and hiring.

The obstacles women encounter along their circuitous route are many, and they come in different forms. In the following sections, we discuss a few of them.

THINK MANAGER, THINK MALE

The automatic tendency of both sexes to "think manager, think male" (TMTM) is well documented. And the linkage presents obvious problems for women. They must swim against the tide of skepticism, whereas men don't have to.

The good news is that while it's still pervasive, TMTM is not as rigid as was once thought. The bad news is that the change doesn't always work to women's advantage.

Results from studies done in the United States and abroad suggest that the strength of the link depends on whether you are describing a manager who is running a successful or an unsuccessful company.[8] The TMTM association is quite strong when you ask people about a manager of a successful company. A very different picture emerges when people are asked to describe a manager of a company that is *not* performing well.

Guess what? In that situation, a "think crisis, think female" association emerges.

It is generally believed—by males and females alike—that qualities considered more female than male are desirable when managing a poorly performing company. These desirable female qualities include intuitiveness, tactfulness, sympathy and being aware of the feelings of others.

Sounds encouraging, right? Well, not exactly. Female qualities are valued *only* if the person is expected to steer the company's employees through the crisis and then, presumably, take a powder.

Female qualities are also desired when "the manager is required to take on a much more passive, and arguably career-damaging, role. More specifically, when the manager was required to stay in the background and endure the crisis, or become a scapegoat for poor company performance."

Read between the lines and you see that women are considered to be ideal martyrs for the company cause, willing to sabotage their own careers for the good of everyone else. That behavior might be fine for achieving sainthood, but how many women want to end up as Joan of Arc—though shoved off the glass cliff instead of put on a flaming pyre.

In addition to whether the company is doing well or is in crisis, preference for having a male or a female leader depends on whether the company has a history of being male- or female-led. If the company has been led by men and is doing well, 62 percent of the study participants chose the male candidate for the leadership job. In contrast, when the male-led company was in crisis, 69 percent chose the female candidate.

But—and here is the best news—when the company has been led by women in the past, there was no difference. The glass cliff disappeared. "Perhaps as people become more used to seeing women at the highest levels of management, female leaders won't be selected primarily for risky turnarounds—and will get more chances to run organizations that have good odds of continued success."[9]

DOWNSHIFTING?

Many leaders in American life come from Ivy League schools. So it seemed like very good news indeed when these once all-male elite bastions opened their doors and women flooded through. Their graduates include such household names as Supreme Court Justices Elena Kagan, Sonia Sotomayor (Princeton), and Ruth Bader Ginsburg (Harvard); Hillary Clinton (Yale); Wendy Wasserstein (Yale); and Madeleine Albright (Columbia).

But recently, a disturbing trend has been playing out in these top schools. A presidential committee at Princeton University reported in 2011 that while women undergraduates are providing leadership in many organizations across campus, they have been less prominent in some major campus posts in the past ten years than they were in the earlier decades of coeducation.[10]

As Evan Thomas puts it in the Daily Beast, "During the 1980s and 1990s, a growing percentage of women took top leadership positions on campus. But then, over the last decade or so, something unexpected happened. The percentage of undergraduate women in top campus positions began to decline."[11]

Female representation in these résumé-building campus roles climbed steadily from the 1970s to the 1990s, then plunged by nearly half in the 2000s, from 31.4 to 17.1 percent.

"Today men are overwhelmingly elected chair of the Honor Committee or president of one of Princeton's eating clubs," Thomas writes.

"Surprisingly, though women win more honors and high honors, men dominate 'highest' honors—as well as academic prizes and postgraduate scholarships. Princeton has endorsed more men than women for the Rhodes Scholarship, and more than twice as many men have won them (10 to 4) over the last decade."

Nan Keohane, the former president of Duke University, has conjectured that female students at Princeton and other elite schools have "shifted into a downward gear."[12]

We are seeing the recurrence of an old pattern. Women are just as busy as men in campus activities, but—as in the days before Betty Friedan published *The Feminine Mystique*—more young women are stepping back to let the men take the visible leadership positions.

Washington Post columnist Ruth Marcus says the situation at Princeton has left her "rattled."[13] She writes, "During the 1990s, for instance, 22 women served in such résumé-burnishing roles. In the following decade, that number fell by nearly half, to 12—even as the proportion of women in the class grew to nearly equal numbers. Only one woman has been elected president of the student government since 1994. This backsliding is not a Princeton-specific phenomenon. Harvard hasn't had a woman head of its undergraduate council since 2003. Yale has elected one woman as student body president in the past decade. Despite the stellar credentials required for admission, women arrive at Princeton, as at similar colleges, reporting lower levels of self-confidence and less likely to think of themselves as leaders than equally qualified men."

Male students seek out the sort of positions that can lead to the fast track in government, politics and business, while women keep busy behind the scenes. It is not rare, according to the presidential committee report, for a Princeton organization to have a male president and a female vice president, secretary and treasurer. "The women did more community service and were more likely to be advisers in the residential colleges," Thomas notes.

At a 2011 conference on women in leadership at Harvard, Keohane said, "We want to make clear that both high-profile jobs and jobs behind the scenes are important leadership positions. But we also wanted to point out the important advantages of high-profile jobs."[14]

Harvard student Beverly E. Pozuelos, the president of Latinas Unidas and a *Harvard Crimson* design editor, said at the conference, "In high school I was a go-getter, but when I got to college I was very intimidated." She added that seeking out student leadership positions "helped me find my voice."

Young women were not being discriminated against, but they themselves pulled back. Why? The answers are complex, but among them are notions that are part of the New Soft War. Women are aware that, as one Princeton undergrad puts it, "People, including faculty, are turned off if we seem over-zealous. They've said, 'slow down, step back.' Would they say the same thing to males?"[15]

Shirley Tilghman, the former Princeton president, suggested that female students felt they must fit a "narrower range of expectations" than men. They felt they were supposed to "dress more carefully" and not to appear "too aggressive," she says, "while at the same time achieving something close to perfection."[16]

One graduate told the commission, "Women are expected to do everything, do it well, and look hot while doing it."[17]

Julie Zeilinger, a nineteen-year-old undergraduate at Barnard College, says on a Forbes.com blog, "My peers and I, the young women of today, may not face the type of *Mad Men*–esque sexism that once prohibited women from leading. . . . But the reasons we fail to lead are still sexist in nature: they're just far subtler than they once were. The truth is many young women today fail to lead because of the pressure put on young women to be perfect and moreover the disparity in what we teach our sons as opposed to our daughters."[18]

Young women, Zeilinger says, were acutely aware of the coverage of both Hillary Clinton and Sarah Palin. "Not only were these women abused and constantly criticized for attempting to lead, they were again reduced to the way they looked, for how they achieved or failed to achieve a ridiculous standard of perfection and ultimately femininity."

She asks, "So, why don't women want to lead? The answer is in the pages of the magazines we read and now even in the news coverage of the political debates we watch, which promote cultural standards that destroy women's confidence and prescribe unattainable standards in all areas of our lives. In order for women to lead—for women to want to lead, to feel that we are capable of leading—we need to redefine leadership altogether. We need to define leadership not as perfection but as intelligence, honesty and doing the right thing. It is also essential that we question and change a society that sets the standard for achievement impossibly high for women and upsettingly low for men."

Women we interviewed found the conflict between appearance and leadership goes far beyond college. A human resources executive in the oil and gas industry told us, "You need to be smart and competent, ready to take on the next dragon. You have to be well groomed and attractive so that the boys will want you around. You have to be able to hold your liquor. Smoking is fine, as is the occasional cursing. But you can't be too pretty or too sexy in appearance, because then it is assumed you've slept your way to the next assignment or promotion. Finding a way forward to a corporate leadership position while diffusing the virgin-whore paradigm is difficult."

An investment manager said, "Aging gracefully in the workplace is like walking a tightrope. If you look too old or matronly, you risk looking too motherly. You must guard your demeanor and appearance."

THE TOKEN TRAP

How can it be that women earn only 77 cents to the dollar when it seems that so many successful women are earning big bucks? Oprah Winfrey makes $275 million annually, and her earnings are likely to go up from there, according to Forbes. Other female celebrities also bring home hefty paychecks.

Top female executives in Fortune 500 companies are also high earners; and for some, their earnings are commensurate with those of their male counterparts. Among this top-tier of executives, Irene Rosenfeld, CEO of Kraft Foods, was the highest female earner, with a total compensation package (salary, bonus, stock and options) of $22 million in 2012.[19] And her compensation was on par with her male peers at other food companies such as Kellogg and General Mills.

Very-high-level corporate women are a rare breed. As McKinsey notes, "The number of women CEOs in Fortune 500 companies appears stuck at 2–3%. . . . At this point women are doubly handicapped because, as our research of the largest US corporations shows, 62 percent are in staff jobs that rarely lead to a CEO role."[20]

These jobs—such as in human resources—don't have profit and loss (P&L) responsibility and involve mainly support functions. Men in contrast, gravitate toward line jobs, which are central to the company and usually have more power and higher pay. In fact, 65 percent of men on executive committees hold line jobs. This difference helps explain the very low percentage of women senior managers.

When women do get to top jobs, they are very well compensated by their boards, and they are seen as exceptionally competent, even when they are in male-dominated fields. These women include, for example, Ginni Rometty of IBM, Ellen Kullman of DuPont, Meg Whitman of Hewlett-Packard, Ilene Gordon of Ingredion, Patricia Woertz of Archer Daniels Midland and Ursula Burns of Xerox.

You'd think this would be great news for all women. Doesn't a rising tide raise all boats? In this case, the answer is no. The financial success of top-tier women seems to have little effect on the earnings of most other women.

Why is this so? It may be that these "stars" are viewed as just that—luminous bodies far, far above the corner of the cosmos that all other women inhabit. The competence of these shining stars is so phenomenal that they are treated as "exceptions to the rule"; their success has little impact on the gender stereotypes that hold most women back.

A study of 51 high-level females and 56 high-level males, all of whom held critical positions within their organization, supports the idea that competence can trump gender stereotypes.[21] Management researchers Karen Lyness and Donna Thompson, both of Baruch College, City University of New York, studied gender differences in compensation and opportunities for professional development among these outstanding executives.

In contrast to their expectations, the researchers found that in these areas, there were no significant gender differences. The literature on gender stereotypes had led them to expect that the men would have higher compensation packages and more opportunities for professional development than the women.

With these women, a different dynamic seems to be at work. It is as if their superiors placed these successful female executives "in a *subcategory* of women," while the stereotype of women as being less able, and incompetent, especially in male-dominated fields, remains unchanged.

These stars become "honorary" men. One successful scientist, for example, is often told, "You're not like other women," or "You think like a man." They are not mere women, but rather, "special" women.

Getting into the star category gives a precious few women distinct advantages. Their superiors have a lot of information about them—enough to override the usual stereotypes. A study by Brian Welle, formerly a Harvard research fellow and currently a manager at Google, and NYU's Madeline Heilman shows that when decision makers have unambiguous information about women's performance or competence, they are less likely to rely on stereotypes that undervalue and hold back "average" women.[22]

But the high visibility of token women gives a false impression of how level the playing field really is. In truth, only 6 percent of CEOs of Fortune 100 companies are women, and there are only a handful of women in the U.S. Congress. The elevation of a few females doesn't have much relevance to most of us—but it can make us think things are better than they are. We look at a Nancy Pelosi or a Ruth Bader Ginsburg, at a Sally Ride or a Drew Gilpin Faust (the president of Harvard), and we can see our future possible selves.

Or maybe not. Are we seeing reality, or a shimmering mirage in the desert that vanishes when we draw close?

There is a good chance that the latter is true.

Even where tokenism is the rule, when they know that only a few women "make it," most women *still* believe that their hard work will pay off. In several studies, women knew that a tokenism policy was in place, but they still clung to the belief that they had a realistic chance to move up.[23]

This belief can undercut any sense of unfairness (which is a prime driver of women's fight for equality) and weakens their sense of solidarity with other women. Unfortunately, the sense that feminism is an outdated artifact of the past leads women to laser-focus on their own careers, believing that the world is fair. Joining with other women to uncover and battle discrimination within organizations often doesn't occur to them. It should. The world of work is far from equal.

To make matters worse, star token women may discourage—rather than encourage—other women.

One strategy employed by many companies, consultants and schools of management is to bring in older, highly successful female leaders (think Oprah Winfrey) to send the message to younger women that if these stars can do it, so can you. The hope is that young women will identify with these highly successful women, decouple the successful leader–male link and strengthen their own leadership aspirations.

But the strategy may backfire. The stars may be too intimidating, too good to be true. New research finds that female undergrads are more likely to identify with mid-level women than with high-level leaders.[24] The superstars' success may seem so unattainable that novices do not identify with them and see them as a group apart—not as women just like them.

Indeed, presented with these stars, young women's feelings of inferiority *increased*, their leadership aspirations *decreased* and the strength of the leader-male link remained as strong as it was prior to the intervention. Marquee women were seen as exceptions to the female stereotype and therefore did not challenge it. Far from the desired effect, "exposure to these leaders did more harm than good to women's self-perceptions."

One participant in a leadership program remembers, "On the final day of our program, a woman was invited to present her tips for getting ahead to a group of aspirational young female leaders. She was in her mid-forties, a professor and dean of a business faculty, and had just given birth to twins through IVF. She was immaculately put together, on stilettos all day. Can we do all that? Why do so many women's leadership programs send out this unrealistic and exhausting message? There is a lack of women leaders as role models, but sustaining stereotypes of the superwoman is no solution."[25]

In contrast, when females were presented with moderately successful women leaders, the effects were positive. The women could identify with those leaders, whose success seemed attainable to them, and their own leadership aspirations increased. Moreover, they began to challenge the traditional leader-male link.

It appears that the mere presence of superstar women in high positions of leadership (i.e., tokens) will not shatter the glass ceiling for all women. Female role models can be inspiring *only* if women can identify with them and see their achievements as possible for themselves.

DIFFERENT EXPLANATIONS FOR SUCCESS AND FAILURE

People tend to explain women's and men's success at masculine endeavors differently—and the differences matter. Because many believe women don't naturally have what it takes to succeed in management, which is considered a male task, their successes are usually attributed to hard work or luck rather than to high ability. For example, "She puts in long hours, doesn't let herself get distracted and is always well prepared."

For men, success in management is more likely to be attributed to high ability than to hard work or luck: "He's got what it takes. He's a born leader." This difference is important because "hard work or luck" explanations reflect less confidence in a person's competence.

Reactions to men's and women's failures in management also differ in ways that favor men. According to Eagly and Carli, "Reactions to failure are different . . . it is the common perception that women fail on masculine tasks because they can't handle the challenges of the work but that men fail on them because they are lazy or merely unlucky."

This difference may help explain why, as we discussed in Chapter 5, men who fail are often given a second chance, whereas women are not.

And if women themselves internalize these ideas, they may well succumb to the well-known "impostor syndrome." Researchers Pauline Rose Clance and Suzanne Imes of Georgia State University say that in our culture, high-achieving women are likely to fall into this pattern. "Despite their earned degrees, scholastic honors, high achievement on standardized tests, praise and professional recognition from colleagues and respected authorities, these women do not experience an internal sense of success. They consider themselves to be 'impostors.' Numerous women graduate students state that their high examination scores are due to luck, to misgrading, or to the faulty judgment of professors. Women professionals in our sample feel over evaluated by colleagues and administrators. One women professor said, 'I'm not good enough to be on the faculty here. Some mistake was made in the selection process.' Another, the chairperson of her department, said, 'Obviously I'm in this position because my abilities have been overestimated.' Another woman with two master's degrees, a Ph.D., and numerous publications to her credit considered herself unqualified to teach remedial college classes in her field."[26]

Women are more vulnerable to impostor symptoms than men are. Too often, they undercut their rightful success in the following ways:

- Feeling like a fake: You don't believe that you earned your own success, and you always worry that any day you will be unmasked as a fraud.

- Attributing success to luck: You don't take personal credit for success, thinking, "I just got lucky this time." And you fear that you can't keep it up.
- Making light of your success: Because you doubt your own ability, you downplay what you've achieved and of course have a hard time being complimented for it.

LINGERING DOUBTS

For women, the weight of history as well as gender stereotypes constitute an "attitudinal penalty" that men never have to bear. For as long as anyone can remember, men have held the major leadership roles in all sectors of public life.[27] And we accept that they should. Even the Bible agrees: "Women must not have authority over men: I do not permit a woman to teach or to have authority over a man" (1 Timothy 2:12–14). Wariness about women moving into leadership positions has deep historical roots. The Roman senator Cato the Elder said, "Once [women] have achieved equality, they will be your masters."[28]

It's no wonder then that leadership is perceived as a male preserve. In addition, as we've noted, cultural stereotypes reinforce the connection between men and leadership. As a result, women face pervasive uncertainty about their ability to lead.

According to Eagly and Carli, this uncertainty leads to lower evaluations: When women are "agentic" (assertive, independent, competent), they are marked down for not being sufficiently "communal"; when they are communal; they are marked down for not being sufficiently agentic.[29] When male leaders act forcefully, they are applauded, not critiqued for any lack of niceness and friendliness. Indeed, male leaders can show "their warm, feminine side, without penalty." But forceful women leaders, who exert their authority over others, may be met with hostile reactions for failing to be more feminine.

A female Wall Street executive says, "You have to be strong and assertive without offending people. So you push a little and then back off, push a little and back off. You're always testing the waters to see how far you can go, trying not to get angry, trying not be confrontative, trying to think of other ways to say, 'You're not right,' without attacking the person. It's getting more and more difficult the higher I go."[30]

The double bind caused by lingering doubts generates considerable pressure. In addition to being under heightened scrutiny by others, women may second-guess their own behavior. *Was I too assertive? Was I too much of a pushover? Did I offend? Was I sufficiently attentive to my group's concerns?* Monday-morning quarterbacking can lead to indecisive behavior, which may well fuel concerns about women's ability to be effective leaders.

Nowhere is this bind more obvious than in the realm of politics. When women run for high office, the full weight of stereotypes comes crashing down on them. When Hillary Clinton became the first serious female candidate for president of the Unites States, she received a degree of scrutiny unprecedented in American politics. With no familiar images of women as high-level political leaders, we tend to fall back on extreme stereotypes bordering on caricature.

When Boston University journalism student Melissa Nawrocki examined campaign coverage, she found that the media accused Clinton of being insane, murderous, witchlike, depressed and egomaniacal.[31]

On the December 20, 2007, edition of MSNBC's *Hardball*, host Chris Matthews said that Clinton's political goal was "to smother the young senator [Obama] in his crib," using the visual of a murderous Clinton killing an infant Obama.[32] Matthews has also referred to Clinton as "witchy" and a "stripteaser."

In a February 27, 2008, *New York Times* column, Maureen Dowd wrote that Clinton "has turned into Sybil," referencing the book and movie about a woman with multiple whiny personalities.[33]

Sexist language was over the top. In the course of her public life, Clinton has been compared to Glenn Close's murderous-career-woman character in *Fatal Attraction*. During the campaign, her "cackle" became the subject of countless media reports, as if she were indeed stirring a pot and chanting, *"Double, double, toil and trouble; Fire burn and cauldron bubble."* Patrick Healy of the *New York Times* dubbed it the "Clinton Cackle," and pundit Dick Morris called Clinton's laugh "loud, inappropriate, and mirthless. . . . A scary sound that was somewhere between a cackle and a screech."[34]

When women run for high office, they step out of their "proper" role as keepers of the hearth, and they pay a price. Signs hoisted by hecklers at Clinton rallies read "Stop Running for President and Make Me a Sandwich" and "Iron My Shirt"—and show the ugly underside of that sentimental idea.

As we noted earlier, when Elizabeth Warren threw her hat into the ring to become the first woman senator from Massachusetts, there was a torrent of criticism. It wasn't her policies that were challenged; it was her appearance, her manner of speaking, her warmth—or lack of it—and even the kind of glasses she wore.

Comedian Bill Maher wrote, "New Rule: Elizabeth Warren has to stop dressing like the 'before' woman in a beer ad. Granny glasses, check; hair in a bun, got it."[35]

A political analyst for Boston radio station WBUR said, "You hear words like 'preachy' or 'lawyer-like' to describe how she comes across on TV. . . . She's got to stop the finger wagging; it adds to her strict schoolmarm appearance and bossy manner." He suggested, "Lose the granny glasses; they're 40 years late and add about 10 years to her age on TV."[36]

Men who have run for office in Massachusetts usually do not get this type of criticism. As *Globe* columnist Joan Vennochi notes, "Bay Staters are tough on sisters who run for political office. . . . Over a span of 25 years, they were dismissed as too shrill, too stiff, too fat, too rich, or simply too uppity to shake hands with the average Sox fan. Such concerns never kept John Kerry, Ted Kennedy, Mitt Romney, or Bill Weld out of office."[37]

On the other hand, what happens when a woman is considered too good-looking, too glamorous? Many right-wing political women such as Sarah Palin and Michele Bachmann have been applauded for their looks. In fact, that's a way *not* to take them seriously. As critic Julia Baird points out, "It's odd to see how some men insist that when women start to grasp power, we should think of them primarily as playthings and provocateurs. Is this the best way to explain their success? They aren't challenging the status quo. They're being wild! They're not trying to lift the ban on offshore drilling. They're being naughty."[38]

Politics is the art of self-promotion, so women, whether they are on the right or left, have to grab the spotlight. That's not "correct" female behavior. Self-promotion can be risky for women, say Eagly and Carli. "People may accept boastfulness in men, but more often dislike boastful women and consider them less deserving of recognition or support than more modest women. As a result, self-promoting women risk having less influence than women who are more modest, even though people who self-promote are considered more competent than their more modest counterparts."

All of these attacks on political women for something other than their ability, their competence or their policies are aimed at pushing them out of the public sphere. If we let these anti-woman forces win by reducing the number of females who put themselves forward, then the New Soft War will have succeeded in silencing women.

ELEVEN

THE PARENT TRAP

Women today get distinctly mixed messages: Those who are childless hear, "You go, girl. Aim high. There is nothing you can't do if you put your mind to it. The world is your oyster."

But when you have children—the message changes. If you *do* aim high, your children will be emotional wrecks, won't get good grades, will get into trouble, won't get into the right college and will probably face a world of troubles as they progress through life.

Mothers are the canary in the coal mine as far as our social anxieties are concerned; that's been true for a very long time.

Today, it is our anxieties about our children's chances in life's economic lottery that seem to be kicking off the latest mommy debate, whereas in the past, other issues twisted us into knots.

BAD MOMMY, GOOD MOMMY

In the 1940s, the worry was how to shove all those women occupying the war jobs they had taken on—and come to love—out of the workforce. The answer? Convince them that they could never be mommies—or were bad mommies if they kept working.

The 1947 bestseller *Modern Woman: The Lost Sex* came up with an intriguing notion: "Male-emulating careerists have such anxiety about pregnancy that their glands secrete chemicals that destroy fertility."[1] Baby-killing chemicals—now there's an idea to make a woman's blood run cold! But have no fear, women. A return to a "normal" role in society would soothe ovaries that spew defective eggs.

In the 1950s, when we worried about the Soviet threat and the coming triumph of Communism, it was all Mom's fault. Bestselling author Philip Wylie claimed that women had so emasculated their sons that these boys broke under torture in Korea.[2] He created the term "momism" and decried the American worship of mothers: "Satan, we are told, finds work for idle hands to do. There is no mistaking the accuracy of this proverb. Millions of men have heaped up riches and made a conquest of idleness so as to discover what it is that Satan puts them up to. Not one has failed to find out. But never before has a great nation of brave and dreaming men absent-mindedly created a huge class of idle, middle-aged women."

Women in the 1950s, said economist John Kenneth Galbraith, occupied subservient and unrewarding posts as "managers of consumption" and kept "the affluent society" humming.[3] But as women became more educated and began to move into the workforce in large numbers, the alarm bells began to clang with abandon. Fifty-some years later, they are still ringing loudly.

The media narratives about working women, we have noticed, are generally negative and often introduced by headlines or sound bites that seem hysteric. One favorite theme is that women are taking part in an ongoing catfight over motherhood. One camp advocates child-destroying careerism and the other promotes soul-destroying twenty-four-hour sacrificial motherhood.

This narrative was in sharp focus after the *Atlantic* cover article "Why Women Still Can't Have It All" created a huge buzz in 2012.[4] Author Anne-Marie Slaughter's actual article was a thoughtful analysis of the pressures women face in top-level jobs in a society that makes few accommodations for parenting or family life. (Slaughter was the first female director of policy planning at the State Department under President Barack Obama.)

But the packaging by the magazine, with the hyperbolic title, undercut the author's serious tone. "The women who have managed to be both mothers and top professionals," reads the article blurb, "are superhuman, rich, or self-employed." (Which is, of course, nonsense. Women hold good jobs in a wide variety of fields, and very few of them are superhuman or rich.)

The *New York Times* responded quickly to the *Atlantic* cover with a story headlined "Women Are in a Catfight over Motherhood."[5] The *Times* pits Slaughter's call for less pressure and more options against Facebook executive Sheryl Sandberg, who worries publicly that women may be giving up too much too soon. Here's how the *Times* framed that discussion:

"The conversation came to life in part because of a compelling face-off of issues and personalities: Ms. Slaughter, who urged workplaces to change and women to stop blaming themselves, took on Ms. Sandberg, who has somewhat unintentionally come to epitomize the higher-harder-faster school of female achievement."

It's the O.K. Corral, with two women, guns drawn.

Stories pitting careerist mothers against the "opt-outers" proliferate, in which, respectively, the "good-enough" mothers jostle with the "perfectionists." The media join the New Soft War by presenting nearly impossible and conflicting scenarios for working women. Discord and angst are the hallmark of many stories. Women are battling each other, torn apart by guilt, opting out or dropping back.

One disturbing trend is the rise of hype about "intensive" parenting, which bolsters the myth that mothers must be with their children at all times, totally immersed in their lives from birth onward; co-sleeping to intensify the mother-child bond; using only washable diapers; preparing only natural and organically grown baby foods, lovingly peeled, diced and strained by mom; and being always ready to fulfill a child's every need.

"We've ratcheted what it means to be a good mother way above what our own mothers or grandmothers had to do," Jennifer Glass, a University of Iowa sociology professor who studies work and family life, told the Working Mother Research Institute.[6] "Even if you're staying at home, it isn't like Monday is wash day and Tuesday is baking day. You're ferrying junior to gymnastics and mommy-and-me activities."

Elizabeth Badinter, a historian and philosophy professor who is sometimes called France's "most influential intellectual," touched off a controversy in the United States with the English translation of her 2010 book, *The Conflict: How Modern Motherhood Undermines the Status of Women*.[7] In it, Badinter argues that the cult of the perfect mother turns child rearing into a full-time occupation that tethers women to the home and creates "mommy tyrants." "Crushing" is her word for a new style of motherhood marked by doing the "right" thing even if it means childbirth without an epidural for the "natural" experience and from then on living for your child and your child alone.

Badinter says that "the irony of this history is that it was precisely at the point that Western women finally rid themselves of the patriarchy that they acquired a new master in the house." Who is that new master? The child.

"[Women's] increased responsibility for babies and young children has proved just as restrictive, if not more so, than sexism in the home or in the workplace. . . . We have agreed to this regression in the name of moral superiority, the love we bear our children, and some ideal notion of child-rearing, all of which are proving far more effective than external constraints. As everyone knows, there is nothing quite like voluntary servitude."

While it's probably a small number of mothers who are actively embracing intensive motherhood, all of us, she says, "are nonetheless influenced by the trend." The widespread media attention to this notion can make women doubt their choice to stay in the workforce, where they obviously can't be "perfect" mothers. "It's almost impossible for a woman to work if she completely follows the dogma of intensive mothering," Badinter says. If working women embrace these ideas, they themselves are loading yet another rock into the heavy backpack they are already carrying.

But some young mothers try. One busy lawyer we know peels and grinds all of her toddler daughter's baby food. She could ask her daughter's babysitter to do it, but she worries it wouldn't be done right. A social worker irons her children's clothes on school days, and another working mother has a goal of breastfeeding until her child reaches the age of two, even though her workplace does not provide a room where she can have privacy.

A recent example of the pressure to be perfect is a 2012 *Time* cover with the headline "Are You Mom Enough?"[8] The cover photo shows a young mother breastfeeding her three-year-old son. The article focuses on Dr. William Sears, an internationally known pediatrician whose baby books sell millions of copies around the world. He believes that babies must be with their mothers at *all* times, even sleeping in the parents' bed, and that mothers should carry them constantly and breastfeed for several years. He also believes that babies' every whimper is a plea for help, so they should not be allowed to cry. He warns on his website that "excessive" crying over "prolonged periods" can damage an infant's brain. He mentions that the cry-it-out approach has the potential to cause "harmful neurologic effects that may have permanent implications on the development of sections of their brain."

An examination of the research, however, doesn't actually provide evidence that bouts of crying affect brain development. There's also no evidence that children turn out better with this kind of parenting. But, as *Time* notes, "it is easy for a mother reading Sears to . . . believe she is doing irreparable harm by not holding her baby constantly and ensuring the infant never cries for more than a moment."

The pressure to increase the chores involved in mothering is enormous, says Linda Hirshman, a retired distinguished professor at Brandeis.[9] Like Badinter, she sees the idea that mothers must live only for their babies' welfare as a new form of sexism that keeps women—if not exactly barefoot and pregnant—pushed back to home and hearth. Throughout history, women have been kept out of the public sphere because of their duties at home. One argument against women's getting the vote in the United States was that exposing the "queens of the home" to the rough and tumble of politics would render them less motherly.

That same fear, though less bluntly stated, rears its head in today's overwrought dialogue about the need for intensive, or "attachment," parenting. Harm to children is routinely exaggerated, Hirshman says. "For years, women have been on the receiving end of negative messages about parenting and working. . . . When the National Institute of

Child Health and Human Development reported recently that long hours in day care added *but a single percentage point* [italics ours] to the still-normal range of rambunctious behavior in children, newspaper headlines read, 'Day Care, Behavior Problems Linked in Study.'"

Rigid prescriptions for mothering are hardly new, however. In Mary McCarthy's novel of 1930s women, *The Group*, one new mother exhausts herself with trying to breastfeed her newborn baby. Her pediatrician husband insists that the baby be fed on demand. When it doesn't work, and the baby still screams for food, the young mother is ordered to just try harder. She's tired, tense and unhappy, but she feels she must succeed or that she'll have failed as a woman.[10]

As for Sears, he suggests that mothers quit their jobs and borrow money so that they can spend all their time parenting. But again, there is simply no evidence that the children of working mothers are in trouble—quite the opposite. And as we'll see, there's a great deal of evidence that a happy, fulfilled woman is a good mother—whether she's at work or at home.

In Sears's world, when a woman has a child, she becomes a mommy and is expected to exhibit a laser focus on her children: Are they happy? Loved? Eating well? Playing nicely with other children? Are their verbal skills adequate? Are they firmly attached? Are they underperforming in preschool? Will they get into Harvard?

As Susan J. Douglas and Meredith W. Michaels point out in *The Mommy Myth*, these ideas "redefine all women, first and foremost, through their relationships to children. Thus, being a citizen, a worker, a governor, an actress, a first lady, all are supposed to take a backseat to motherhood. (Remember how people questioned whether Hillary Clinton was truly maternal because she had only one child?)"[11] The new models of perfect motherhood insist that women always have to be adoring, flawless mothers before they do anything else. As critic

Letty Cottin Pogrebin puts it, "You can go be a CEO, and a good one, but if you're not making a themed birthday party, you're not a good mother."[12]

In fact, children do well with many types of parenting. When the renowned Harvard child psychologist Jerome Kagan studied the Mayan Indians of northwest Guatemala, he was startled by what he found.[13] The Mayans swaddle their infants in pieces of cloth and leave them suspended in a hammock in the darkness of their houses for many hours of the day. Kagan initially thought that these practices would have severe negative effects on the children's later development. His own follow-up work proved him wrong. By later childhood, these children are as alert and psychologically well developed as children from other cultures who are raised very differently. In Mayan society, parents demonstrated their care and protection for their children by swaddling, and gave them love and affection as well.

The Guatemalan experience should have given the lie to the idea that children cannot thrive unless they are parented by constantly doting adults. But it didn't. Too many mothers today fear that anything short of 24-7 interaction with their children will cause psychological damage. Research shows that the orphanage studies have no relationship to working women and their babies. Why not? Maybe because of a scientific misunderstanding of "maternal deprivation" and what it really means. During World War II, the influential psychologist John Bowlby studied children in orphanages.[14] What the researchers found was indeed frightening, because those children spent hours in a barren environment with no loving care or human contact. Not surprisingly, they suffered from emotional problems and the impairment of many of their skills. The term for this loss became "maternal deprivation." However, these children were deprived not only of their mothers but also of any true human contact and stimulation.

This bears no resemblance to what happens in the routine daily separation of children and working mothers. In fact, in addition to the orphanage studies, Bowlby studied children between ages two and four who were cared for in day nurseries while their mothers worked. While the orphans suffered from serious developmental delays, the children from the nurseries were *absolutely normal.*

But the latter study fell right off society's radar screen, while the orphanage studies get repeated over and over.

One stunning example of a "maternal deprivation" scare story was a 1998 *New York Times Magazine* cover article highlighting the problems facing parents who adopt Romanian orphans.[15] On the magazine cover: a stark photograph of a young boy, his mouth open in a scream of anguish. The headline blares in white letters: "Disturbed, detached, unreachable." The chilling text beneath reads, "Children adopted by Americans from the worst European orphanages may be telling us not only about the extreme trauma of parental deprivation but also about the more routine separation of parent and child."

A terrifying warning—but one that is completely misleading. The problems of children adopted from the most miserable orphanages of Eastern Europe have *no* connection with the lives of children of American working mothers. The *Times* itself even says so, buried deep in the article: "The most recent and reliable studies that have looked at the attachment security of children in child care have found that while there are some negative effects, they are quite small—statistical flutters. The ambitious National Institute of Child Health and Human Development Study of Early Child Care . . . concluded, for example, that 'there were no significant differences in attachment related to child-care participation.'"[16]

In other words, no connection, no real story.

The power of the mommy myth is astonishing. No matter how

many women succeed at both work and motherhood, no matter how many happy, thriving children bond with their employed mothers, the idea remains fixed that women simply cannot manage both motherhood and serious work. We call this the "receding goalpost problem." A mother can never be good enough—she can always do more. When someone like Sears—with his medical degrees and his international reputation—insists that women can't really be anything other than full-time mothers, women tend to believe it. Who could blame them?

And working mothers not only have to deal with their own guilt, but also have to contend with their coworkers, who may see them as "bad mommies." A 2012 study finds that these problems are especially severe for full-time working mothers in male-dominated occupations.[17] Coworkers question both their competence on the job *and* their competence as parents. Mothers who are successful, especially when they are seen as working out of "choice," suffer most intensely from this assumption. It creates an additional source of stress, adding to women's already heavy burden. Interestingly, fathers get a pass; there is no evidence that they suffer from a "bad-father assumption."

You can barely dent these mommy myths, even with a howitzer fired at point-blank range. Always-available mommy may be an old idea, but it's a mainstay of the New Soft War. Both of us grew up fighting this notion, and our daughters still hear its echoes. Our granddaughters probably will, too, unless we are able to finally win this war. Roz Barnett remembers that when her son Jonathan was an infant, her mother came to visit. When Roz asked her mother if she'd like to hold the baby, she was taken aback by her mother's reaction. Her mom said, "You're not home enough, so why don't you hold him?" Her mother didn't realize that a working mother is not a neglectful mother. It was the beginning of a fruitful discussion between mother and daughter.

Caryl Rivers often felt guilty when she thought she was asking too much of her husband, Alan. On one January winter day, she was on assignment covering the Virginia Slims tennis tournament in Florida, and Alan was home with the kids. Meanwhile, a nor'easter was hitting Boston. When she called home to say "We just played a round of tennis and then went to the hot tub," that may have been one bridge too far. But the couple managed over the years to share parenting very evenly. In the end, both of us ended up with children who are happy and successful in their adult lives.

LET'S GET REAL

While the media repeatedly chant about the decline of the family, scientific research continues to paint a very different picture. The Families and Work Institute, drawing on a nationally representative sample of more than 3,000 full-time employees, found that mothers are spending the same amount of time with their children today as mothers did in the 1960s—even though most mothers now are working full-time.[18] They also have fewer children. Sociologist John Sandberg says, "Contrary to popular belief, the increase in female labor force participation has not led to a decrease in the amount of time parents spend with their children. Even though parents, and especially mothers, may be busier than ever before, many seem to be managing to fit in more time with their children than an earlier generation of parents did."[19] How do today's moms do it? They sleep fewer hours, do less housework and spend more time with their children when they're home.

Married fathers in two-earner couples have dramatically increased the amount of time they spent in both child care and housework over the past twenty-five years. The net effect is that children are getting *more* time with their parents today than at any time in the past four decades. The fact that parents' overall time with their kids went up significantly over the past twenty years gives the lie to the notion that today's parents are so harried or otherwise absorbed that they slight their children. It's hard to make a case for a nation of selfish parents with these data.

Ellen Galinsky, author of *Ask the Children: The Breakthrough Study That Reveals How to Succeed at Work and Parenting* and president of the Families and Work Institute, put another nail in the coffin of the "bad working mothers" mythology.[20] Galinsky surveyed 1,023 children in grades three through twelve and found that the kids gave their working mothers and fathers high marks for their parenting. While the parents assumed that their kids would say they wanted more time with them, that wasn't the case. "Only 10 percent wish for more time with their mothers and 15.5 percent for more time with their fathers," Galinsky writes.

Whether a mother worked or not made no difference in kids' assessments of parenting skills, Galinsky found. FamilyTLC, a network of early childhood educators, says: "These findings, in particular, should go a long way toward reducing the guilt of working moms. . . . There is now much more evidence showing that a mother's work is not, in itself, the most important variable that influences children's positive development. Rather, it is a combination of other factors including: the mother's comfort level with her choice to work, the income her job brings in, the quality of child care she uses, the resources available from her family and neighborhood, and the warmth, sensitivity, and responsiveness she shows to her children."[21] But complex explanations and real data get lost when we stray into the realm of motherhood mythology.

Surprisingly, Galinsky found that while the mothers expected that their children would want more time with them, the children did *not* say that. So here are working women racked by "mommy guilt" when they don't need to be. Cultural memes about what it takes to be a good mother may be everywhere, but being omnipresent doesn't make them true.

THE MOTHERHOOD PENALTY AND THE FATHERHOOD BONUS

Imagine a woman who is smart, ambitious, organized, a good leader and a fine communicator. Now imagine that this woman has a child. Would you assume that she has suddenly become disorganized, unable to cope, a terrible manager and an unambitious slug to boot? Of course not.

Employers, however, often *do* make such assumptions. The competence, drive and commitment that get a woman to the top of the corporate hierarchy are all called into question when she has a child. Doubts are raised about her commitment and her drive. Will she be willing to take challenging assignments? Travel? Meet tight deadlines?

According to Ann Crittenden, author of *The Price of Motherhood: Why the Most Important Job in the World Is Still the Least Valued*, for those under age thirty-five, the pay gap between mothers and non-mothers is larger (as much as 20 percent larger) than the pay gap between men and women.[22]

Crittenden said in an interview, "When you've been home raising children, you are looked at (by employers) as if your brain has been on ice, so you take a hit in your income, in the kind of wages you can command. I put a name on it: The Mommy Tax. In other words, what is your lifetime loss of income if you have a kid, in terms of lowered income for the rest of your life? There's a lot of variation, but you can say, in general, that if a college-educated woman has one child, she will lose about a million dollars in lifetime earnings. I didn't have my child until I was over 40, and I already had a number of years working. But my Mommy Tax is close to a million."[23]

This is not just hyperbole. Cornell sociologists Shelley Correll, Stephen Benard and In Paik conducted a two-part study to go beyond the anecdotes.[24] First, in the laboratory portion, they asked male and female subjects to rate application materials for pairs of fictitious job applicants who were equally qualified but differed on parental status.

The results of this experiment provided clear evidence that mothers are discriminated against in the hiring processes—and most likely in subsequent evaluations and promotions. Their findings were nothing less than startling:

- Both males and females rated mothers as less competent, less committed, less suitable for hire, promotion and management training, and more deserving of lower salaries than females who were not mothers and males, regardless of their parental status. Astonishingly, childless women were *8.2 times more likely than mothers* to be recommended for management training.
- With respect to salary, the recommended starting salary for mothers was $11,000 (7.4 percent) *less* than that offered to non-mothers—a significant difference.
- With respect to the likelihood of being hired, childless women were especially advantaged compared with mothers; they were over *six times more likely* to be recommended for hire.
- In sharp contrast, men were not penalized for, and sometimes benefited from, being a parent. Fatherhood often means more money for men!
- The mere fact of being married confers a benefit on men's wages—a "marriage premium"—which, according to peer-

reviewed research, is "one of the most robust empirical findings in labor economics."

- Male and female raters recommended that fathers receive a
  significantly *higher* salary than childless men. (Compared
  with fathers, mothers were offered approximately 8.6 percent
  lower salaries.) And fathers were 1.83 times more likely to be
  recommended for management than childless men.

But perhaps the most striking example of the fatherhood bonus
comes from a study of gender inequality on Wall Street by Louise Marie Roth. In her book *Selling Women Short: Gender and Money on Wall
Street,* she notes that women find Wall Street's frenetic pace and impossible hours out of synch with family demands. And since all women
are expected to be mothers at some point, their devotion to their careers was viewed with suspicion. As a result, women are often not
considered for career-building assignments, because they *might* have
children. When they did become mothers, managers and peers believed that they had less commitment to their jobs—despite the fact
that these women did not significantly cut back their work hours.
"Mothers received an average of 53 percent as much money as fathers
while working 92 percent as many hours."[25]

The real-world situation of fathers validated the research. On the
face of it, you'd think that childless men would be the most prized
employees, because they'd be seen as totally dedicated to their work.
But surprisingly, Wall Street fathers worked 90 percent as many hours
as their childless male colleagues and received *more* money—122 percent as much money as childless men.

Why do men get this bonus? Because married men and fathers are
seen as being highly productive, motivated and committed, whereas
married women and mothers are seen as conflicted, divided in their

loyalties and unable to perform at a high level. In short: Men benefit from being married and enjoy a fatherhood bonus as well.

Why should employers so harshly penalize mothers? Cultural beliefs about motherhood, such as the ones we discussed above, may hold the answer. A mystical and totally captivating mother-child bond is at the heart of these beliefs.

Joanne Brundage, director of the nonprofit group Mothers and More, says the assumption that "motherhood dumbs women down" has serious consequences.[26] She notes that people believe that "women have less commitment to their paid work once they become mothers, that a 'good' mother does not/should not have personal ambitions. Part of the problem is that many mothers themselves are conflicted about whether they deserve to be penalized in the paid workplace for having this second full-time job. One of the most tenacious cultural assumptions many of us share is that motherhood equals selfless/self-sacrificing; that once one becomes a mother, caring for yourself and caring for your children are mutually exclusive."

To the extent that employers share these beliefs, they will, perhaps unwittingly, view mothers as less committed to or less competent in workplace settings. In these ways, employers will subtly discriminate against mothers. Research suggests that employers do, in fact, share this belief and discriminate against mothers in a range of settings.

As a result, mothers, in addition to managing the real demands that young children make on them, have to contend with unparalleled levels of scrutiny and skepticism from their colleagues and superiors. Because cultural beliefs about the good father—those who work hard and do all that they can to provide for their family—are totally in synch with our ideas of what it means to be a good worker, fathers are spared the doubt and surveillance that mothers have to contend with.

After these anti-mother biases surfaced in their laboratory study, Correll, Benard and Paik wondered whether real-world employers do indeed discriminate against mothers, but not fathers. So, they decided to respond to actual job ads in newspapers, using résumés and cover letters that were identical except for first names and clues as to parental status.[27] Application materials were sent to more than 600 employers. The team then tracked how many of these "applicants" were called back, by phone or e-mail, for interviews.

This time, the people who were deciding whom to call back were real managers who had the power to hire and fire. Once again, mothers were at a disadvantage. They were significantly *less likely* than non-mothers to get called back. In fact, childless women received twice as many callbacks as equally qualified mothers. Because, by design, the applicants had identical qualifications, it was clear that employer discrimination was responsible for the "mommy applicants" losing out.

What happened to the "fathers" in this experiment? Being a parent had scant impact on men. Fathers and non-fathers were equally likely to be called back. But for women, motherhood was the kiss of death. They couldn't even get a foot in the door.

WHAT, YOU'RE PREGNANT?

According to the website the Glass Hammer, an attorney heard these unsolicited comments from coworkers during her two pregnancies: "My wife stayed home when our kids were little," "I'm sure you'll be checking in from home," and "We need to stick with business attire here" (even though she was wearing appropriate maternity clothes, her coworkers drew unwanted attention to her pregnancy with such comments).[28]

"Countless other women find themselves bombarded with unwanted—and sometimes downright rude—questions about their pregnancy once coworkers learn about their condition.

"Jennifer Wong, founder and CEO of Alt12, which creates mobile apps for pregnancy, health, and parenting, worked for a corporation when she had her first child. Wong says her announcement was met with a 'Congratulations. Now how are you going to get your work done?' attitude."

Wong says, "Because I was very career driven and 34 years old when I was pregnant—an age many consider to be 'old' to be having kids—I got comments from coworkers like, 'I never thought you would have kids' or that I would probably need more time to recover because I'm older. The most annoying comments came from those who assumed I was going to give up my career and not come back after my maternity leave."

Pregnancy can be a charged issue for women at work today. The reactions of employers and coworkers can range from mildly insulting comments to outright harassment.

When an employee of Bloomberg LP told her supervisor she was pregnant, she says that she was advised to have an abortion. She brought an action against the company through the U.S. Equal Economic Opportunity Commission (EEOC), which detailed a hostile attitude toward mothers in the workplace. According to Joan Williams in the Huffington Post, the EEOC brief claims that the CEO reportedly insisted managers "'get rid of these pregnant bitches' (referring to two women on maternity leave). The Head of Global Human Resources reportedly commented that mothers 'belong at home' and that 'women [do] not really [have] a place in the workforce.' The Head of News is said to have commented that 'half these f**king people take the [maternity] leave and they don't even come back. It's like stealing money from Mike Bloomberg's wallet. They should be arrested.' The Head of Global Data allegedly asked, 'Who would want to work with an office full of women?'"[29]

Unlike most other developed countries that mandate paid maternity leave, the United States has only the Family and Medical Leave Act (FMLA), which guarantees unpaid leave for some workers. Many companies in fact don't regard maternity leave as legitimate for their workers. The attitude is, *You chose to get pregnant. It's your problem.*

One employee at a television station tells us that several of her pregnant coworkers were extremely anxious about telling their superiors. They feared that their careers could take a nosedive—and research suggests they may be right. The number of pregnancy-related discrimination charges has jumped by 35 percent in the past decade; one in five charges of discrimination brought by women involve pregnancy, according to the EEOC.[30] Since 2001, the EEOC has handled 52,000 pregnancy complaints that totaled $150.5 million in damages. "Pregnancy discrimination persists in the 21st century workplace, unnecessarily depriving women of the means to support their families," EEOC chairwoman Jacqueline Berrien says.

The federal Pregnancy Discrimination Act mandates that companies treat pregnancy in the same way as any other medical condition. But women fear they will be seen as less committed employees and discriminated against. They are all too often greeted with such comments as "'Have you figured out how this happened yet?' from coworkers, or 'Do you feel you're up to this project?' from supervisors."[31]

When Yahoo! CEO Marissa Mayer announced that she was pregnant shortly after she took on the job, there was a media feeding frenzy. Some said that she was bound to fail, while others said that she would regret being a CEO *and* a new mom. Still others were upset that she planned to take only a two-week maternity leave.

It's interesting that such concern was lavished on Mayer, whose high position (and $129 million pay package) gave her benefits that few other pregnant women could ever hope for. As Amy Keyishian says in *Forbes*: "She's a CEO and can give herself work-from-home days if she needs to. She can hire a nanny, a nurse, a courier, a cook. She can set her company policy so that infants are allowed in the workplace (which has benefits like higher morale in the office!). Her hot-ass husband is a venture capitalist with a flexible schedule who can take the kid to doctor appointments and whatnot. You know who's not a CEO? Almost everyone else. Marissa Mayer is an outlier, and while her actions may make splashy headlines, her situation doesn't apply to the rest of us."[32]

The average working mother gets zero attention from the media. As Keyishian notes, "The vast majority of women going back to work after two weeks have nothing in common with Marissa Mayer. They're dragging their weary butts back to work, and wrapping up their boobs because there's no place to pump at work. They're getting paid by the hour.

"Or they're military women, like Robyn Roche-Paull, the author of *Breastfeeding in Combat Boots*, who went back to work after six weeks because it was required. When her son wouldn't take a bottle, she co-slept with him so he could nurse all night and sleep all day while she was at work."

Mayer is unquestionably an elite woman, with two degrees from Stanford in computer science; the average woman is very different. For example, as Keyishian says, among women whose education ended with high school "16% had paid maternity leave in 1971. And these days? . . . The number hasn't improved at all."

THE TIME-OFF BIND

Many of us applauded the passage of the FMLA, requiring that any company with fifty or more employees provide twelve weeks of unpaid parental leave for their workers. Some companies even put in more generous policies, with more time and some pay.

The good news is that the FMLA requires companies to provide job protection to employees who take family leave. So, a new mother on maternity leave knows that she can have her old job or one equivalent to it when she returns to work. In its way, the FMLA allows women (and men) to retain their connection to their companies.

The bad news is that there are major hidden costs for employees who take a leave. A leave of absence for illness or family responsibilities is associated with *significantly fewer subsequent promotions and smaller salary increases* for both men and women managers. This is true whether the leave is long or short.

But these costs are borne much more heavily by women, who are far likelier than men to be leave-takers, say researchers Michael Judiesch and Karen Lyness, both of Baruch College, the City University of New York.[33]

Judiesch and Lyness looked at a whole range of possible reasons to explain these results. Only one explanation worked: Managers who took any kind of leave were regarded as less than fully committed to their work. Any leave—even a brief leave to travel for a family funeral—seems to raise serious doubts about a manager's loyalty and commitment.

All managers, male and female, who deviate from "masculine norms" are punished. The corporate ethos resembles that of an NFL football team—you "play hurt." Even taking sick leave may be "seen as a violation of masculine norms, in that an aggressive, masculine manager would not allow anything to get in the way of work commitments."

Of the managers who took a leave of absence over a two-year period, 89 percent were women. So the drawbacks associated with these leaves applied primarily to women. The availability of a leave of absence can help women deal with managing their family responsibilities while remaining in the workforce. But women pay a price. They need to be aware that taking a leave of absence is likely to mean lower chances of promotion and smaller salary increases in the future.

Before the passage of the FMLA, women were often forced to drop out of the workforce when they got pregnant. We know that the long-term consequences of such a career interruption are huge. Women with twenty years of continuous work since their last career interruption had not fully caught up with their counterparts who had no such gaps in their work history. Quite a price to pay!

As a society, we've taken some baby steps toward the idea that people need time to deal with family issues such as parenthood, sickness, death, life crises. But we've stopped there. What we haven't done is to see such leaves as a normal part of the lives of companies and people. Fathers as well as mothers are looking for more flexibility. As a 2012 Pew Research Center report found, for the first time, men see having time with their families as central to their lives.[34] In Great Britain, the Equality and Human Rights Commission found the majority of working fathers unhappy with their work-life balance.[35] Sixty-two percent of fathers thought that they should spend more time caring for their children.

Is it true that dads want to cut back on working hours so that they can spend more time with their children? "Yes they do," says Duncan Fisher, who left a position in international development to spend more time with his daughters and manages a website called Dad.info.[36] "It's a very slow process because there are lots of things blocking them—workplace cultures and pay—but the impulse is definitely there."

In much of Europe, the situation is quite different from that in the United States. The idea of leaves of absence for family issues has become so "normal" that workers rarely pay a price. Hardly anyone even thinks that such a leave would affect his or her long-term career prospects. We need to learn this lesson here in the United States if women are ever going to have a fair shot at the jobs for which their talent and their training qualify them.

WHAT DOES "HAVING IT ALL" MEAN?

The idea of "having it all" has confused women for decades. One memorable image of this notion is the hugely popular Enjoli perfume commercial of the 1980s. A gorgeous blond woman first dons her power suit and goes to work, then hefts a frying pan and finally appears in slinky, clinging lingerie while singing this catchy ditty: "I can bring home the bacon, fry it up in a pan, and never let you forget you're a man."

Is this what women are really supposed to do? Must they be all things at all times to themselves—and to their husbands and children?

In her *Atlantic* cover article "Why Women Still Can't Have It All," which we discussed earlier, Anne-Marie Slaughter said that she felt she had to leave her high-powered State Department job because her teenage son was having a crisis, and she was commuting between her home in Princeton, New Jersey, and Washington, D.C. (Her husband, also an academic, handled the children.)

When she left D.C., she returned to her old job—University Professor at Princeton. As she describes it, "I teach a full course load; write regular print and online columns on foreign policy; give 40 to 50 speeches a year; appear regularly on TV and radio; and am working on a new academic book."

In what world does a woman with a husband and children and this powerful position *not* have it all? If this accomplished, highly successful woman who was able to choose between two great jobs is a "failure," what chance is there for the rest of us? Have we defined "having it all" upward to the point where it's become an impossible dream?

Debora Spar, president of Barnard College, thinks this is exactly the case. She says in the Daily Beast, "Indeed, rather than leaping with glee at the liberation that has befallen women since the 1960s, we are laboring instead under a double whammy of impossible expectations—the old-fashioned ones (to be good mothers and wives, impeccable housekeepers and blushing brides) and those wrought more recently (to be athletic, strong, sexually versatile, and wholly independent). The result? We have become a generation desperate to be perfect wives, mothers, and professionals—Tiger Moms who prepare organic quinoa each evening after waltzing home from the IPO in our Manolo Blahnik heels. Even worse, we somehow believe that we need to do all of this at once, and without any help."[37]

She knows of what she speaks: "I have sprinted through airports in the futile hope of catching an earlier flight home and tried to comfort a sobbing child when, inevitably, the plane was late. I delivered my first lecture in a suit that reeked of infant throw-up from earlier that morning and crashed the minivan into a tree as I raced to retrieve the correct ballet costume.

"Through all this chaos I have become increasingly convinced of two interconnected points. First, that there is undeniably still a 'women's problem' in the United States, a problem that relates deeply and intimately to the bleak roster of numbers that tell this story. And second, that part of this intractable problem is tied to the fact that women in this country are struggling far more than is necessary not only to have that ephemeral 'all,' but to do it all alone."

If the problem were simply overt discrimination, we could find a direct remedy. But women are affected by a "culture of perfection" that they didn't create, that can't be legislated against and that too frequently shapes their behavior. This issue is especially salient for women who are mothers. They don't want to be seen as slackers or to confirm the stereotype that working mothers can't hack it, so what do they do? They double down, push harder and take the shortest possible leaves both before their delivery date and after. Oddly, women in high-paid jobs, who could afford to cut themselves some slack and take a breather, don't. They take the shortest leave of all.

"But at the end of the day," Spar says, "women who juggle children and jobs will still face a discrete and serious set of tensions that simply don't confront either men (except in very rare cases) or women who remain childless. . . .

"Which brings me to my final point. The only way that American women will ever fully solve the 'women's problem' is by recognizing the quest for perfection for what it is: a myth. No woman can have it all, and by using all as the standard of success, we are only condemning ourselves and our daughters to failure."

AIMING HIGH?

As we noted earlier in this chapter, the message to women who are mothers is that aiming high can be dangerous—to themselves, their children and their marriage. Why do we believe this? Because while there are a great many women who aim high and make it, for the most part we are unaware of them. We may know about a few highly successful, prominent women—but not about the vast majority who are managing well at having both work and family. These folks are not of much interest to the media—they only become stories when they fail. For example, when Brenda Barnes left as CEO of PepsiCo, the media narrative was that she couldn't manage both the job and her children.

But when she resurfaced in an even bigger job—as president of Sara Lee—it wasn't news, outside of the business pages. She still had the same husband and the same kids, but she wasn't failing, so nobody cared. It's not surprising that few people know that women can handle high-level positions and a family—they don't hear much about these women. So it's easy to conclude that mothers can't hold down high-level jobs. Not true. As we noted in Chapter 8, high-achieving women are just as likely to marry as are women in less-demanding jobs, and married high-achieving women are exactly as likely to have had kids by ages thirty-six to forty as are all other married women who work full-time.

While we obsess about achieving women who fail, we often ignore the price women pay when they aim too low. The nearly exclusive focus on the costs of aiming high does not serve women well. They are still being urged to trim their sails when they have kids; no one ever says, "Aim low." But that's the real message.

It's easy to believe that by aiming low, your life will be all that you want it to be—time for making the best birthday parties, attending yoga classes, preparing gourmet meals, being the class mother, going to every soccer game. On the other hand, by aiming high, some say, you will automatically experience frayed marriages, stressed-out kids, a harried lifestyle and a litany of other horrors. But as full-time working mothers who have raised happy and healthy children while we did work that we loved, we know this picture is completely bogus. This isn't just our experience. In our book *She Works, He Works*, based on a major study of working couples, we found that working women enjoyed better emotional health than those who didn't work. And among working women, those in high-prestige jobs who had children had the best mental health of all.

Another version of aiming low is settling for a job that pays very little but promises "mommy benefits." You may actually be getting a really bad deal. Women need to be wary when they are led to believe that although the salary they are being offered is low, the benefits that go along with the job (flexible hours, a part-time option, etc.) make up for the loss of pay. This message is often sent to women in female-dominated fields. Research shows that women who work in such jobs pay a *higher* penalty, in terms of lower hourly wages, than do women who work in occupations that are more integrated by gender or even in male-dominated jobs.[38]

At the same time, the promised flexible hours may not materialize. Research shows that they often don't—surprise, surprise. In fact, women in integrated and male-dominated fields are paid more and have *better* access to such benefits. Another lose-lose scenario for women, especially mothers.

People often advocate for these "mommy hours" jobs, but such jobs have serious drawbacks. In fact, part-timers are paid on a lower scale, have few if any benefits and no career ladder and are unlikely to ever again achieve full-time employment commensurate with their previous employment. Take, for example, couples in which both partners are doctors.[39] If the wife reduces her work hours while her husband does not, they both experience distress. She's unhappy because she isn't working up to her capacity, while *he* is. Her unhappiness makes him miserable as well.

The new facts of women's lives make it imperative for them to set their sights high. A woman who is twenty today has a good chance of living until she is ninety. She may well have to support herself through-out her life. Once upon a time, women spent most of their lives in-volved in intensive childrearing. No longer. Today, women spend only a fairly short period of their long lives raising young children. Men's incomes have been flat or declining for more than thirty years. Most men today expect their wives to be partners in breadwinning.

If a woman plans to have a family, the financial facts are daunting. The cost of raising a child from birth to age seventeen for a middle-income two-parent family averaged $234,900 in 2012 (not including college), according to the U.S. Department of Agriculture.[40] That's up nearly 40 percent—or more than $60,000—from ten years ago. Just one year of spending on a child costs up to $13,830 in 2010, compared with $9,860 a decade ago.[41] If you add college costs into this picture, the figure escalates hugely. One estimate puts the total at a staggering 1.1 million dollars.[42]

Gone are the days when high-wage manufacturing jobs provided a secure family income. White-collar and professional jobs are increas-ingly moving offshore. Old-style lifelong pensions hardly exist. The middle class is shrinking. Fifty percent of marriages end in divorce, so that a woman who expects to be supported for life by a husband is making a fool's bet.

Cultural memes about motherhood seem to tell women, "Stay at home or your children will be damaged." At the same time, mothers who aren't in the workforce are called lazy drones who are not carrying their weight. Neither extreme is accurate. Women have to make deci-sions based on their own needs and desires—illuminated by the facts that good research can provide.

Whatever choices women do make, they need to be aware of the costs and benefits of those choices—in the present and in the future.

TWELVE

WINNING THE NEW SOFT WAR

'm sick of hearing how far we've come," writes Harvard Kennedy School professor Barbara Kellerman, an expert on women's leadership.[1] "I'm sick of hearing how much better situated we are now than before. I'm sick of hearing how women are closing the gaps (in health outcomes, educational attainment, and economic participation), how in some cases women are superseding men, and how in the present more than in the past women are progressing to positions of middle and upper management. Above all I'm sick of hearing about the pipeline, about the path to the top supposedly thick with women who will, in the fullness of time, be rewarded for their patience and virtue.

"The fact is that so far as leadership is concerned women in nearly every realm are nearly nowhere—hardly any better off than they were a generation ago."

Kellerman doesn't mince words, and as the previous pages may have convinced you, she is absolutely right. It's hard to find a better summary of the consequences of the New Soft War. It's here, it's real, and it puts a brake on the ambitions, hopes and dreams of millions of women.

Of course, women have made gains. As we've seen, a really big deal is being made of young women's educational success. Break out the champagne! Women are winning; their success has led to the end of men; everything is wonderful. But the strong focus on preparing girls and women for their future work is not matched by an equally strong focus on what happens *after* they get their degrees. We can all clap our hands when women get into law school, med school or garner top-notch scientific credentials. But then what? Like the MIT and Harvard women who discovered to their dismay that they were being short-changed despite their accomplishments, many of us make the same mistake. We haven't kept a vigilant eye on the ways in which women are increasingly losing out.

School is not life. In school, the rules are clear, you know when you're succeeding or failing because you get a grade that spells it out. And if you are failing, you know that you can study hard and get back on track. Whether you pass or fail a class is primarily dependent on what you have or have not done. The criteria for getting good grades are set out in detail in the syllabus. In school, students have direct access to information about exactly what constitutes success.

(But there's a downside even to women's success in school. Thanks to the fact that they increasingly lag behind men in the workplace, reports Hilary Lips of Radford University, "a higher percentage of women [47%] than men [39%] find themselves with a high student debt burden, paying more than 8% of their earnings toward student loan debt."[2])

Unfortunately, we have focused too intensely on what happens in school and on getting the first entry-level job and not enough on the challenges of building a lifelong career. Because of this skewed focus, women are at risk of not being able to build on their successes—or to reap the rewards their education and accomplishments should bring them.

It's clear that no one policy or set of actions will win this war. What's needed is a multipronged approach: on the personal, corporate and state and federal levels. Let's look at some critical steps individual women can take to help themselves as they try to advance in their careers.

ARM YOURSELF
WITH INFORMATION

Women need to be vigilant in finding out what's really going on and standing up for themselves. The good news is that women can arm themselves to fight the New Soft War and win victories in the quest for a level playing field. Knowledge can indeed be power, if it's used strategically to escape the "no second chances," "no credit where credit is due," "receding goalposts," "hard-won but easily lost" and other dilemmas.

In the workplace, especially at higher levels, the clarity found in schools is hard to come by. In most major sex discrimination cases, the problem has been that a lack of objective criteria for promotions opens the door for subjective judgments, and women suffer as a result. Unconscious bias plays a much larger role in the boardroom than it does in the classroom.

Reasons for hiring, firing and promotions can be totally subjective. You need to gather information, talk to other women, read salary surveys and question the status quo. Be prepared!

You may not even know when you are being discriminated against, so it's important to maximize your chances of getting a fair shake. But there are things you can do. First, be sure you clearly understand what your job entails and the criteria for evaluating your performance. What do you have to do to get a promotion? A raise? To get ahead? If you aren't sure, ask. If you do what's suggested and you're still not moving up the ladder, ask again, forcefully. At least you won't be flying in the dark. Then, if you are still not advancing—but rather watching the goalposts recede—consider moving on, like the medical academic who kept seeing the goalposts recede. You too may find a better opportunity elsewhere.

DON'T BE THE STEREOTYPE

One of the most chilling facts to emerge from the evidence we've examined is that if people (male and female) have no information about a woman, they make their judgments on the basis of the female stereotype. That stereotype casts women as emotional, not rational, as unsuited for analysis or leadership, and as good at caring but not at decision making.

It may come as a shock to smart young women that they may be judged so unfairly. In all likelihood, they are thinking, "I'm not like the stereotype at all." But people *do* have this stereotype in their heads, so you have to defang it.

Back in the early days of the second wave of the women's movement, feminist lawyer Bella Abzug remarked that she wore wide-brimmed hats in the courtroom so no one would think she was a secretary and ask her to get the coffee. Those were the bad old days, right? Would that that were true. But so powerful is the grip of stereotypes that they retain their ability to shape reality even today.

Not long ago, the vice president of a company walked down to the lobby of her building to greet the CEO of another company who was arriving for an important meeting. All she knew was the CEO's name: Leslie R. As a group of people entered the lobby, the VP strode up to a well-dressed man and said, "So nice to meet you, sir." To her embarrassment, she had just grasped the hand of the executive assistant to the CEO, *Ms.* Leslie R. The vice president, who had always considered herself a feminist, realized that someplace in her head was anchored the image of a CEO: tall, attractive, well groomed—and male.

There's a lot of that going around. In a Gallup–*Wall Street Journal* survey, a startling 61 percent of the female executives reported having been mistaken for a secretary at a business meeting.[3]

It's hard for many of us to wrap our minds around the notion that "leadership" and "female" can go together. A major part of male privilege is that men get a free pass in this area. The male stereotype leads us to expect men to be leaders, forceful, good at analysis, competent. Of course, many of us can instantly bring to mind a man we've met who was incredibly impressive at first sight—imposing, confident, certain he knew the truth and not hesitant to pronounce it—who turned out to be a complete idiot. History is replete with such men. Warren G. Harding seemed right out of central casting for the role of U.S. president. He ran one of the most incompetent, corrupt administrations in history. Spiro T. Agnew was tall, attractive and forceful, but he is on everybody's list of the worst VPs in history.

If you're a woman and you aren't proactive about defining exactly who you are, the female stereotype will do it for you. Women of color often face a double whammy in this regard. Negative stereotypes of blacks, Hispanics, Arabs, South Asians and others are still powerful in the United States.

TALK YOURSELF UP

What's the take-away message? It is absolutely essential that women let their bosses and colleagues know about their accomplishments. Often, superiors don't know about the achievements of their female employees—the very things that men get rewarded for. You can't just blame your supervisor for not promoting you if you haven't given him or her the relevant information.

But there is a catch, as we have noted: Self-promoting women, research shows, while being seen as competent, are considered to be stepping beyond the bounds of "proper" female behavior and risk being disliked.

This is the classic catch-22. Damned if you do, damned if you don't.

Although there are risks, we believe it's better to offend than to be sidelined forever.

Knowing the risks, it's possible to devise strategies. It's not fair that women have to strategize about ways to present their accomplishments while men can just do it straightforwardly, but that's life.

Some ideas: Make sure that information about you gets to decision makers before they pigeonhole you into a "female" box. Take seriously the notion that you have to provide information about your accomplishments and find ways to do that. Seek a high-placed colleague to introduce you and speak glowingly about your credentials. Use social media and e-mail to get information to your superiors and to people who are friends and colleagues of your superiors. Knowing that competent women may be viewed as unlikable, you should be sure to acknowledge those who have helped you and praise the contributions of colleagues. Use self-deprecating humor to show that you can laugh at yourself. (Watch the press conferences of John F. Kennedy to see a master at this tactic.)

Unfortunately, too many young women take themselves out of the game before they even get to the stage of planning how to make a name for themselves.

This can be a real problem. Harvard Law professor Nancy Gertner, in a recent talk in Boston, told the story of a young female law student who had approached her, saying that she planned a career in wills and trusts.[4] This was an area, she told Gertner, that would enable her to combine a job with having a family. Gertner asked the student if she was married or had children. The student said no, that she didn't even have a boyfriend. Then Gertner asked if she liked the area of law she was planning to practice. The student said no, and in fact she found it boring!

This is an example, Gertner said, of women sabotaging their careers even before they've gotten their feet wet in the fields they are studying.

Facebook CEO Sheryl Sandberg weighed in on this issue, making a big media splash in 2013 with *Lean In: Women, Work, and the Will to Lead*, her book urging ambitious women in their twenties and thirties to "lean in" to their careers, especially when they have children.[5] Instead of pulling back and aiming low, Sandberg wants them to move full-steam ahead. Unfortunately, she says, too many women are letting up.

She proposes that women attend "lean in" circles, in which they follow a curriculum she developed to help them succeed on the job. "Don't leave before you leave" is a mantra she advocates, cautioning women about giving up and limiting themselves too soon.

Sandberg has indeed put her finger on a real problem. At the same time, she's been criticized for addressing mainly elite women and putting little emphasis on structural changes needed at the corporate and government levels.

As Maureen Dowd puts it in her *New York Times* column, "She seems to think she can remedy social paradigms with a new kind of club—a combo gabfest, Oprah session and corporate pep talk. (Where's the yoga?) . . . People come to a social movement from the bottom up, not the top down. Sandberg has co-opted the vocabulary and romance of a social movement not to sell a cause, but herself."[6]

True, Sandberg is encouraging elite women to get to the top. But the top is where the power is, and the research we've cited shows that all women do better with more females in the C-suite. As we've documented, it's not easy for women to get to the seat of power, given all the roadblocks they face.

As for us, we're delighted to see a top-level executive embrace feminism in such a full-throated way. While she focuses on what individual women can do, she readily admits that corporate culture and public policy must change.

Sandberg opened a discussion that we are now adding to in a very serious way. We must note that because she is such a high-powered superstar, she can soar right over many of the obstacles that would trip up most of us. As we've noted, marquee women transcend the "feminine" stereotype. She's probably not going to be penalized for being too competent and thus not likable enough. Neither is she likely to see credit for her successes go to men. She probably doesn't have to worry about "no second chances," since she owns part of the company. Her road is surely easier than that of most other women, but it's good to have her on our side.

AVOID THE DISEASE TO PLEASE

Keep in mind that you can't always be liked by everybody. Women tend to be overly sensitive to being liked—not surprisingly, because the feminine stereotype includes an imperative to take care of everybody else. That mandate often conflicts with the requirements of leadership.

If you buy into the stereotype that women are natural caretakers and being nice is what you're supposed to do, there is a downside you may not be aware of. For example, you may hesitate to confront an employee who really needs to be brought up short for the good of the company—and for that person's own benefit. You may not stand your ground when someone with a bad idea challenges your good idea. You can't be a good decision maker if you always prioritize someone else's plans and second-guess your own well-thought-out ones. You sell yourself short if you are overly modest. Why should others pay attention to your ideas when you yourself seem unsure of them? You may put yourself under too much stress by always worrying about what other people think about your actions. Chances are, some people will agree with you and others will not. That's the nature of leadership. Step up to these challenges and you will discover that you can beat the "please disease," and that not being "nice" all the time is really OK.

STAKE YOUR CLAIM

Information—or the lack of it—is at the heart of the no-credit-where-credit-is-due dilemma. As we've noted, if a woman is part of a male-female team and doesn't speak up, her accomplishments will likely be credited to the man on her team—even when she does most of the work. Many of the women we interviewed had encountered this problem and found it very frustrating.

It's not a simple ego boost that's involved in speaking up. Some women who had done the heavy lifting found out that their male colleagues had gotten a promotion or a raise that they did not get. Not claiming credit can set in motion a downward spiral that robs women of deserved promotions, as well as many thousands of dollars.

Managers at Google report that special efforts must be made to persuade female engineers to nominate themselves for promotions.[7] Laszlo Bock, a senior vice president, told the *Wall Street Journal* that all employees are encouraged to nominate themselves for promotions, and men jump at the chance, often before they are ready. But women have to be pushed. Bock says he tells women, "For God's sake, nominate yourself for promotions. You're holding yourself back." Women who do make the leap usually get promoted. "By the time a woman says she is ready, she was probably ready a year ago."

Female Google employees who put off asking for promotions are not atypical. Many women are overqualified for the jobs they take; men assume they will learn on the job. Women all too often hesitate to apply; men go after jobs they do not yet know how to do.

Even though today's young women are better educated than ever before, many doubt their worth in the workplace, say Alice Eagly and Linda Carli.[8] "They feel they don't deserve success or think, 'I should be happy with what I have.'"

This kind of thinking shows that women themselves get trapped by the female stereotype. It's "nice" to take what you're offered and not complain.

Sadly, deference gets you nowhere. Speaking up *can* get you into trouble, but *not* speaking can also get you in trouble—and make you seem weak, uninformed and unable to make a contribution. Those young women in the Ivy League schools who are working behind the scenes in campus organizations and not taking credit up front can be setting themselves up for second-class citizenship in later years.

Wanting to avoid risk, many women simply put their heads down, cross their fingers and "overdeliver," as former General Electric CEO Jack Welch suggested. This course of action is unlikely to succeed, unless women both overdeliver *and* demand rewards for doing so. (If Welch and other powerful men don't see that they are part of the problem, little will change.)

If, after doing your best, you still aren't seeing the results you want, you may have to look elsewhere. The "receding goalposts" dilemma may be operating at your workplace.

One woman in academic medicine was told that in order to get promoted, she had to receive grants and publish more scholarly papers. She did both successfully, only to have her supervisor tell her exactly the same thing at her next review. After this scenario was repeated several times, it finally dawned on her that she was never going to get promoted and that she needed to find a more receptive work environment. Scary as it was to leave, she found a high-level job where she has been incredibly successful; she's no longer just spinning her wheels.

In addition, it can be hard for women to ask for a raise. Research finds that women who ask for a raise not only are disliked but also are seen as not competent. And women often have little experience with negotiating, which may explain why their pay packages lag behind those of their male colleagues.

One female full professor in an academic department at a large midwestern university found, to her surprise, that she was being paid less than the average assistant male professor. (She found this out from a list, published by the university, of the faculty's average salaries by rank.) She noticed that men were getting raises every year while women weren't. Her department chair told her that the younger men really needed the money, since they had families to support. Somehow, he failed to notice that all the women in the department *also* had children to support. She took her case to the president of the university and discovered something she hadn't known: that he was determined to improve conditions for women. Had she not been proactive, she might still be making less than a man of lesser rank.

A woman can also get stuck if she compares herself with other women. And indeed, it may be that, relative to other women, she is doing great. This sort of thinking can sidetrack her motivation to advance her own cause. Women need to measure themselves against people who have the same qualifications as they do, and those people are usually male. Females have to gather as much information as they can about how the guys are doing and what their salaries and benefits are. Clearly, this can be very difficult—perhaps even impossible. But there may be avenues to get the information, such as asking people who have left the company about their compensation packages. Or asking people at similar companies what the going rates are. Social media networks like LinkedIn and the Glass Hammer, and women's professional organizations may make this difficult task a bit easier. Serendipity also may play a part. When Roz Barnett was at a major business school, a female colleague happened to find out what the men were earning and told Roz that she was making much less than her male peers. Roz made an appointment with the director of research, who told her he had assumed that she, a young married woman with a child, wasn't serious about a career and so could be paid less. Roz told him forcefully that he was wrong, and she got a raise.

If you are leading the female pack in the race but are not catching up with your male peers, you are losing. And the further behind you drop, the more you lose and the harder it is for you to negotiate a fair deal for yourself.

GO AHEAD AND GET ANGRY . . . BUT DON'T FORGET TO EXPLAIN WHY YOU'RE MAD

Historically, female anger has been portrayed as irrational. The Furies of Greek mythology had snakes for hair and blood streamed from their eyes as they ripped asunder their enemies. To perform bloody murder, Shakespeare's Lady Macbeth implored, "Come, you spirits / That tend on mortal thoughts, unsex me here, / And fill me, from the crown to the toe, top-full / Of direst cruelty." More recently, in presidential politics, Hillary Clinton was pictured as both a witch and Lady Macbeth, and Michelle Obama was often labeled as "angry" or "mad."[9]

In contrast, male anger is often portrayed as just and righteous: an angry Jehovah, expelling Adam and Eve from Eden after their sin; Christ driving the moneychangers from the temple; Patrick Henry thundering, "Give me liberty or give me death"; FDR after Pearl Harbor decrying, "a date which will live in infamy"; and Ronald Reagan saying, "Mr. Gorbachev, tear down this wall!"

So it's not surprising that women's anger in the workplace is often seen as troubling. As we noted, angry women are thought to be out of control and not worthy of a high salary, while men don't suffer the consequences of their anger. Even when they're mad, men are considered just as competent, just as likable, as when they're not angry.

Here again, women have to explain themselves, while men don't. Yale's Victoria Brescoll and HEC Paris's Eric Uhlmann found that a woman's anger makes her seem uncontrolled and irrational *unless* she gives a good explanation of why she was angry in the first place.[10]

So, women can do something to manage the way their anger is perceived. They can help their own cause by explaining their anger as a response to understandable circumstances. For example, when a woman explained that she was angry because a coworker had lied to her, her colleagues then saw her anger as legitimate, not as a sign of her being out of control. They were able to put themselves in her shoes, and were not so quick to pass judgment.

Men, too, need to understand that they may easily jump to a wrong conclusion about women's anger. Instead of a knee-jerk reaction that an angry woman is overly emotional, they can give her the benefit of the doubt, as they would a male colleague. A simple question like "What's ticking you off?" might shine a light on what's really happening.

CLEARING THE HURDLES

How many thousands of articles have asked "Have we broken the glass ceiling, or haven't we?" The idea that women smash up against an invisible barrier as they near the top has a lot of appeal, and is endlessly discussed. But new research has found that the glass ceiling is clearly not the main problem.

Women don't sail right along and suddenly crash into an invisible barrier. A better image comes from the world of track and field: "the hurdles." It's not one obstacle that women confront near the end of the race but rather a whole series of them all along the course. Women can get knocked out anywhere along the way. As Phyllis Tharenou, executive dean of social and behavioral sciences at Australia's Flinders University, reports in an important 2012 paper, "current research and theories on the gender pay gap have focused little on the *cumulative economic disadvantage* [italics ours] that may accrue to women over a lifetime of lower pay than men."[11] In other words, it's the hurdles that really make the difference.

Imagine a world in which workplace gender discrimination doesn't exist. Then, take a hiring pool of 500 equally qualified female and male employees. They'd be hired at a fifty-fifty ratio. Next, imagine that both sexes do equally well and work equally hard. At the first promotion decision—and at every subsequent one—men and women would be equally represented.

Now, imagine a workplace in which gender discrimination has a very minor negative effect—0.1 percent. What would this mean at the entry level? That 51.8 percent of men would be hired, compared with 48.2 percent of women.

This very small initial male advantage increases over time. "When later promotion decisions are made, the impact of gender stereotypes is compounded." In this scenario, the first group of women hired is less than 50 percent, and the group "will shrink again at each step of advancement as the 'small' impact of gender stereotypes has its effect."

By the fourth promotion decision, the percentage of women will shrink to 41.9 percent—while the percentage of men promoted will be 58.1 percent. So, an early gap of 3.6 percent favoring males balloons up to a stunning 16.2 percent advantage.

Tharenou makes her point very conservatively. As we've said, the real-world male advantage is closer to 5 percent than it is to 0.1 percent—an enormous difference.

So the hurdles really need sustained and thorough attention. We have to see clearly—and early—the scope of the problem. If women fail to clear the hurdles in the early stages of the race, they will never achieve gender equity in senior positions. So women shouldn't hang back, not asking for promotions, blaming themselves if they don't get them, and explaining away disappointments as unlucky accidents. If we don't understand the layout of the battlefield, then we can't win the war. Don't make the assumption that it's your fault if you're not moving fast enough. And speak up early. If you don't, nothing will change.

WHAT SHOULD CORPORATIONS AND GOVERNMENTS DO?

As we've just discussed, there are steps individual women can take to advance their cause, but they can't win the New Soft War on their own. Systemic changes are needed to give women a fair chance. This is a global problem, and new, dramatic evidence shows how pervasive it is. The World Economic Forum issued a report in 2012 showing that in *no* country in the world do women earn more than 82 cents for every dollar a man who is doing comparable work earns.[12]

To get to gender equity, corporations will have to play a large role, as will the federal and state governments. While formal, overt gender discrimination at the corporate level is explicitly prohibited by federal law, particularly by Title IX, subtle and covert discrimination is not. And given the current status of women, companies have a long way to go to create conditions where women can flourish free from the constraints of gender stereotypes.

For a long time, the argument for moving women up the job ladder was one of equality, of "fairness"; it was the moral and righteous thing to do. The problem, according to a 2011 report by Deloitte, is that morality and righteousness have barely moved the needle: "The actual participation rate of women at the top of corporate structures remained largely unchanged."[13]

Goodness and fairness are not working. Happily, something else may do the trick: the bottom line. The Deloitte report establishes a link between productivity and the proportion of women on boards or in senior management. It cites an Australian investment banking study, for example, that found "an increase of up to 12 percent in productivity of Australian businesses could be achieved if the gender gap were eliminated." Research conducted by both Deloitte and McKinsey demonstrates that companies with significant numbers of women in management have a much higher return on investment than companies that lag on this front. In addition, productivity goes up when work teams have an equal number of women and men.

What might be called the gender-and-greenbacks connection is changing the way companies think about business, especially in the European Union. The EU hadn't been doing well with respect to gender diversity. From 2007, when McKinsey's first *Women Matter* study was released, to 2012, women's representation on executive committees in very large companies in nine major countries had risen to only 10 percent.[14]

That slow progress was a wake-up call, and now the EU is paying attention. Michel Barnier, a member of the European Commission, says, "It's not only a question of fairness. The presence of women in the leadership of a country or a region or a business is a question of good governance."[15]

So far, we are not seeing the same enthusiasm in the United States. Once upon a time, what foreign companies did was of little interest to us. Today, as countries in Europe and beyond are our trading partners and competitors in a globalized world, the U.S. government and U.S. companies would be well advised to pay attention. The *Wall Street Journal* reports, "There is evidence that the U.S. is losing ground. Women are making huge strides in emerging economies such as India and China; in India, 12 percent of chief-executive slots at the 250 biggest companies are held by women"—compared with *less than 5 percent* in the United States.[16]

Why is the United States lagging so far behind the rest of the developed world? Whatever the reasons, corporate leaders, policymakers and women themselves need to be acutely aware of this problem. If no action is taken, the United States will fall even further behind. Such a failure will be bad not only for women's advancement but also for the pocketbooks of all Americans.

TARGETS VS. QUOTAS

The productivity argument is having an appreciable effect elsewhere in the world. The Australian Securities Exchange "now requires gender ratios to be reported by listed companies and action plans to be developed to address gender imbalances," the Deloitte report notes.[17] This isn't about fairness; it's about letting investors know which companies are probably going to do well. Governments elsewhere are tackling this issue. "Malaysia has set a target of 30 percent of women on boards of listed companies within 5 years; Norway has imposed quotas and a number of countries in the EU are threatening quotas if business does not lift its game in this respect."

Recognizing that voluntary efforts have failed, Britain now requires that women make up half of the slate of candidates for board of directors seats, and any company that has a board made up of fewer than 30 percent women has to detail the steps it is taking to remedy the situation. Britannia is about ruling the waves again (even if now they are electronic pulses), not about being nice to women.

With this new initiative, England joins a growing number of European countries that have set gender quotas. In 2011, France approved a law forcing some 2,000 large companies to reserve at least 40 percent of their boardroom positions for women within six years. As a result, by 2012 the number of women on French boards increased from 12 percent to 22 percent.[18] Norway introduced a quota for women on boards a decade ago, which catapulted their share from 9 percent in 2003 to the required 40 percent today. Several EU countries have recently followed suit.[19]

Women are of two minds about quotas. "Some think any way of getting in through the door is fine as long as they can do the job. Others say they would never want to be chosen for a job on the basis of their gender, regardless of their ability."[20] "If you think you are good enough, take the job and run with it," advises Patricia Bellinger, executive director of executive education at Harvard Business School, adding, "Worry about what people think later."[21]

The need to win the competitive war for productivity may move other countries, such as the United States, toward gender targets or quotas. While most countries have not imposed quotas, many have set out specific gender targets with associated penalties for failure to comply. Indeed, Deloitte concludes that the threat of quotas for noncompliance may be sufficient to stimulate action.

Today, competition isn't just for productivity or for customers; it is also for talent. Why would rising stars from countries that are committed to gender equity choose to work in the United States, where few women make it to the top and the commitment to remedy the situation is more conversational than action-based?

Among the strongest arguments against quotas is that they may result in the appointment of unqualified women. The fear is that if quotas were instituted, there wouldn't be enough eligible women in the pipeline and it would lead to "token" appointments. Yet according to Deloitte, these fears haven't materialized. And, as we have noted, there are far more women in the pipeline than there are women in top positions. In fact, in Norway, which has quotas, such fears have proved groundless.[22]

Nevertheless, many countries have not embraced quotas, the United States among them. The consensus seems to be that "intervention or compulsion should only be imposed where absolutely necessary."

Short of quotas, many companies are implementing policies that have teeth, such as tying senior executives' compensation to their diversity programs' performance. Such steps may not be necessary in the future if companies come to fully realize the economic benefits of gender diversity. Striking an optimistic note, the Deloitte report says, "We are finally seeing an increase in the pace of change in many countries around the world." Moreover, it notes that "gender balance is likely to benefit the companies that do adopt it. It is increasingly being recognized as a badge of good governance and therefore desirable. Investors should demand it. If this progress continues and disclosure and targets work, then there may be no need to impose quotas."[23]

BY THE NUMBERS

Whether women get in by quotas, targets or company policies, their numbers matter. It is said that one woman is a token, two are a presence and three are a voice.

As we've noted, the goal of gender diversity must be to have enough women in senior positions to create a critical mass. When you have a token woman or two, the most important fact about them is that they are female. When women become the norm at high levels, people see them for their individual strengths, not as "the females."[24]

For example, a study of 7,711 executives at 831 U.S. firms found that women CFOs were paid notably less than similarly qualified men *except* when there were at least three women on the compensation committee.[25] For now, the salaries of female CFOs have less to do with their qualifications and more to do with the speed with which their companies get behind policies to improve gender equity on their boards.

The inescapable conclusion is that companies that want to succeed on the new international playing field need more women on their boards and in senior management.

WHEN DIVERSITY PROGRAMS JUST DON'T WORK

One of the most distressing facts to emerge from research is that the majority of companies around the globe have diversity programs on their books, but they are ineffective. Across Europe and Asia, 90 percent have such programs, as do 75 percent of Fortune 500 companies in the United States. Yet too often these programs lack clear goals, evaluation and enforcement, and less than half have criteria that allow for them to be evaluated.[26]

Critically, there's little commitment to the programs in the C-suite, and it gets weaker as you go down the organizational ladder. At lower management levels, a paltry 17 percent of managers support diversity programs. It can be disastrous for a young woman if early in her career she runs into a manager whose mind-set, conscious or otherwise, is that women don't have what it takes.

Moreover, there's been poor implementation and a lack of monitoring of existing programs, according to Brian Welle and Madeline Heilman.[27] The situation is depressing, but fortunately there are concrete steps companies can take.

- Companies need to educate middle managers so that they recognize gender discrimination as a problem. They need to know "what it is, how it happens, and how they can prevent their own stereotypes from biasing their actions." Stereotypes are a major barrier to women's success, and confirmation bias works in many and often subtle ways. Nothing will change until mind-sets change. Welle and Heilman say that education about stereotypes is critical for companies and will "have a positive impact on the bottom line of their businesses."
- The nature of jobs and the skills required for success must be spelled out in detail. When job descriptions are specific and focus on the skills needed to do them, candidates will be selected and judged on those criteria. These steps will reduce the edge men get by virtue of the often unconscious belief that success at "male" jobs requires certain masculine characteristics. Clarity and transparency are powerful tools for fighting the New Soft War.
- Well-intentioned programs that have the unanticipated effect of actually promoting discrimination must be jettisoned. Companies need to realize that "women-only" solutions don't work, and may end up re-segregating the workplace. For example, if "mommy hours" are only being taken by mommies—and not by daddies—the policy has to be rethought. Why? Because women but not men will be sidelined as less committed, less valued workers. Also, these policies need a name change. How about "parent hours"?
- Programs have to be constantly monitored to see whether they are having the intended effect. For example, while 69 percent of companies said they had a mentoring program for women, only 16 percent of these programs were judged to be

well implemented.[28] It's not enough to get programs on the books, they have to be enforced.

It may take several tries to get a program right. If a well-intentioned program is not having the desired effects, it needs to be reworked, as Sweden learned.[29] A major goal of that nation's child-care leave policy was to encourage fathers to take leaves so that their wives could maintain their connections to their workplaces. However, not many fathers took up this policy in its original form. Today after several redos, more than 80 percent of Swedish dads take paternity leave. And some politicians are arguing that those benefits should become even more generous. Such policies would be good for most economies. For example, a new study from Cornell of fathers in Canada found that those who took parental leave spent more time caring for their children and doing household chores, even years later. Equally important, their wives spent considerably more time developing their own careers and thus boosting the economy.

The United States is taking a few baby steps in this direction. Some big companies, Ernst & Young and Bank of America for instance, are financing such leaves for employees, as are a few states, including California and New Jersey. But progress is fitful and slow.[30]

GETTING EQUAL PAY

"Our journey is not complete until our wives, our mothers and daughters can earn a living equal to their efforts."[31] These words, spoken by President Obama during his second inaugural address in 2013, are a strong reminder that pay inequity is still a fact of life in the United States. So far, the gender pay gap has defied solution. A recent American Association of University Women report put it this way: The pay gap is "real, it's persistent, and it's undermining the economic security of American families."[32]

Despite endless pleas for fairness and several legislative initiatives, women still earn only 77 cents for every dollar that men earn. At a 2012 White House Forum on Women and the Economy, Obama said this figure hadn't changed in the past year.

President John F. Kennedy signed into law the Equal Pay Act of 1963. A year later, Title VII of the Civil Rights Act outlawed discrimination against women in the workplace. All of this happened fifty years ago! Talk about a snail's pace.

In 2009, President Obama's first legislative initiative was the Lilly Ledbetter Fair Pay Act. The Paycheck Fairness Act, which aims to give women additional and much-needed equal pay protections by requiring employers to demonstrate that any salary differences between men and women doing the same work are not gender-related, was blocked by Senate Republicans in 2012. Can it be true that we've been having this argument for half a century? Obviously, the pay gap is not going to go away by itself.

Sadly, companies have not taken up the goal of gender pay equity. They have been unresponsive to the call for parity on moral or even legal grounds. "Companies like Home Depot, Novartis, and Smith Barney have paid hundreds of millions of dollars to settle cases of gender pay discrimination brought by women employees under the Equal Pay Act and Title VII of the Civil Rights Act. Wal-Mart recently spent billions of dollars defending what would have been the largest class-action lawsuit in history, brought by female employees alleging systemic pay and promotion discrimination" according to the American Association of University Women.[33]

Evidence suggests that pay equity has a positive effect on the bottom line. Fair pay is linked to high morale, reduced absenteeism and productivity. "A worker who believes that she or he is paid fairly is more likely to contribute her or his best effort to the job," according to the AAUW. Here, too, a focus on heightened productivity and shareholder benefit may put pressure on corporate America to do the right thing.

Some skeptics argue that the gender pay gap does not reflect gender discrimination at all, arguing instead that women's life choices result in their lower pay. If the issue is life choices, then no remedy is required.

But research finds that not all of the pay gap can be "explained away" by life choices.[34] Even after taking into account a staggering array of factors, such as college major, occupation, industry, sector, hours worked, workplace flexibility, experience, educational attainment, enrollment status, GPA, institution selectivity, age, race and ethnicity, region, marital status and number of children, there is *still* an unexplained difference of 5 percent in the earnings of male and female college graduates one year after graduation. And as we have noted, the gap widens over time. The gender pay gap of full-time workers ten years after college graduation is 12 percent. Stated differently, "Just one year after college graduation, women earned only 80 percent of what their male counterparts made. Ten years after graduation, women fell further behind, earning only 69 percent of what men earned."[35]

The pay gap is ongoing and demoralizing for women, affecting their productivity and depressing the corporate bottom line.

Also, sunshine—the free discussion of wages and the availability of data—makes a difference. As long as employees are in the dark about the wages and salaries of their coworkers, inequities will likely persist. Fully half of the employees surveyed by the Institute for Women's Policy Research reported that they "worked in a setting where discussions of wages and salaries are either formally prohibited or discouraged by managers."[36] Pay secrecy was much more prevalent in the private sector (61 percent of employees) than in the public sector (14 percent of employees). Transparency undoubtedly contributes to the greater gender pay equity among federal employees. Among federal workers, women earned 89 percent of what men earned, compared with 78 percent in the workforce as a whole.[37]

DON'T PLAY IT AGAIN, SAM!

"Hard-won and easily lost" is, as we've said, a recurring problem for women. In 2013, a new danger reemerged in an area where we'd thought the battles were over: workplace flexibility. This was one area where real progress benefitting both workers and companies had gotten solid traction. But shockingly, the progressive trend may be coming to a screeching halt. In 2013, Yahoo! CEO Marissa Mayer stunned the business world by announcing, just after the birth of her first child, that she was ending work-at-home hours for all employees.

Over the past three decades, evidence has been growing that flexibility in the workplace is an asset to companies. It took a very long time to persuade businesses to give up on the idea that "face time" in the office was the best indicator of productivity. But thanks to research showing that flexibility is good for companies, they came around. Flexibility, it turns out, enhances recruiting and retention of employees.

In a Daily Beast article, Ellen Galinsky of the Families and Work Institute cites a 2010 survey that found that human resource professionals were more likely to cite flexibility (58 percent) as the most effective way to attract talent.[38] Galinsky says that according to the institute's 2012 National Study of Employers, almost two-thirds (63 percent) of companies allow some employees to work from home. Other studies found that flexible policies cut costs and boosted productivity.[39] This figure is even more remarkable when you realize that in 2005, only 34 percent reported employees working at home.

Flexibility is not just a women's issue. Both men and women find flexible hours attractive, Galinsky says.[40] "When asked about what they would look for in a new job, 87 percent of men and women alike said that flexibility was extremely or very important." In fact, research finds that today men are *more* likely than women to report work-family conflict.

Then Mayer dropped her bombshell. Critics noted that she had a well-appointed nursery for her baby built right next to her office, an option no other employees had. Work-family conflict is certainly not a problem for a CEO with a nursery at the office!

Shortly after Mayer's announcement, Best Buy, a company that had been at the forefront of flexible work arrangements, suddenly announced that it too was making a U-turn. No more flexibility for workers. Face time was back—big-time.

Astonishingly, the company took this step even though its highly touted flexible-work program—the Results-Only Work Environment (ROWE), which evaluated employees only on performance, not on how many hours they work or where they work—was a success.

According to the company's own research, ROWE helped Best Buy save $2.2 million over three years by reducing turnover by 90 percent and boosting productivity by an average of 41 percent.[41] Other big companies, including Gap, Banana Republic and H.B. Fuller, followed suit.

But now, are we seeing the beginning of a stampede back to the bad old days, in which women will especially suffer because they are the ones typically forced out of jobs by rigid policies? For a time, it seemed as if the workplace was finally adapting to the realities of the twenty-first-century two-earner family. We are going back to a twentieth-century workplace—but today's dual-earner family is not going away.

Mayer explained her decision with the claim that Yahoo! employees weren't productive enough. Galinsky retorts that flexibility is not the problem—but a solution. "It is clear that *wherever* employees work—in the office, at home, or at remote locations, they need to be well managed and engaged in making the company a success. Yes, it is about creating an engaged work culture, but in the global economy, it's not only about bumping into other colleagues around the water cooler. It is about taking direct steps to create a culture of collaboration and innovation. If Yahoo has a problem with employees not being productive, they need to address that problem directly."[42]

But face time died hard, and it now looks like the patient is being resuscitated. The corporate stereotype that the best worker is the one at the desk from sunup to sundown has proved amazingly hardy.

Will all the research on the tangible benefits of flexibility now go out the window on the heels of a "hot" new-old theory that face time is the only way to energize flagging companies? Rigidity didn't work so well in the past. Why is it now being touted as the next big thing in business?

Jennifer Glass of the University of Texas at Austin, coauthor of a major report on the U.S. workforce, says she was "flabbergasted" by the Yahoo! decision.[43] "This seems to be trying to bring Yahoo in line with corporate America, not high-tech industries. . . . the idea that this is going to promote more innovation seems bizarre. Promoting the value of interactions in hallways and canteens seems strange at a time when face-to-face contact within the office is decreasing. I frequently e-mail someone without getting up to see if they are there."

Glass says that managers can be biased toward those they can actually see working. "There is this attitude that managers need to see people are close by and that those workers are more productive. It is a natural tendency to want to control things."

Alas, this urge may override the best information that science can provide. Confirmation bias can be found everywhere in business.

If this new face-time movement turns turn out to have deep roots, it will escalate the New Soft War. The trend will be a huge blow not only for all men and women workers but also for gender equity in the workplace. These policies will re-segregate both the family and the home—with more and more women having to give up their careers, and more men having to abandon highly valued time with their families.

Bad for the bottom line, bad for families—will this runaway train keep going? Those who value gender equity need to watch carefully, lest yet another hard-won gain disappear.

THE WAY FORWARD

Are we serious about realizing the economic potential of women? From a look at the data, you have to conclude that we are not. The United States as a nation has to decide whether we will change this situation or will simply let the rest of the world pass us by. Do we *really* want to win the New Soft War?

We hear lots of talk, but little gets done. Let's stop pretending that women are the richer sex, that the end of men is coming, that the nation is turning into a middle-class matriarchy, that gender discrimination is a thing of the past and that women are soaring. As the *Chronicle of Higher Education* puts it, "women may flood into previously male-dominated fields of endeavor, but when they do, there's no magical inevitability to improved circumstances. . . . Women take orders on the line and men surveil them from offices; women serve as nurses and office staff while men serve as doctors; women serve as general practitioners but not specialists; as accountants but not managers; as teachers but less commonly as principals."[44]

Sylvia Ann Hewlett points out that there has been only a modest success of just a few programs. "No matter how laudatory, these programs are outliers and the women who take advantage of them the fortunate few," she says. "What's needed to truly enable all women to exploit their full potential is something far more pervasive, something that becomes the law of the land."[45]

Fifty years is far too long for the United States to have moved such a short distance toward gender equality in the workplace. As we've said, companies can take steps right now to get the ball rolling. They can initiate company-wide programs to educate both men and women about the power of gender stereotypes—making sure to monitor the anemic gender-diversity programs already on their books to ensure that they are working. And they can tie managers' performance reviews to gender diversity.

On the policy front, Congress should immediately pass the Paycheck Fairness Act and reopen debate on the Equal Rights amendment that failed in 1982. If the ERA passed, all forms of discrimination against women would be illegal.

Also, the United States is scandalously remiss when it comes to policies that—elsewhere in the world—make it possible for women (and men) to both care for families and pursue meaningful careers.[46] Women too often "choose" low-level jobs because there is simply no adequate child care or other family supports available to them. Here's how we are doing vis-à-vis the rest of the world:

- Working mothers in the United States have far fewer supports than mothers in other countries.

- Thirty-seven countries guarantee parents some type of paid leave when children fall ill, and 163 countries offer paid maternity leave. The United States does neither. (California was the first state to offer partially paid parental leave. Despite worries about its price tag, a study of the program found few costs to employers and, in fact, some savings.)[47]
- All industrialized countries except Australia and the United States offer paid family and medical leave. Australia guarantees a full year of unpaid leave, while the United States offers twelve weeks.
- Sixty-five countries offer paternity leave. The United States does not.
- Ninety-six countries mandate paid annual leave. The United States does not.
- At least 145 countries require paid sick days, with 127 providing a week or more annually. U.S. federal law requires no paid sick days.
- The United States is tied for thirty-ninth place, with Ecuador and Suriname, for enrollment in early-childhood education for three- to five-year-olds.

"Our work/family protections are among the worst. It's time for a change," says Jody Heymann, dean of UCLA's Fielding School of Public Health and director of the first global initiative on health and social policies in all 193 countries of the United Nations.[48]

Winning the New Soft War has to be an urgent national priority, for all the reasons we've discussed. There is cause for optimism. A confluence of national and international currents is flowing together to create the right climate for change. The United States is losing ground in the new global economy, and our competitors have gotten the message and are acting on it. The realization is dawning that we can't lag behind much longer. At the same time, U.S. men are invested more than ever before in their family lives, and since they are overwhelmingly in two-earner families, they are committed to their wives' economic success. And women themselves are increasingly unlikely to hang back and forfeit the monetary and personal success they have worked hard for and deserve.

At long last, we must move from rhetoric to action, from mythology to hard reality. The New Soft War can be won if we can summon the will to battle.

ACKNOWLEDGMENTS

We want to thank our editor, Sara Carder, for her insights and advice that helped to shape the book. And we are deeply grateful to our agent, Joelle Delbourgo, who believed in the project from the start and was a major factor in bringing it to fruition.

We are indebted to the Glass Hammer, an online weekly blog that covers many issues confronting women at work. The mission of the blog overlaps that of this book, and we have benefited from its coverage. We also want to pay special thanks to its editor, Melissa Anderson, who was generous enough to host two versions of our survey that generated so many responses from working women about their day-to-day struggles.

Roz is especially grateful to the director of the Women's Studies Research Center, Dr. Shula Reinharz. Shula has been an encouraging and supportive voice throughout this project. And the Center, through its Student-Scholar Partnership Program, has brought her into contact with several outstanding undergraduates whose contributions and enthusiasm have been hugely important to this book. In particular, Anushka Aqil and Clara Gray deserve special thanks for their efforts.

Caryl wishes to thank the College of Communication at Boston University, especially Dean Tom Fiedler and journalism chair Bill McKeen, for their unfailing support.

NOTES

Chapter 1. Where the Battle Lines Are

1 http://intentionalworkplace.com/2012/04/19/women-and-men-the-dignity-of-work

2 Corbett, C., & Hill, C. (2012). Graduating to a pay gap: The earnings of women and men one year after college graduation. American Association of University Women. http://www.aauw.org/research/graduating-to-a-pay-gap

3 http://www.nytimes.com/2012/12/16/business/to-solve-the-gender-wage-gap-learn -to-speak-up.html? pagewanted=1

4 http://www.incontext.indiana.edu/2009/mar-apr/article1.asp

5 Estimates of the pay gap between female and male physicians vary widely from a high of 36 percent (http://www.pay-equity.org/PDFs/ProfWomen.pdf) to a low of 12 percent (http://well.blogs.nytimes.com/2012/06/28/among-doctors-too-women -are-paid-less), depending on how many factors are taken into account.

6 http://www.catalyst.org/blog/catalyzing/mind-gap

7 Schmitt, M. T., Spoor, J. R., Danaher, K., & Branscombe, N. R. (2009). Rose-colored glasses: How tokenism and comparisons with the past reduce the visibility of gender inequality. In M. Barreto, M. K. Ryan, & M. T. Schmitt (eds.), *The glass ceiling in the 21st century: Understanding barriers to gender equality*. Rockville, MD: American Psychological Association.

8 http://www.freakonomics.com/2010/01/22/superfreakonomics-book-club-ask-claudia -goldin-and-larry-katz-about-the-male-female-wage-gap

9 http://www.bloomberg.com/news/2012-04-02/female-cfos-in-u-s-paid-16-less-than -men-study-finds.html

10 http://www.catalyst.org/media/latest-catalyst-census-shows-women-still-not-scaling
-corporate-ladder-2010-new-study-indicates

11 http://www.mckinsey.com/client_service/organization/latest_thinking/unlocking_
the_full_potential

12 http://www.forbes.com/sites/davechase/2012/07/26/women-in-healthcare-report
-4-of-ceos-73-of-managers

13 http://www.huffingtonpost.com/2012/05/14/fewer-women-in-top-us-tech-jobs_
n_1514196.html

14 http://www.ncwit.org/sites/default/files/file_type/ncwit_computing_jobs_women
.jpg

15 Schmitt, M. T., Spoor, J. R., Danaher, K., & Branscombe, N. R. (2009). Rose-colored glasses: How tokenism and comparisons with the past reduce the visibility of gender. In M. Barreto, M. K. Ryan, & M. T. Schmitt (eds.), *The glass ceiling in the 21st century: Understanding barriers to gender equality.* Rockville, MD: American Psychological Association.

16 http://www.huffingtonpost.com/dr-philip-zimbardo/post_3387_b_1543693.html

17 Dawkins, R. (1976). *The selfish gene.* London: Oxford University Press.

18 http://www.mckinsey.com/client_service/organization/latest_thinking/unlocking_
the_full_potential

19 http://apolloresearchinstitute.com/news-releases/workforce-preparedness/leap-new
-career-four-educational-and-job-opportunities-2012; accessed February 18, 2013

20 http://www.w2t.se/se/filer/adler_web.pdf

21 Freeman, R. B. (2000). The feminization of work in the USA: A new era for (man) kind? In S. S. Gustafsson & D. E. Meulders (eds.), *Gender and the labour market.* New York: St. Martin's Press.

22 http://www.pewsocialtrends.org/2012/04/19/a-gender-reversal-on-career-aspirations

Chapter 2. Doing Well May Not Work Out So Well

1 http://blogs.hbr.org/cs/2011/10/women_dont_go_after_the_big_jo.html

2 Ibid.

3 http://online.wsj.com/article/SB10001424052748704415104576250900113069980
.html

4 http://www.economist.com/node/21539930

5 http://www.catalyst.org/media/catalyst-study-explodes-myths-about-why-women's
-careers-lag-men's

6 http://www.catalyst.org/knowledge/myth-ideal-worker-does-doing-all-right-things-really
-get-women-ahead

7 http://www.nationaljournal.com/magazine/washington-s-women-we-still-face-discrimination
-20120712

8 Heilman, M. E., & Haynes, M. C. (2005). No credit where credit is due: Attributional rationalization of women's success in male-female teams. *Journal of Applied Psychology*, 90(5), 905–916.

9 http://www.huffingtonpost.com/jacki-zehner/why-are-goldmans-women-in_b_139650.html

10 http://hbr.org/2010/09/why-men-still-get-more-promotions-than-women/ar/1

11 http://blogs.hbr.org/ideacast/2010/08/women-are-over-mentored-but-un.html

12 http://blogs.hbr.org/cs/2011/10/women_dont_go_after_the_big_jo.html

13 http://hbr.org/2010/09/why-men-still-get-more-promotions-than-women/ar/1

14 http://www.marieclaire.com/career-money/sallie-krawcheck-interview

15 Eagly, A. H., & Carli, L. L. (2007). *Through the labyrinth: The truth about how women become leaders*. Boston: Harvard Business School Publishing.

16 https://members.weforum.org/pdf/gendergap/corporate2010.pdf

17 http://blogs.hbr.org/ideacast/2010/08/women-are-over-mentored-but-un.html

18 http://hbr.org/2010/09/why-men-still-get-more-promotions-than-women

19 http://hbr.org/2010/09/why-men-still-get-more-promotions-than-women/ar/2

20 http://hbr.org/2010/09/why-men-still-get-more-promotions-than-women/ar/1

21 Ibid.

22 http://www.washingtonpost.com/national/on-leadership/why-women-need-more-hot-jobs/2012/11/14/567d65c8-2e73-11e2-beb2-4b4cf5087636_story.html

23 Silva, C., Carter, N. M., & Beninger, A. (2011). Good intentions, imperfect execution? Women get fewer of the "hot jobs" needed to advance. Catalyst. http://www.catalyst.org/knowledge/good-intentions-imperfect-execution-women-get-fewer-hot-jobs-needed-advance

24 http://web.mit.edu/faculty/reports/overview.html

25 Personal communication to Rosalind Barnett, 2010.

26 http://www.insidehighered.com/news/2005/12/07/gender

27 http://www.nytimes.com/2012/09/25/science/bias-persists-against-women-of-science-a-study-says.html

28 Ibid.

29 Wenneras, C., & Wold, A. (1997). Nepotism and sexism in peer-review. *Nature*, 387 (May 22), 341–343.

Chapter 3. Competent but Unlikable?

1 http://thecaucus.blogs.nytimes.com/2012/09/12/elizabeth-warren-softens-her-image-in-new-ad

2 http://bostonglobe.com/opinion/2012/09/12/elizabeth-warren-must-sell-substance-over-scott-brown-flash/0LWWgzbidAmQtaI8oGTiNP/story.html

3 http://scholarship.law.marquette.edu/facpub/529

4 http://mediamatters.org/research/2008/01/09/media-figures-claimed-clintons-emotional-moment/142093

5 http://www.nytimes.com/2008/01/09/opinion/08dowd.html?pagewanted=all

6 http://abcnews.go.com/Politics/Vote2008/story?id=4097786&page=1

7 http://www.thefiscaltimes.com/Articles/2010/10/26/California-Races-Getting-Tepid-Response.aspx#page1

8 Fiorina, C. (2006). *Tough choices: A memoir*. New York: Portfolio.

9 http://www.businessweek.com/stories/2000-11-19/as-leaders-women-rule

10 http://www.apa.org/monitor/julaug04/women.aspx

11 http://www.dukechronicle.com/articles/2004/03/30/heilman-outlines-reasons-female-discrimination

12 Ibid.

13 http://dyn.politico.com/printstory.cfm?uuid=281B5C89-EC5A-42B5-939F-B279164C567A

14 http://www.thedailybeast.com/articles/2013/04/24/leave-jill-abramson-alone-you-sexists.html

15 http://www.marieclaire.com/career-money/sallie-krawcheck-interview

16 Rudman, L. A. (2004). Implicit power brokers: Benevolent barriers to gender equity. In C. S. Crandall & M. Schaller (eds.), *Social psychology of prejudice: Historical and contemporary issues* (35–55). Lawrence, KS: Lewinian Press.

17 http://www.womensmedia.com/lead/88-women-and-leadership-delicate-balancing-act.html

18 http://www.businessweek.com/1998/21/covstory.htm

19 Oppenheimer, J. (2009). *Toy monster: The big, bad world of Mattel*. Hoboken, NJ: John Wiley & Sons.

20 http://www.people.com/people/archive/article/0,,20108046,00.html

21 http://money.cnn.com/magazines/fortune/fortune_archive/1999/06/21/261701/index.htm

22 http://www.womensmedia.com/lead/88-women-and-leadership-delicate-balancing-act.html

23 http://www.nbcnews.com/id/17345308/ns/business-careers/t/men-rule-least-workplace-attitudes/#.UW1XixzX_vU

24 http://www.nytimes.com/2012/07/25/us/25iht-letter25.html

25 Brescoll, V. L., & Uhlmann E. L. (2008). Can an angry woman get ahead: Status conferral, gender, and expression of emotion in the workplace. *Psychological Science*, 19(3), 268–275.

26 Brescoll, V. L. (2012). Who takes the floor and why: Gender, power, and volubility in organizations. *Administrative Science Quarterly*, 20, 1–20.

27 http://www.elle.com/life-love/society-career/whos-the-boss-19718

28 Rikleen, L. S. (2006). *Ending the gauntlet: Removing barriers to women's success in the law.* Eagan, MN.

29 Ibid.

30 Karpowitz, C. F., Mendelberg, T., & Shaker, L. (2012). Gender inequality in deliberative participation. *American Political Science Review, 106*(3), 533–547.

31 http://www.theglasshammer.com/news/2012/10/31/women-and-power-do-we-get-it

Chapter 4. The Glass Cliff and the Glass Escalator

1 Ryan, M. K., & Haslam, S. A. (2005). The glass cliff: Evidence that women are overrepresented in precarious leadership positions. In B. Schyns & J. R. Meindl (eds.), *Implicit leadership theories: Essays and explorations* (173–199). Greenwich, CT: Information Age.

2 http://www.psychologytoday.com/blog/benign-bigotry/201001/are-katie-couric-and-diane-sawyer-perched-glass-cliff

3 http://www.forbes.com/sites/helaineolen/2012/07/16/marissa-mayer-and-the-glass-cliff

4 http://www.thedailybeast.com/articles/2012/07/18/marissa-mayer-stares-down-glass-cliff-at-yahoo.html

5 http://money.cnn.com/magazines/fortune/most-powerful-women/2012/snapshots/3.html

6 Ibid.

7 http://www.theglasshammer.com/news/2008/05/07/last-woman-standing-the-firing-of-zoe-cruz

8 http://www.forbes.com/sites/nathanvardi/2012/05/13/jamie-dimon-we-took-far-too-much-risk

9 http://www.nytimes.com/2012/05/14/business/jpmorgan-chase-executive-to-resign-in-trading-debacle.html?pagewanted=all&_r=0

10 http://nymag.com/news/business/46476/index7.html

11 http://www.nytimes.com/2011/04/11/business/media/11couric.html?pagew

12 http://www.people.com/people/article/0,,1088791,00.html

13 http://newsbusters.org/node/13368

14 http://articles.baltimoresun.com/2012-06-28/news/bs-ed-reimer-curry-20120628_1_ann-curry-matt-lauer-credibility-deficit

15 http://observer.com/2011/04/cathie-black-speaks-it-was-like-having-to-learn-russian

16 http://www.forbes.com/sites/brycecovert/2012/05/15/was-jp-morgan-chases-cio-ina-drew-pushed-off-the-glass-cliff/2

17 http://www.huffingtonpost.com/2012/08/28/katie-couric-cbs-constrained-liberated_
n_1835799.html

18 Fiorina, C. (2006). *Tough choices: A memoir.* New York: Portfolio.

19 http://blogs.hbr.org/hbr/hewlett/2008/08/are_women_leaders_often_set_up.html

20 Ryan, M., Haslam, A., & Kulich, C. (2010). Politics and the glass cliff: Evidence that
women are preferentially selected to contest hard-to-win seats. *Psychology of Women
Quarterly,* 34, 56–64.

21 http://www.theatlantic.com/politics/archive/2012/10/50-shades-of-terrible-heres
-what-an-awful-debate-question-looks-like/263808

22 http://www.nytimes.com/2012/05/21/business/increasingly-men-seek-success-in
-jobs-dominated-by-women.html?pagewanted=1&_r=2

23 http://womensenews.org/story/economyeconomic-policy-labor/120526/wage-gap
-womens-median-wages-compared-mens-in-the-same#.UKanNBy7nNQ

24 Ibid.

25 Smith, R. A. (2012). Money, benefits and power: A test of glass ceiling and glass
escalator hypotheses. *The Annals of the American Academy of Political and Social Science,*
639(1), 148–171.

26 Williams, C. L. (1992). The glass escalator: Hidden advantages for men in the "female"
professions. *Social Problems,* 39(3), 253–267.

27 http://womensenews.org/story/equal-payfair-wage/120601/%E2%80%98glass
-escalators%E2%80%99-move-pink-collar-guys-ahead#.URFKE_GrDi8

28 http://www.dol.gov/wb/factsheets/QS-womenwork2010.htm

29 http://www.bls.gov/opub/ooq/2009/winter/art1fullp1.htm

Chapter 5. Hard-Won and Easily Lost

1 Brescoll, V. L., Dawson, E., & Uhlmann, E. L. (2010). Hard won and easily lost: The
fragile status of leaders in gender-stereotype-incongruent occupations. *Psychological
Science,* 21(11), 1640–1642.

2 Ibid.

3 http://hbr.org/product/the-athena-factor-reversing-the-brain-drain-in-sci/an/10094
-PDF-ENG

4 http://hbswk.hbs.edu/item/3711.html

5 Heilman, M. E., & Haynes, M. C. (2005). No credit where credit is due: Attributional rationalization of women's success in male-female teams. *Journal of Applied
Psychology,* 90(5), 905–916.

6 http://blogs.hbr.org/cs/2011/10/women_dont_go_after_the_big_jo.html

7 http://www.theatlantic.com/national/archive/2012/06/im-not-your-wife-a-new
-study-points-to-a-hidden-form-of-sexism/258057

8 http://papers.ssrn.com/sol3/papers.cfm?abstract_id=2018259

9 http://www.theatlantic.com/national/archive/2012/06/im-not-your-wife-a-new-study
   -points-to-a-hidden-form-of-sexism/258057

10 http://www.forbes.com/2009/08/06/sexual-harassment-office-forbes-woman-leadership
   -affairs.html

11 http://www.equalrights.org/professional/sexhar/work/workplac.asp; Oppenheimer,
   D. (1995). Exacerbating the exasperated—Title VII liability of employers for
   sexual harassment committed by their supervisors. *Cornell Law Review*, 81(1),
   66–153.

12 http://www.sdinjuryfirm.com/specialties/sexual-harassment

13 http://www.military.com/daily-news/2012/08/13/sex-assault-cases-flood-military
   -courts.html

14 http://www.theglasshammer.com/news/2012/06/25/lgbt-progress-and-problems
   -in-the-workplace-part-1

15 http://www.theglasshammer.com/news/2010/07/14/is-sexual-harassment-on-the
   -decline-in-the-finance-industry

16 http://www.cnn.com/2012/05/21/opinion/stepp-conservatives-contraception

17 http://www.huffingtonpost.com/2012/02/15/rick-santorum-contraception-birth
   -control-women_n_1279944.html

18 http://www.washingtonpost.com/national/health-science/birth-control-exemption
   -bill-the-blunt-amendment-killed-in-senate/2012/03/01/gIQA4tXjkR_story_1
   .html

19 http://www.feminisms.org/4677/rush-limbaughs-slander-of-sandra-fluke

20 http://www.motherjones.com/politics/2012/08/americans-united-for-life-anti-abortion
   -transvaginal-ultrasound

Chapter 6. Females and Math: Strange Bedfellows?

1 http://www.nytimes.com/2012/12/14/opinion/roger-cohen-american-bull.html?_r=0

2 http://www.nytimes.com/2011/07/19/science/19google.html

3 http://web.mit.edu/facts/enrollment.html; http://www.brown.edu/Administration/
   Provost/Advance/Hopkins%20Mirages%20of%20Equality.pdf

4 http://articles.washingtonpost.com/2012-09-20/national/35495422_1_powerful
   -women-ginni-rometty-sheryl-sandberg

5 Ibid.

6 Hill, C., Corbett, C., & St. Rose, A. (2010). Why so few? Women in science, technology, engineering, and mathematics. American Association of University Women.

7 Quoted in http://www.thecrimson.com/article/2005/1/14/summers-comments-on
   -women-and-science

8 http://www.boston.com/news/education/higher/articles/2005/01/17/summers_remarks
_on_women_draw_fire/?page=full

9 http://www.thecrimson.com/article/2005/1/14/summers-comments-on-women
-and-science

10 http://www.theatlantic.com/magazine/archive/2005/02/why-feminist-careerists-neutered
-larry-summers/303795

11 Parker, K. (2006, September 21). Larry Summers and the thought police. *Washington Post*.

12 http://www.washingtonpost.com/wp-dyn/articles/A40073-2005Jan26.html

13 http://www.nytimes.com/2013/01/01/science/the-life-of-pi-and-other-infinities.html?
pagewanted=all

14 Gornick, V., & Moran, B. K. (1971). *Woman in sexist society: Studies in power and powerlessness*. New York: Basic Books.

15 Ibid.

16 Benbow, C. P., & Stanley, J. C. (1980). Sex differences in mathematical ability: Fact or artifact? *Science*, 210(4475), 1262–1264.

17 Kolata, G. B. (1980). Math and sex: Are girls born with less ability? *Science*, 210(4475), 1234–1235.

18 Are boys better at math? (1980, December 7). *New York Times*.

19 The gender factor in math. (1980, December 15). *Time*.

20 Eccles, J. S., Barber B., et al. (1999). Linking gender to educational, occupational, and recreational choices: Applying the Eccles et al. model of achievement-related choices. In W. B. Swann, J. H. Langlois & L. A. Gilbert (eds.), *Sexism and stereotypes in modern society: The gender science of Janet Taylor Spence*. Washington, D.C., American Psychological Association, 153–191.

21 Fausto-Sterling, A. (1985). *Myths of gender: Biological theories about men and women*. New York: Basic Books.

22 Fox, L. (1984). Sex differences among the mathematically precocious. *Science*, 224, 1293–1294.

23 Spelke, E. S. (2005). Sex differences in intrinsic aptitude for mathematics and science? A critical review. *American Psychologist*, 60(9), 950–958.

24 Boswell, S. L. (1985). The influence of sex-role stereotyping on women's attitudes and achievement in mathematics. In S. F. Chipman, L. R. Brush & D. M. Wilson (eds.), *Women and mathematics: Balancing the equation* (175–198). Hillsdale, NJ: Lawrence Erlbaum Associates.

25 Ibid.

26 Ibid.

27 Beilock, S. L., & Gunderson, E. A., et al. (2010). Female teachers' math anxiety affects girls' math achievement. *Proceedings of the National Academy of Sciences of the United States of America*, 107(5), 1860–1863.

28 Glasser, H. M. (2011). Arguing separate but equal: A study of argumentation in public single-sex science classes in the United States. *International Journal of Gender, Science and Technology*, 3(1), 70–92.

29 Huguet, P., & Régner, I. (2007). Stereotype threat among schoolgirls in quasi-ordinary classroom circumstances. *Journal of Educational Psychology*, 99(3), 545–560.

30 Cvencek, D., Meltzoff, A.N., & Greenwald, A.G. (2011). Math-gender stereotypes in elementary school children. *Child Development*, 82(3), 776–779.

31 http://psycnet.apa.org/index.cfm?fa=search.displayrecord&uid=1997-04591-001

32 Huguet, P., & Régner, I. (2007). Stereotype threat among schoolgirls in quasi-ordinary classroom circumstances. *Journal of Educational Psychology*, 99(3), 545–560.

33 Weisgram, E. S., Bigler, R. S., & Liben, L. S. (in press). Gender, values, and occupational interests among children, adolescents, and adults. *Child Development*.

34 http://www.dailymail.co.uk/news/article-483707/Only-men-geniuses—far-stupid-men-women.html#axzz2K9mTUBF2

35 Siegel, E. (2012). Surprise! Gender equality makes everyone better at math! Science-Blogs. http://scienceblogs.com/startswithabang/2012/01/06/surprise-surprise-gender-equal

36 Kane, J. M., & Mertz, J. E. (2012). Debunking myths about gender and mathematics performance. *Notice of the American Mathematical Society*, 59(1).

37 http://www.girlscouts.org/research/pdf/generation_stem_summary.pdf

38 Hill, C., Corbett, C., & St. Rose, A. (2010). Why so few? Women in science, technology, engineering, and mathematics. American Association of University Women.

39 Bryant, S. D. (2011). It's nothing personal: Competing discourses for girls and women in mathematics. University of Massachusetts–Amherst: Open Access Dissertations and Theses.

40 Ibid.

41 Beede, D., Julian, T., Langdon, D., McKittrick, G., Khan, B., & Doms, M. (2011). Women in STEM: A gender gap to innovation. U.S. Department of Commerce Economics and Statistics Administration, 1–11.

42 Hill, C., Corbett, C., & St. Rose, A. (2010). Why so few? Women in science, technology, engineering, and mathematics. American Association of University Women.

43 Fisher, J. Margolis, & Miller, F. (1997). Undergraduate women in computer science: experience, motivation, and culture, *ACM SIGCSE Bulletin*, 29(1), 106–110.

44 http://www.esa.doc.gov/sites/default/files/reports/documents/womeninstemagaptoinnovation8311.pdf; http://www.forbes.com/sites/work-in-progress/2012/06/20/stem-fields-and-the-gender-gap-where-are-the-women/

45 http://www.businessweek.com/news/2012-08-31/romney-s-lbo-world-is-boys-club-with-few-top-women

46 http://www.nytimes.com/2012/07/25/us/25iht-letter25.html

47 http://blogs.wsj.com/economics/2012/04/14/number-of-the-week-finance-job-losses
    -hit-women-harder

48 http://www.businessweek.com/articles/2012-12-11/at-elite-b-schools-the-gender-wage
    -gap-grows

49 http://www.learningfirst.org/visionaries/DanicaMcKellar

50 http://www.usnews.com/opinion/articles/2012/06/15/stem-education-is-the-key-to-
    the-uss-economic-future

51 Ibid.

52 Hyde, J. S., Lindberg, S. M., et al. (2008). Gender similarities characterize math
    performance. *Science*, 321, 494–495.

53 http://www.amandagoodall.com/IHEAHGOct05.pdf

54 http://www.imf.org/external/about.htm

55 Martinot, D., & Desert, M. (2007). Awareness of a gender stereotype, personal be-
    liefs and self-perceptions regarding math ability: When boys do not surpass girls.
    Social Psychology Education, 10, 455–471.

56 Huguet, P., & Régner, I. (2007). Stereotype threat among schoolgirls in quasi-ordinary
    classroom circumstances. *Journal of Educational Psychology*, 99(3), 545–560.

Chapter 7. Risk Takers, No; Caretakers, Yes

1 http://www.edge.org/3rd_culture/debate05/debate05_index.html

2 Pinker, S. (2002). *The blank slate: The modern denial of human nature*. New York:
   Viking.

3 http://www.fact.on.ca/newpaper/nw990329.htm

4 http://connection.ebscohost.com/c/articles/9411157519/feminists-meet-mr-darwin

5 Power: Do women really want it? (2003, October). *Fortune*.

6 http://www.forbes.com/sites/womensmedia/2012/08/27/do-women-fear-power-and
   -success

7 Iggulden, H. (2006). *The dangerous book for boys*. London: HarperCollins.

8 http://www.thedailybeast.com/newsweek/2011/01/26/disney-princesses-and-the
   -battle-for-your-daughter-s-soul.html

9 Baron-Cohen, S. (2003). *The essential difference: The truth about the male and female
   brain*. New York: Basic Books.

10 Spelke, E. S. (2005). Sex differences in intrinsic aptitude for mathematics and sci-
    ence? A critical review. *American Psychologist*, 60(9), 950–958.

11 Powell, G. N. (1993). *Women and men in management* (2nd ed.). Newbury Park, CA:
    Sage.

12 Ibid.

13 http://www.businessweek.com/careers.old/content/jan1990/b3670071.htm

14 Carter, N. M., & Silva, C. (2011). The myth of the ideal worker: Does doing all the right things really get women ahead? Catalyst.

15 http://www.nytimes.com/2003/10/26/magazine/26WOMEN.html?pagewanted=all

16 http://www.mothersmovement.org/features/mhoodpapers/printpages/least_worse_ choice.html; U.S. Census Bureau, Current Population Survey, *Fertility of American Women: June 2002.*

17 Stroh, L. K., Brett, J. M., & Reilly, A. H. (1992). All the right stuff: A comparison of female and male managers' career progression. *Journal of Applied Psychology*, 77(3), 251–260.

18 http://www.worklifelaw.org/pubs/OptOutPushedOut.pdf

19 http://www.nytimes.com/2007/04/25/opinion/25hirshman.html

20 Ibid.

21 http://www.slate.com/articles/news_and_politics/the_highbrow/2006/06/a_working _girl_can_win.html

22 http://www.workingmother.com/research-institute/what-moms-choose-working-mother -report

23 http://www.nytimes.com/2006/03/15/opinion/15goldin.html

24 http://www.theatlantic.com/past/docs/issues/2002/09/flanagan.htm

25 http://www.nytimes.com/roomfordebate/2011/12/01/save-america-shop-at-work/taking -back-personal-time

26 https://old.catalyst.org/publication/94/women-take-care-men-take-charge-stereotyping -of-us-business-leaders-exposed

27 http://www.catalyst.org/knowledge/double-bind-dilemma-women-leadership-damned -if-you-do-doomed-if-you-dont-0

28 Gilligan, C. (1982). *In a different voice: Psychological theory and women's development.* Cambridge, MA: Harvard University Press.

29 Belenky, M. F., Clinchy, B. M., Goldberger, N. R., & Tarule J. M. (1986). *Women's ways of knowing: The development of self, voice, and mind.* New York: Basic Books.

30 http://www.kuscholarworks.ku.edu/dspace/bitstream/1808/4079/1/35-56.pdf. See also http://www.positivebodyimage.org.uk/culture.html

31 http://www.businessweek.com/careers.old/content/jan1990/b3670071.htm

32 Crosby, F. (1993). *Juggling: The unexpected advantages of balancing career and home for women and their families.* New York: Free Press.

33 Harter, S., Waters, P. L., Pettitt, L. M., Whitesell, N., Kofkin, J., & Jordan, J. (1997). Autonomy and connectedness as dimensions of relationship styles in men and women. *Journal of Social and Personal Relationships*, 14, 148–164.

34 Rudman, L. A., & Glick, P. (1999). Feminized management and backlash toward agentic women: The hidden costs to women of a kinder, gentler image of middle managers. *Journal of Personality and Social Psychology*, 77(5), 1004–1010.

35 Heilman, M. E., & Chen, J. J. (2005). Same behavior, different consequences: Reactions to men's and women's altruistic citizenship behavior. *Journal of Applied Psychology*, 90(3), 431–441.

Chapter 8. Miserable Achievers?

1 http://www.theatlantic.com/magazine/archive/2008/03/marry-him/306651
2 http://www.theatlantic.com/magazine/archive/2011/11/all-the-single-ladies/308654
3 http://www.nytimes.com/2010/06/27/opinion/27Paglia.html?_r=0
4 http://www.nytimes.com/2009/05/26/opinion/26douthat.html
5 http://www.econstor.eu/bitstream/10419/35564/1/605352836.pdf
6 http://www.theatlantic.com/magazine/archive/2005/04/primary-sources/303836
7 http://www.nytimes.com/2005/10/30/magazine/30feminism.html
8 http://www.theatlantic.com/magazine/archive/2005/04/primary-sources/303836
9 Hewlett, S. (2004). *Creating a life: What every woman needs to know about having a baby and a career.* New York: Miramax.
10 http://prospect.org/article/creating-lie
11 http://www.boston.com/jobs/news/articles/2008/03/02/want_to_have_a_baby_nows_the_time
12 http://www.dailymail.co.uk/health/article-186451/Career-womens-baby-hunger.html
13 Rivers, C., Baruch, G., & Barnett, R. (1983). *Lifeprints.* New York: McGraw-Hill.
14 http://www.prospect.org/article/creating-lie
15 http://www.cato-unbound.org/2008/01/14/stephanie-coontz/the-future-of-marriage
16 Oppenheimer, V. K. (1997). Women's employment and the gain to marriage: The specialization and trading model. *Annual Review of Sociology*, 23, 431–535.
17 http://www.nytimes.com/2012/02/12/opinion/sunday/marriage-suits-educated-women.html?pagewanted=all
18 http://www.forbes.com/2006/08/23/Marriage-Careers-Divorce_cx_mn_land.html
19 http://www.nytimes.com/2006/08/28/technology/28forbes.html?pagewanted=all&_r=0
20 http://psycnet.apa.org/journals/fam/12/3/354
21 Morgan, M. (1990). *The total woman.* New York: Pocket Books.
22 Gray, J. (1992). *Men are from Mars, women are from Venus: The classic guide to understanding the opposite sex.* New York: Harper.
23 Doyle, L. (1999). *The surrendered wife: A practical guide to finding intimacy, passion, and peace with your man.* New York: Fireside.

24 http://www.foxnews.com/opinion/2012/11/24/war-on-men

25 http://www.nytimes.com/2007/04/01/education/01girls.html?pagewanted=all

26 http://www.dailyprincetonian.com/2009/03/11/23057

27 http://www.villagevoice.com/2010-06-01/news/is-this-woman-too-hot-to-work
-in-a-bank

28 http://www.seventeen.com/health/tips/demi-lovato-pressure-to-be-perfect?click=main
_sr#slide-1

29 http://www.sirc.org/publik/mirror.html

30 http://videomind.ooyala.com/blog/more-time-ever-spent-facebook-watching-tv-video

31 http://www.nytimes.com/2012/11/18/magazine/girls-love-math-we-never-stop-doing-it
.html?pagewanted=all

32 Goffman, E. (1979). *Gender advertisements*. New York: Harper & Row.

33 http://link.springer.com/content/pdf/10.1007%2Fs11199-012-0223-6.pdf

34 http://www.counterpunch.org/2010/08/02/the-stepford-sluts

35 http://yaledailynews.com/magazine/2012/04/27/thinking-aloud. Accessed February
8, 2013

36 http://www.apa.org/pi/women/programs/girls/report.aspx. The quotations from the APA
that follow are taken from this report.

37 http://www.buffalo.edu/news/releases/2011/08/12769.html

38 http://rutgerssocialcognitionlab.weebly.com/uploads/1/3/9/7/13979590/rudmanheppen
2003pspb.pdf

39 http://www.huffingtonpost.com/melissa-lafsky/misogyny-for-sale-the-new_b_22313
.html

40 http://www.tuckermax.com/other/pass-the-beer-in-defense-of-fratire

41 http://216.22.0.192/images/maddox_pri.mp3

Chapter 9. Straw Women, Straw Men?

1 http://www.bls.gov/opub/mlr/2012/06/precis.htm

2 http://www.npr.org/2011/07/12/137790381/financial-recovery-looks-more-like-man
-covery

3 http://www.time.com/time/magazine/article/0,9171,2109140,00.html?pcd=pw-op

4 http://www.americanprogress.org/issues/labor/report/2012/04/16/11377/the-new
-breadwinners-2010-update

5 Winkler, A. E., McBride, T. D., et al. (2005). Wives who outearn their husbands: A
transitory or persistent phenomenon for couples? *Demography*, 42(3), 13.

6 http://www.time.com/time/magazine/article/0,9171,2109140,00.html?pcd=pw-op

7 Rosin, H. (2012). *The end of men: And the rise of women*. New York: Riverhead Books.

8 Benatar, D. (2012). *The second sexism: Discrimination against men and boys*. New York: Wiley-Blackwell.

9 http://www.economix.blogs.nytimes.com/2012/10/29/the-end-of-men-revisited

10 http://www.msnbc.msn.com/id/41928806/ns/business-us_business/t/men-falling-be hind-women/#.UPglmhy7nN

11 http://www.thedailybeast.com/newsweek/2006/01/29/the-trouble-with-boys.html

12 http://www.usatoday30.usatoday.com/news/education/2005-10-19-male-college -cover_x.htm

13 http://www.npr.org/templates/story/story.php?storyId=5246877

14 http://www.diversityweb.org/digest/sp01/research2.html

15 http://www.time.com/time/nation/article/0,8599,90446,00.html

16 http://www.prb.org/articles/2007/crossoverinfemalemalecollegeenrollmentrates .aspx?p=1

17 http://www.prospect.org/article/its-not-end-men-0

18 http://www.catalyst.org/c-news%E2%80%94february-2012

19 http://www.pewsocialtrends.org/2008/09/25/women-call-the-shots-at-home-public -mixed-on-gender-roles-in-jobs

20 http://www.washingtonpost.com/wp-dyn/content/article/2008/09/25/AR2008092 504167.html

21 http://www.nytimes.com/2012/09/11/opinion/brooks-why-men-fail.html

22 Brizendine, L. (2006). *The female brain*. New York: Broadway Books.

23 Fisher, H. (1999). *The first sex: The natural talents of women and how they are changing the world*. New York: Ballantine.

24 MacGeorge, E. L., Graves, A. R., Feng, B., Gillihan, S. J., & Burleson, B. R. (2004). The myth of gender cultures: Similarities outweigh differences in men's and women's pro-vision of and responses to supportive communication. *Sex Roles*, 50(3/4), 143–175.

25 Balliet, D., Li, N. P., Macfarlan, S. J., & Vugt, M. V. (2011). Sex differences in coop-eration: a meta-analytic review of social dilemmas. *Psychological Bulletin*, 137(6), 881–909.

26 http://www.news.harvard.edu/gazette/story/2012/02/feminism-now-stalled

27 http://www.contemporaryfamilies.org/gender-sexuality/gender-revolution-sympo sium-keynote.html

28 womenintvfilm.sdsu.edu/research.html

29 http://www.thewrap.com/tv/column-post/number-women-working-behind-scenes -prime-time-rises-56851

30 http://www.thestar.com/entertainment/movies/2012/11/23/niagara_falls_film_critic _battles_with_publisher_over_movies_with_strong_women.html

31 http://www.monthlyreview.org/2002/09/01/feminist-consciousness-after-the-wom ens-movement

Chapter 10. Leading the Way

1 http://www.forbes.com/sites/nickmorgan/2012/10/17/blarney-benghazi-and-binders-takeaways
-from-the-second-presidential-debate

2 http://new.wellesley.edu/news/stories/node/26669

3 Adler, R. D. (2001). Women in the executive suite correlate to high profits, *Harvard Business Review*, 79, 3.

4 Eagly, A. H., & Carli, L. L. (2007). *Through the labyrinth: The truth about how women become leaders*. Boston: Harvard Business School Publishing.

5 http://online.wsj.com/article/SB100014240527023038776045773823213648039 12.html

6 Ibid.

7 Catalyst (2005). Women "take care," men "take charge": Stereotyping of U.S. business leaders exposed. New York.

8 Ryan, M. K., Haslam, S. A., Hersby, M. D., & Bongiomo, R. (2011). Think crisis–think female: The glass cliff and contextual variation in the think manager–think male stereotype. *Journal of Applied Psychology*, 96(3), 470–484.

9 http://hbr.org/2011/01/how-women-end-up-on-the-glass-cliff/ar/1

10 http://www.princeton.edu/main/news/archive/S30/05/88Q71

11 http://www.thedailybeast.com/articles/2011/03/21/why-princetons-women-take-second
-place-on-campus.html

12 Ibid.

13 http://www.commercialappeal.com/news/2011/apr/05/ruth-marcus-victims-of-the-ambition
-gap/?print=1

14 http://www.thecrimson.com/article/2011/4/26/positions-leadership-harvard-women

15 http://www.thedailybeast.com/articles/2011/03/21/why-princetons-women-take-second
-place-on-campus.html

16 Ibid.

17 Ibid.

18 http://www.forbes.com/sites/deniserestauri/2012/07/16/why-millennial-women-do-not
-want-to-lead

19 http://www.telegraph.co.uk/finance/newsbysector/retailandconsumer/9973070/
Cadburys-chief-given-4.5million-pay-rise.html

20 http://www.mckinsey.com/client_service/organization/latest_thinking/unlocking_
the_full_potential

21 Lyness, K. S., & Thompson, D. E. (2000). Climbing the corporate ladder: Do female and male executives follow the same route? *Journal of Applied Psychology*, 85, 86–101.

22 Welle, B., & Heilman, M. E. (2007). Formal and informal discrimination against women at work. In S. W. Gilliland, D. Steiner & D. P. Skarlicki (eds.), *Managing*

social and ethical issues in organizations (229–252). Charlotte, NC: Information Age Publishing.

23 Schmitt, M. T., Spoor, J. R., Danaher, K., & Branscombe, N.R (2009). Rose-colored glasses: How tokenism and comparisons with the past reduce the visibility of gender inequality. In M. Barreto, M. K. Ryan, & M. T. Schmitt (eds.), *The glass ceiling in the 21st century: Understanding barriers to gender equality.* Rockville, MD: American Psychological Association.

24 Hoyt, C. L., & Simon, S. (2011). Female leaders: injurious or inspiring role models for women? *Psychology of Women Quarterly,* 35(1): 143–157.

25 http://ffbsccn.wordpress.com/tag/womens-leadership-programs-are-necessary-to-accelerate-womens-leadership-aspirations

26 http://www.suzanneimes.com/wp-content/uploads/2012/09/Imposter-Phenomenon.pdf

27 Eagly, A. H., & Carli, L. L. (2007). *Through the labyrinth: The truth about how women become leaders* (96). Boston: Harvard Business School Publishing.

28 http://educationforum.ipbhost.com/index.php?showtopic=14702

29 Eagly, A. H., & Carli, L. L. (2007). *Through the labyrinth: The truth about how women become leaders* (102). Boston: Harvard Business School Publishing.

30 Ibid., 103.

31 Personal communication to Caryl Rivers, 2010. See also http://mediacrit.wetpaint.com/page/Sexist+Language+in+Media+Coverage+of+Hillary+Clinton

32 http://mediamatters.org/research/2007/12/21/matthews-clinton-campaigns-goal-is-to-smother-t/142022

33 http://www.nytimes.com/2008/02/27/opinion/27dowd.html?_r=0

34 http://mediacrit.wetpaint.com/page/Sexist+Language+in+Media+Coverage+of+Hillary+Clinton; http://mediacrit.wetpaint.com/page/Sexist+Language+in+Media+Coverage+of+Hillary+Clinton

35 http://www.hbo.com/real-time-with-bill-maher/episodes/0/258-episode/article/new-rules.html

36 http://www.wbur.org/2012/09/11/warren-campaign-problems

37 http://www.highbeam.com/doc/1P2-33638850.html

38 http://www.thedailybeast.com/newsweek/2010/07/03/too-hot-to-handle.html

Chapter 11. The Parent Trap

1 Lundberg, F., & Farnham, M. F. (1947). *Modern women: The lost sex.* Harper & Brothers.

2 Wylie, P. (2007). *Generation of vipers* (2nd ed.). London: Dalkey Archive Press.

3 Galbraith, J. K. (1998). *The affluent society.* New York: Mariner Books.

4 http://www.theatlantic.com/magazine/archive/2012/07/why-women-still-cant-have
-it-all/309020

5 http://www.nytimes.com/2012/06/22/us/elite-women-put-a-new-spin-on-work-life-de
bate.html?_r=0

6 http://www.workingmother.com/research-institute/what-moms-choose-working-mother
-report

7 http://www.nytimes.com/2012/05/13/books/review/the-conflict-and-the-new-feminist
-agenda.html?pagewanted=all&_r=0

8 http://www.time.com/time/magazine/article/0,9171,2114427,00.html

9 http://www.nytimes.com/2007/04/25/opinion/25hirshman.html

10 McCarthy, M. (1954). *The group*. New York: Harcourt, Brace, Jovanovich.

11 Douglas, S., & Michaels, M. (2004). *The mommy myth: The idealization of mother-hood and how it has undermined all women*. New York: Free Press.

12 Quoted in Douglas, S., & Michaels, M. (2004). *The mommy myth: The idealization of motherhood and how it has undermined all women*. New York: Free Press.

13 http://www.nytimes.com/1984/11/18/books/not-the-father-of-the-man.html?pagewanted
=all

14 Bowlby, J. (1951). *Maternal care and mental health*. New York: Shocken.

15 http://www.nytimes.com/1998/05/24/magazine/the-disconnected-attachment-theory
-the-ultimate-experiment.html?pagewanted=all&src=pm

16 Ibid.

17 Okimoto, T. G., & Heilman, M. E. (2012). The "bad parent" assumption: How gender stereotypes affect reactions to working mothers. *Journal of Social Issues*, 68(4), 704–724.

18 http://familiesandwork.org/site/work/workforce/2002nscw.html

19 http://www.ns.umich.edu/Releases/2001/May01/r050901a.html

20 Galinsky, E. (2000). *Ask the children: The breakthrough study that reveals how to suc-ceed at work and parenting*. New York: Quill.

21 http://www.familytlc.net/working_parents.html

22 http://www.anncrittenden.com/wydk.htm

23 http://life.familyeducation.com/working-parents/family-time/36305.html

24 Correll, S. J., Benard, S., & Paik, I. (2007). Getting a job: Is there a motherhood penalty? *American Journal of Sociology*, 112(15), 1297–1338.

25 Roth, L. M. (2006). *Selling women short: Gender and money on Wall Street*. Princeton, NJ: Princeton University Press.

26 http://www.theglasshammer.com/news/2010/02/10/debating-the-motherhood
-penalty

27 Correll, S. J., Benard, S., & Paik, I. (2007). Getting a job: Is there a motherhood penalty? *American Journal of Sociology*, 112(15), 1297–1338.

28 http://www.theglasshammer.com/news/2012/10/30/what-not-to-say-to-a-pregnant-co -worker

29 http://www.huffingtonpost.com/joan-williams/bloomberg-case-open-seaso_b_934232 .html

30 http://healthland.time.com/2012/02/16/pregnant-at-work-why-your-job-could-be-at -risk

31 http://www.theglasshammer.com/news/2012/10/30/what-not-to-say-to-a-pregnant-co -worker

32 http://www.forbes.com/sites/learnvest/2012/07/19/the-pregnant-ceo-should-you-hate -marissa-mayer/2

33 Judiesch, M. K., & Lyness, K. S. (1999). Are women more likely to be hired or pro-moted into management positions? *Journal of Vocational Behavior*, 54, 158–173.

34 http://www.pewsocialtrends.org/2012/04/19/a-gender-reversal-on-career-aspirations

35 http://www.guardian.co.uk/lifeandstyle/2009/oct/20/working-fathers-report-ehrc

36 http://www.guardian.co.uk/lifeandstyle/2009/oct/21/men-work-paternity-leave

37 http://www.thedailybeast.com/newsweek/2012/09/23/why-women-should-stop -trying-to-be-perfect.html

38 Glauber, R. (2011). Women's work and working conditions: Are mothers compen-sated for lost wages? *Work and Occupations*, 39(2), 115–138.

39 Gareis, K. C., & Barnett, R. C. (2002). Under what conditions do long work hours affect psychological distress? *Work and Occupations*, 29(4), 483–497.

40 http://business.time.com/2012/06/26/million-dollar-babies-what-it-really-costs -to-raise-a-child

41 http://money.cnn.com/2011/09/21/pf/cost_raising_child/index.htm

42 http://business.time.com/2012/06/26/million-dollar-babies-what-it-really-costs-to -raise-a-child

Chapter 12. Winning the New Soft War

1 http://blogs.hbr.org/imagining-the-future-of-leadership/2010/04/the-abiding-tyranny -of-the-mal.html

2 Lips, H. M. (2012). Acknowledging discrimination as a key to the gender pay gap. *Sex Roles*, 68, 223–230.

3 http://online.wsj.com/article/SB10001424052702304746604577381953238775784 .html

4 Personal communication to Caryl Rivers, February 2013.

5 Sandberg, S. (2013) *Lean in: Women, work, and the will to lead*. New York: Alfred A. Knopf.

6 http://www.nytimes.com/2013/02/24/opinion/sunday/dowd-pompom-girl-for -feminism.html?_r=0

7 http://online.wsj.com/article/sb10014240527023047466045773819532387755784 .html46; accessed February 18, 2013

8 Eagly, A. H., & Carli, L. L. (2007). *Through the labyrinth: The truth about how women become leaders*. Boston: Harvard Business School Publishing.

9 http://www.washingtontimes.com/news/2011/oct/30/curl-the-very-angry-first -lady/?page=all

10 Brescoll, V. L., & Uhlmann, E. L. (2008). Can an angry woman get ahead: Status conferral, gender, and expression of emotion in the workplace. *Psychological Science*, 19(3), 268–275.

11 Tharenou, P. (2012). The work of feminists is not yet done: The gender pay gap—a stubborn anachronism. *Sex Roles*, 68, 198–206.

12 Hausmann, R., Tyson, L., & Zahidi, S. (2012). *The global gender gap report 2012*. World Economic Forum.

13 http://www.deloitte.com/assets/Dcom-Tanzania/Local%20Assets/Documents/Deloitte %20Article_Women%20in%20the%20boardroom.pdf

14 http://www.mckinsey.de/downloads/publikation/women_matter/20120305_Women_ Matter_2012.pdf

15 Cited in http://www.deloitte.com/assets/Dcom-Tanzania/Local%20Assets/Docu ments/Deloitte%20Article_Women%20in%20the%20boardroom.pdf

16 http://online.wsj.com/article/SB10014240527023047466045773819532387755784 .html

17 http://www.deloitte.com/assets/Dcom-Tanzania/Local%20Assets/Documents/Deloitte %20Article_Women%20in%20the%20boardroom.pdf

18 http://www.reuters.com/article/2011/01/13/us-france-equality-idUSTRE70C5Z A20110113

19 Mullally, M. (2012). *Gender imbalance in corporate boards: European commission con-sultation*. European Commission.

20 http://www.womens-forum.com/meetings/program/session/influencing-female-ad vancement-do-quotas-trump-merit-reframing-the-debate

21 Ibid.

22 http://www.deloitte.com/assets/Dcom-Tanzania/Local%20Assets/Documents/Deloitte %20Article_Women%20in%20the%20boardroom.pdf

23 Ibid.

24 Eagly, A. H., & Carli, L. L. (2007). *Through the labyrinth: The truth about how women become leaders*. Boston: Harvard Business School Publishing.

25 Shin, T. (2012). The gender gap in executive compensation: The role of female directors and chief executive officers. *Annals of the American Academy*, 639, 258–278.

26 women_matter_mar2012_english-3pdf; http://dspace.mit.edu/bitstream/handle/ 1721.1/55933/CPL_WP_05_02_HeilmanWelle.pdf

27 Welle, B., & Heilman, M. E. (2007). Formal and informal discrimination against women at work. In S. W. Gilliland, D. Steiner, & D. P. Skarlicki (eds.), *Managing Social and Ethical Issues in Organizations* (229–252). Charlotte, NC: Information Age Publishing.

28 Ibid.

29 http://www.nytimes.com/2010/06/10/world/europe/10iht-sweden.html?pagewanted =all&_r=0

30 http://www.nytimes.com/2013/04/07/magazine/how-shared-diaper-duty-could -stimulate-the-economy.html?pagewanted=all

31 http://www.whitehouse.gov/the-press-office/2013/01/21/inaugural-address-president -barack-obama

32 Hallman, L. D. (2012). *The simple truth about the gender wage gap.* American Association of University Women.

33 Ibid.

34 Ibid.

35 Ibid.

36 http://www.iwpr.org/publications/pubs/pay-secrecy-and-wage-discrimination

37 Ibid.

38 http://www.thedailybeast.com/articles/2013/02/26/yahoo-has-it-backward-why -working-remotely-is-better-for-everyone.html

39 http://www.scidev.net/en/opinions/family-friendly-policies-must-target-men-too.html

40 http://www.thedailybeast.com/articles/2013/02/26/yahoo-has-it-backward-why -working-remotely-is-better-for-everyone.html

41 http://www.startribune.co/business/195156871.html; accessed February 21, 2013

42 http://www.thedailybeast.com/articles/2013/02/26/yahoo-has-it-backward-why -working-remotely-is-better-for-everyone.html

43 http://www.bbc.co.uk/news/magazine-21588760

44 http://www.chronicle.com/article/Lady-AcademeLabor-Market/135284

45 http://blogs.hbr.org/research/2011/01/paid-family-leave-pays-off-in.html

46 Heymann, J., Earle, A., & Hayes, J. (2007). Implications for U.S. policy of the work, family, and equity index. Institute for Health and Social Policy, McGill University.

47 http://www.cwaunion.org/news/entry/workers_ready_for_battle_in_fight_to_save_ fmla#.UR5-8PGrDi8

48 http://www.inc.com/news/articles/200702/family.html

INDEX

If you enjoyed this book, visit

www.tarcherbooks.com

and sign up for Tarcher's e-newsletter to receive
special offers, giveaway promotions, and
information on hot upcoming releases.

TARCHER
PENGUIN

Great Lives Begin with Great Ideas

Connect with the Tarcher Community

Stay in touch with favorite authors!
Enter weekly contests!
Read exclusive excerpts!
Voice your opinions!

Follow us

 Tarcher Books

@TarcherBooks

If you would like to place a bulk order
of this book, call 1-800-847-5515.